PRECISION
CRUISING

PRECISION CRUISING

by *Arthur Chace*

ILLUSTRATIONS BY
Brad Dellenbaugh

W · W · Norton & Company, Inc.
NEW YORK

The text of this book is composed in Baskerville, with display type set in Palatino. Composition by Vail-Ballou Press, Inc. Manufacturing by The Maple-Vail Book Manufacturing Group. Book design by M. Franklin Plympton.

First Edition

ISBN 0-393-03302-3

W. W. Norton & Company, Inc., 500 Fifth Avenue,
New York, N. Y. 10110
W. W. Norton & Company Ltd., 37 Great Russell Street,
London WC1B 3NU

1 2 3 4 5 6 7 8 9 0

Contents

Acknowledgment

Mary von Conta, Jay Harris, and Robert Hopkins played greatly appreciated roles in bringing the ideas in this book to final form.

Arthur Chace

Preface

Precision Cruising is written to tell the reader of the joy and excitement of cruising in a boat that is sailed as perfectly as possible. Not being constrained by handicap rules, its sails can be chosen solely on the basis of what they do for the boat and its crew without regard for what they do for the time allowance the boat has against other boats. The book tells stories illustrating the joys of maneuvers executed with precision, of sails trimmed to get every last tenth of a knot of speed, of a boat kept in the groove, where sails are trimmed right the first time and adjusted as conditions change, where anchors are solidly set before the boat is secured for the night.

The book uses fictional anecdotes to maintain the readers' interest and to teach by illustration. It is hoped that the readers will read because they enjoy what they read and acquire knowledge and new ideas from every page without having to study. The reader vicariously enjoys good food and drink, uncrowded waters and harbors, and unlimited cruising areas available because the boat is fast, seaworthy, and well sailed. *Dancing Girl* can go farther and with greater safety and pleasure because plans have been carefully worked out to handle all contingencies.

The appendix presents the plans and instructions for the boat so that the prospective crew member coming aboard for the first time will be able to understand and comply with the boat's way of doing things. This appendix presents a standard and a model against which the readers can judge the plans made for their own boat. Because these bills have been carefully thought out and have stood the test of time the thoughtful reader will either accept or reject them, but to ignore them would waste what may be the greatest value the book has to offer.

The book is written primarily for two types of sailors: one is the round-the-buoys racer who is getting a bit tired of the monotony but is wary of cruising because it might prove unexciting. The other is the cruiser who is bored by ill-trimmed sails, long days with short mileage, and the monotony of the cruising areas close to home and easy for all to reach. It is hoped that the book, based on more than 60 years of sailing, will provide the reader with a substitute for personal experience and enhance his or her enjoyment of cruising.

Introduction

Rowing in an eight-oared shell with a well-trained crew is perhaps the epitome of the delight that one can experience when a group of people work together to make a boat move with grace and speed. At the catch the blades drop in unison, the pressure is applied smoothly, and almost all of it results in the shell spurting rapidly ahead. At the finish the oars flick out of the water and move smoothly forward as though connected together while the shell runs out with little diminution of speed. With a poorly trained crew the blades drop in with many splashes over a considerable period of time and the boat wobbles forward almost reluctantly. At the finish the shell has no run and wallows miserably waiting for the next stroke, and the crew works much harder to gain much less. A cruising sailboat responds similarly to the precision, or imprecision, of its handling.

Good seamanship is an essential of the happy cruiser but the boat does not come fully into its own unless the crew cares enough to do its job precisely and well. When sails are set and trimmed, quickly and properly, the boat should respond and move with the grace and speed its designer had in mind. Those abroad should have a sense of exhilaration as it suddenly starts to move rapidly ahead, working with the sea rather than against it. The boat tacks and is squared away and back in the groove while a clumsily handled cruiser plods awkwardly through stays and takes much longer to regain lost speed. A small adjustment in a sheet can make a quarter of a knot difference in speed with the wind's energy converted into forward motion rather than heeling moment. There are times when easing the sheets an inch or two will permit the boat to sail higher and faster to windward. Sail changes made with precision and speed mean less time for the crew to be exposed to the hazards of the foredeck, and the boat is sooner back to full speed with the proper rig and no unnecesssary weight on the bow.

The well-handled boat can arrive in harbor behind one with a sloppy crew and be at anchor with the rum bottle out while *Ineptitude* is still messing around. During the night *Precision* will sleep soundly except for the shouts from *Ineptitude* as they deal with dragging ground tackle. The precision sailor has dinner delayed 5 minutes by a stove fire of a seriousness that might cause the cook on the other yacht to lose the boat.

Good sails well trimmed bring life to any boat, but afloat the more precisely every task is accomplished, the more all hands will enjoy the delights of cruising under sail. Whatever you do, do well. Do not attempt to do more than you can do well.

PRECISION CRUISING

I

~~~~~~~~~~

The Gangster's Girlfriend

Dancing Girl, a tall-rig Ohlson 38 with four of us aboard, was beating south along the east shore of Great Exuma Island in the Bahamas. The water was calm and the winds light and variable, and we were playing the #1 genoa to get as much to windward as possible without dropping speed. We were mostly on port tack, and with delicate use of the barber haul, we were often tacking in 70°, but no matter what we did, we were hard pressed to make 4 knots through the water. The water was so luminous a blue that the sails took on the color of shoal water, the sun so bright that when an occasional puff of cloud obscured it for a moment, it was as though evening had fallen early. All of us were dressed to protect ourselves from the sun. I wore pale blue pajamas and a thick coat of what my cultured young students used to call "sun glop" to minimize our burning. Bliss in the Elysian Sea! None of us could ask for more.

Because we had been able to study the channel carefully coming into Adderly Cut the previous afternoon, we had gotten under way at 0815 when the sun was really not quite

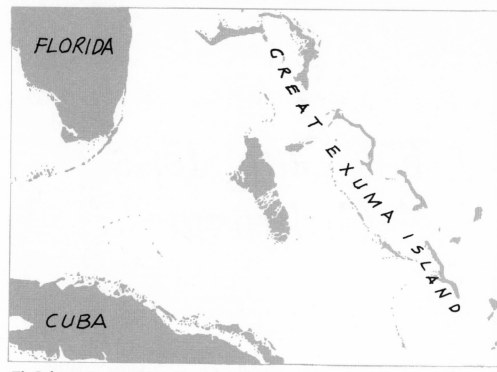

FLORIDA

GREAT EXUMA ISLAND

CUBA

The Bahamas

high enough to permit us to eyeball our way eastward toward open water. We had, however, used the engine and proceeded with great caution to be sure that we did not hang up on an unexpected shoal spot.

When the light is bad it is hard to differentiate between the off-white that means "only 3 feet" and the very pale green that means "7 feet" or to tell the black of grass from the black of coral heads. We had honed our piloting skill, but even the natives waited for good light to enter waters they did not know.

With the depth finder transducer aft in the hull under the cockpit, we always needed an expert pair of eyes forward, wearing Polaroid sunglasses and backed by a ready leadline to prevent us from being fooled by sudden shoaling. Of course, the joy of this type of navigation is that as you become expert in reading the water, you become appreciative of its colors

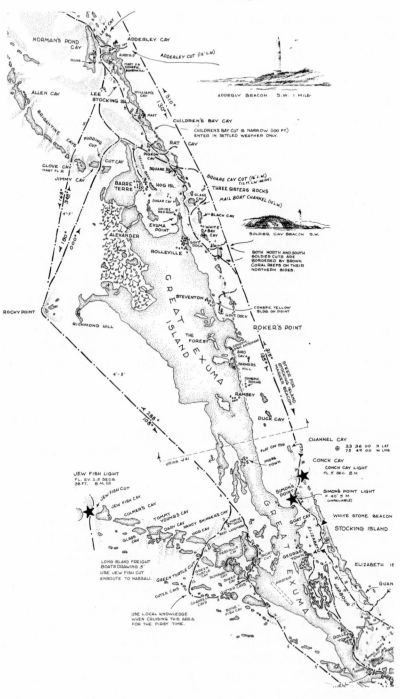

and the changing shapes of the bottom. Instead of pushing down into a dark opaque fluid, the boat is floating over the bottom in water so clear that it sometimes seems not to exist.

The wind was light and variable but we probably could have made it out under sail on starboard tack. Discretion, however, said that as this was our first sortie from this anchorage and as we needed to charge our batteries anyway, it was wiser for us to power out.

At 0915 we came to 130° M and set the main and #1. Once we settled down we were able to make 125°M occasionally but most of the time we were making 135°M on port tack and accordingly having to take an occasional leg out on starboard. It was fascinating to be sailing so delicately that if the wind velocity declined we could not sail as close to the wind and therefore would have to take more tacks to keep off the coral. If the wind freshened we could go a little faster and then by trimming carefully, gain by sailing closer to our desired course. With 16 knots of steady wind we could have the genoa 3 inches off the spreader and the draft about 46 percent back from the luff, the foot against the shrouds and the sheet holding the clew over the block on the 8° track. The main was carrying a luff halfway to the battens with a full flattening reef and 3,700 pounds on the backstay. The groove was narrow and to make it unnecessary for anyone to push himself, we rotated wheel watches every half hour.

We had hoped to make the 32 miles to Georgetown that day but the wind was not making it easy. As we passed Soldier Cay Beacon, the Old Man pointed out a great cumulonimbus anvil cloud building up threateningly ahead, and at 1208 we turned right to go into Steventon so that we could be securely at anchor when the thunderstorm struck. On the chart the twin rocks between which the channel led were shown to be about equal in size but in fact the northern one appeared to be significantly smaller. Immediately we were in doubt as to our position, the accuracy of the chart, and the wisdom of going into Steventon at all. We checked our dead reckoning, tried to identify all the possible landmarks, took careful soundings, and finally decided that the chart was in error.

We changed from the #1 down to our 91 percent working jib to get better visibility and less speed as we threaded our way between the rocks. To be ready in case we grounded and needed to kedge off, we brought two anchors on deck and arranged one on each corner of the counter. The rodes were led outside of everything and through the bow chock on the port and starboard sides respectively with about a boat-length of scope faked out on deck before each was cleated. It was our plan that if it touched we would immediately get one or both anchors over as far from the boat as possible in the hope that we could kedge off before the job got too big. To be prepared to extricate ourselves quickly if we encountered more serious errors in the chart, we started the engine and kept it idling out of gear.

The Old Man took the wheel. David was on the bow wearing his Polaroid glasses. Big Ann (whose name dated from her days 16 years before in the program at the junior yacht club, when she, weighing 86 pounds, pushed aside a big, soft boy and demonstrated that she could handle a loose spinnaker pole in a blow even if he could not) stood by the anchors and handled the sheets in the cockpit. Ann was about the prettiest girl I could remember seeing but she did not seem to realize it. I was on the depth finder, calling every fluctuation. Nothing went wrong and the run between the rocks was easy. When we turned south to head toward our anchorage we had a mile of beautiful white sand bottom interspersed with many clearly visible coral patches. We secured the engine and wove our way in without difficulty.

By 1305 we were anchored in 7 feet with a white sand bottom just off the government dock. We quickly gave the boat a thorough check to be sure that there was nothing that would come adrift in a blow and went below to have lunch out of the hot sun. The Old Man had taken bearings on all useful landmarks and had even gotten a range to be certain that we could tell if our anchors started to drag. When the first puffs of wind batted us we closed all the hatches and were ready when the storm hit. The rain would have made Sadie Thompson homesick and the wind was gusty, but it never blew over 35 in the puffs. Although we were snug and dry, it sounded as though several fire hoses were being played on us at the same time. We watched for signs that the hooks were dragging, but it never became stormy enough for us to doubt our ability to ride safely and securely to our anchors. We were thankful for our decision to anchor early. Warm as the weather was, a tropic downpour is best enjoyed from solid shelter.

Our meal centered around a bowl of conch ceviche, which had been "cooking" in lime juice in the icebox since our mid-day snorkeling the day before. There was also fresh bread. David had baked it in the pressure cooker early in the day so that the cabin would cool down by the time we wanted to use it. The fold-down table was set with a blue checkered table-cloth which was easy to wash in a bucket when we did our laundry. It gave a gala air to meals and kept the table clean.

We each had a napkin ring. The Old Man's was a silver one from his Navy days, engraved with the name of each of the four ships on which he had served in World War II and of his two yachts in later life. David's was an Eskimo carving that he had bought 10 years before at the Grenfell Mission when he had gone down to Labrador in *Dancing Girl.* Mine was of silver, given to me 10 years before by the students in my dormitory at school, on the occasion of my completion of 25 years as House Master. Ann used a hammered silver one dating from her jewelry-making phase. We were drinking Cokes, and since we were through sailing for the day, they were liberally laced with anti-scorbutic dosages of rum.

I leaned back and lifted my glass to toast, "Endless days of beauty and delight." The others joined me. I said, "There is a magic to this. How could you describe cruising to a lands-man who had never seen the sea . . . so that he could under-stand why we are here?"

"I read somewhere," said the Old Man, "and I do not believe it was in the Bible: Cruising is like bedding the gangster's girlfriend. The pleasure is great and the danger adds zest, but there comes the time when the prudent man concen-trates on extrication and survival." His eyes twinkled as he looked around the cabin while we laughed.

"I like the picture," said David, "but I am not sure the sim-ile is true. I've sailed long enough to have seen things go wrong and to have had some dramatic moments . . . but real danger? Almost never! Ever since I was a kid, Old Man, you and I have differed as to the need to preplan our response to every imaginable happening, dangerous or routine. Common sense is all it takes . . . like not lighting a match to see how much gas there is in your car's tank. I don't think that I've ever felt that I've been in genuine danger at sea."

The Old Man glared. "Do you remember an incident 10 years or so ago? I think it was the year you were a senior at school. I can never forget that night off Newfoundland when the wind came up and I did a single-handed spinnaker douse. I handed the sail to you to take below to pack for the next set. The wind caught it and suddenly you were going over the rail with the chute in your arms."

"I was clutching half the sail," said David. "The water filled the other half. I was on my way overboard when Charlie brought me and the sail back into the ship's company. Perhaps he saved me from a dunking, but I don't think I was in danger. The bath probably would have done me good."

The Old Man stood up and surveyed the harbor through a rain-streaked porthole. *Dancing Girl* was swinging to the right on her mooring as the thunder squall peaked in intensity. The wind was fairly whistling through the dorade over my berth, and our voices were to a subtle extent modulated by the rise and fall of the wind outside.

Satisfied that all was still well with *Dancing Girl*, the Old Man replied, "I know you're really rugged. Yet it still makes me sick to think of you going over the side into that dark, cold, rough sea. Our "Man Overboard Bill" was as good as I could make it, and all of us had read it and were seamen, but if Charlie had missed your belt that night, the odds against your being alive today are unpleasantly slim. The thought of trying to relocate and retrieve any one on a night like that makes me feel sick, and that's leaving out the risk of hypothermia."

"Perhaps I am too confident, but I have never been afraid on *Dancing Girl*," said David. "Sure I have seen the mast lying in the water, and a green sea come over the bow and fill the cockpit. I have seen us handle at least one spectacular galley flare up, but I have never seen anything to suggest that the sea could be an enraged hoodlum with newly discovered horns on his head. I am sure that common sense can handle whatever comes up. You make life at sea sound dangerous."

"I hate to disagree with a shipmate of over fifteen years' standing," said Ann after listening to David and the Old Man's well-rehearsed arguments, "but I suspect that the reason the sea does not appear dangerous to us is because the Old Man taught us our common sense in the first place. Things that we consider to be routine difficulties can easily turn into dangers for the mariner who is neither foresighted nor alert. Remember a couple of years ago when we were bringing the boat to Marblehead from Marion with a couple of friends aboard who had talked a good game but later turned out to be pretty inexperienced? One of these jokers had been on the wheel as we were running downwind when a squall hit us and he became confused. You sprinted from the foredeck, where you had been adjusting the chute, to the wheel just in time to prevent a goose-wing jibe. Our friend nearly took the stick out that day. For my money, that was a dangerous moment."

"That," David said, "was a case of a know-nothing who waited until we were at sea to demonstrate his abilities. Perhaps it was our fault for forgetting the rule that you can never trust anybody."

"I suspect that if you found yourself at sea with a bunch of real know-nothings you would run things well," Ann said, "and I bet you would also find yourself telling them that the sea can be dangerous."

The Old Man put a little rum and the rest of his Coke in his glass and, after taking a sip, said, "The dangers of going to sea are not that there are constant hazards to our safety, but rather that threats occur so infrequently that they may find us otherwise engaged and totally unprepared. It's hard to remember danger in the pleasure of the moment. That is why I like the simile of the gangster's girlfriend. We bask in heaven without a care in the world, when suddenly we're in combat with an all-powerful brute in whose domain we are trespassing, in this case the sea. At sea, common sense without proper training behind it can get you only so far. It is, after all, common sense which told the Mediterranean sailors of the Renaissance that the earth was flat. How could the Spanish have plundered the New World with that kind of attitude? Common sense also says that the greatest danger is

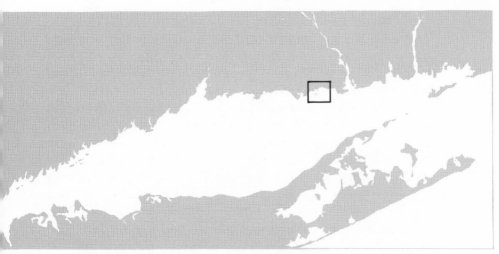

Long Island Sound with Duck Island Roads Outlined

sailing out of sight of land, but the seaman knows that the danger increases the closer to land he gets. There are plenty of Spanish galleons moored permanently under these waters to testify to that.

"The only time that I have really thought that the sea would destroy us," continued the Old Man, "was when I was cruising with a friend on his boat and we got caught on a lee shore in a very nasty unforecast squall. We ran into Duck Island Roads for cover."

Ann interrupted, "Duck Island Rose? Sounds like a sailor's clip joint to me."

The Old Man chuckled and said, "The name is Duck Island Roads, a harbor of refuge on the north shore of Long Island Sound, now silted in so as to be of little interest to us. A roads is a protected place where ships can anchor, but not as protected as a harbor. Coasting schooners once anchored there behind Duck Island to await favorable wind or sit out a blow.

"But that afternoon was different," said the Old Man, returning to the tale. "We had been beating west along the north shore of Long Island Sound when a sudden blackening of the sky warned that a storm was coming soon. We should have run right then for sea room in the center of the sound. The skipper thought that we could gain the shelter of

Duck Island Roads if we drove the boat. It was his yacht, so I agreed. We still had full sail when the blow hit. The boat was on her beam ends and we had to get the sails off to let her up. As the sails came under control the owner attempted with total lack of success to start the engine.

"The lee shore loomed large in our thinking and we got the ready anchor over with lots of scope. It caught south of Menunketesuck Island the first time and the skipper went back to his engine. I started a search for the storm jib and trysail. The trysail turned up in the forepeak and the jib under the after port bunk. By this time I had noticed the anchor jerking through the sand one very wave. A quick check of the depth finder told us that trouble was closing fast. The charts showed us that if we tried to keep going west and did not clear, as seemed more likely by the minute, we were headed for some pretty rocky waters. If we could get off on Starboard tack and head south, we would have more room and a less hostile beach if we did not make it. I bent on the jib and set it just as our keel bounced on the sandy shoal in the trough of a big wave. The trysail was up moments later. The shoal was 50-yards wide and at this tide would have had 3 feet under the keel in calm water. The 4-foot sea meant we would bounce in each trough.

"We hauled the anchor rode aft outside of everything to our starboard quarter and trimmed the jib flat. We eased the trysail sheet and bunched the sail against the mast with a turn around a halyard winch until we got it on the port jib winch. As she swung over, we cast the anchor rode overboard and, like a couple of enraged octopuses, brought the boat up on a starboard tack with both sails drawing. We tried to heel her over in each trough and only smashed down hard on the bottom three times as we worked our way across the shoal to deep water.

"There was unanimous agreement then that what we needed was sea room. We worked our way offshore until the storm ran its course. When the barometer started up and all signs were favorable, we headed in and after a soft twilight sail under full main and #1, we finally anchored behind the breakwater, setting our anchor with an extra heavy slug of rum for each. The next morning, trolling from the dinghy

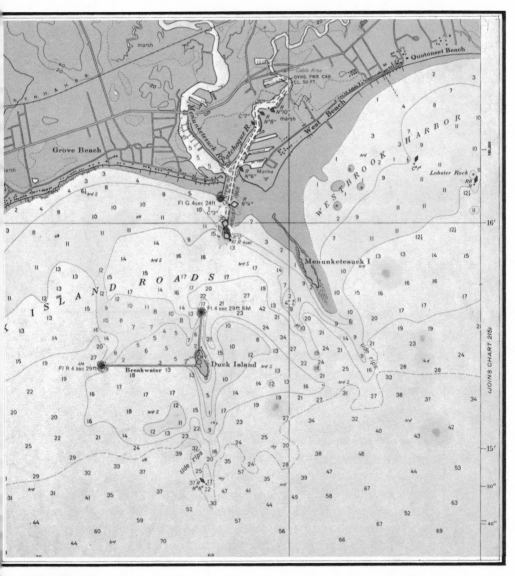

Duck Island Roads

in light zephyrs, we retrieved our abandoned anchor and were on our way rejoicing.

"We are safer afloat than ashore but just as most auto accidents occur within seventeen miles of home, so staying close to the home shore is not the secret of safe cruising." His story was over, and we waited for the Old Man to present its moral.

"David, that time when you saw the mast lying on the water, there was no danger because we had already shut all hatches and ports. We've always stowed and rigged everything on the boat to withstand a 360° roll. That makes for less chaos below. We know galley fires have destroyed many boats, but the reason you were not alarmed by our flare-ups was because all of us have thought a lot about the proper reaction to a flare-up or spill. Planning ahead can make anyone more effective."

The Old Man slid aft until his legs were free of the table, got a hand bearing compass from the rack over the navigator's bunk and took a round of bearings through the ports to make sure we hadn't dragged.

David watched his father until the bearings showed that we had not moved. "As I analyze it, when we're racing we are testing boat and crew. We take almost any chance where skill will gain us a few seconds' advantage. We are all capable, able, and strong, and we're used to working together. We're able to do whatever has to be done smartly. Cruising is best when you have the same kind of crew and do everything with the same precision. You just don't take as many chances, and when you are shorthanded, you have to take that into account."

The Old Man replied, "Remember, David, we cruisers are not like those little birds who feed on scraps of meat caught between the crocodile's teeth. At least we should not be. The cruiser should not be testing crew and ship the way the racer does, but should enjoy the pleasure of a well-sailed boat as he visits interesting places. Cruisers should be able to sail safely into crowded harbors and wilderness coves. Because they are good seamen, they should be able to work their boats into tight little creeks and across wide oceans. The goal is that all hands should finish a cruise physically and spiritually refreshed. To achieve this objective, I believe that you plan ahead, decide the best way to handle each eventuality, and be prepared to act promptly to avoid trouble. Because of my age, I may dwell too much on what can go wrong. Whatever the situation, I am subconsciously running through the defensive and corrective measures. I think it a habit that good seamen all have, but they may not all see as many hazards as

I do. By being prepared, you will be able to enjoy all the wonders of the sailor's world. I love being at sea. I love it all, the escape, the beauty, the places we visit and also the discipline required to deal with the sea's unlimited power. Every bit of the sea I have seen has been beautiful. Not just the bright moonlit nights or the sparkling sunny days, but also the ocean graybeards rolling under black clouds, or the sky veined with lightning, or the sea streaked with spume. I have loved clawing off a lee shore under storm jib and trysail, or tiptoeing through dense fog listening so hard my ears seemed to stretch out like trumpets. I have enjoyed every minute."

II

~~~~~~~~~~~~~~~~

Beating

That July morning we were in the cove at the north end of Allen Island just north of Monhegan Island off the coast of Maine. We had all slept well, and after a quick swim in the icy water to give us a sense of moral superiority we had stuffed down a breakfast built around a mountain of pancakes containing the first of the season's wild blueberries, served with real maple syrup and sausage patties. We ran the engine to charge the batteries as we attended to our chores. The weather was clear. The sling psychrometer gave a wet bulb reading of 62 and a dry of 67, promise that with the water temperature at 63 we would not see fog before sunset. The weather report suggested that it would be a good day to visit Matinicus almost 20 miles to the east of us, well off the coast and often deep in fog. It was too good an opportunity to be wasted on any of the other harbors more often accessible.

The Old Man put me in charge of the sails. At anchor the wind was about 4 knots coming from 090° but I expected it to increase and back as the day progressed. *Dancing Girl's* new and beautiful #1 was 165 percent and made of new 3.7-oz. soft, laminated Mylar and Dacron cloth, which had greater tear strength and overall toughness than the 5-oz. 150 percent it was replacing. This sail is our choice in apparent winds from 3 to 21 knots. Because we do not race, there is no need to be concerned about our handicap and so the Old Man has maximized the sail area for performance in light airs. On the other hand the 3.7 is well designed and can remain dimensionally stable up to 22 knots. In the higher velocities the main must be reefed to keep the boat at maximum speed, but jiffy reefing is so simple that we can use it to keep the boat at the optimum angle of heel as easily as adjusting a windowshade. We have no #2, but when reducing sail go direct to our #3, a Solent jib, which is 91 percent and was made of 7.25 oz. cloth 9 years ago. It is reefable with reef points 12 inches apart to insure a tight enough furl to avoid any catching of heavy wind or water. We also carry a storm jib.

It was an easy decision to start off with the 3.7 and we bent it on and secured it to the top life line to keep it clear of the anchors. We led the sheets inside the life lines for I expected to be hard on the wind for all but the first part of the day. I did not think it worthwhile to rig the sheets outside for the fifteen minutes it would take us to clear Burnt Island and get onto our course for buoy 5MI but I did rig a temporary sheet outside to get proper shape for this short leg. The wider angle permitted by using a temporary sheet even more importantly lets the main be trimmed further to leeward without back-wind, producing more forward force.

The main is a full-cut sail made of 5.0-oz. cloth with an ample shelf. Not being concerned with handicap measure-ments or rating, the Old Man had had it made as large as the mast and the boom would permit. The outhaul brings it to the block at the end of the boom with light tension and the shelf fully open. The halyard brings it as high up the mast as there is room for the head board to clear the backstay and the toppinglift. It has a cunningham and a flattening reef, which is rigged with extra blocks inside the boom to give enough purchase so that the sail can be hauled flat by a mod-erately strong person without a winch.

There are reefing pigtails on each side of the gooseneck and the sail is equipped for three jiffy reefs. We carry the lines led through the blocks on the boom for all three reefs but to cut down on windage and unnecessary spaghetti we only reeve the first two through the reefing grommets. The Old Man says, however, that he has a project for early com-pletion to lead all the reefing lines inside the boom to further reduce the pasta. Rigged in there there would be less chance of fouls and tangles and less windage. The weather seemed to promise that we might well be double reefed during the day but I thought that final preparation for the third reef could wait until the weather developed.

When everyone was set we secured the engine which had gotten the batteries up to 80 percent charge. Ann and David handled the foredeck and mast. I handled the cockpit and O. M. was on the helm. We hoisted the main and sailed up the port anchor, with David hauling in the rode to have it taut when it came up and down. A quick turn around the mooring cleat and the anchor broke ground. We had way enough to tack and did so heading for the starboard anchor. David washed off the port anchor and brought it on deck.

Ann took in the slack in the starboard rode and cleated it when it came up and down. The anchor almost stopped the boat but at the last moment the bow sprang up and we were free. It was 1020. Working well together, they had that anchor washed and on deck before we were going too fast to keep it from banging against the hull.

As soon as the foredeck was clean and the anchor secure we hoisted the genny and slid down the channel to the west of Burnt Island on a close reach on port tack with 8 knots over the deck. Ann and David moved back into the cockpit and I relieved the wheel so that the Old Man could tend to the navigation. We were making about 7.5 knots. In spite of the shortness of the leg, our recollection of the trim settings that had worked in similar circumstances on previous occasions permitted us to come very close to the ideal trim for maximum speed on our first try. Based on our indicated speed through the water and the apparent wind speed and direction as shown by the instruments the navigator made a vector diagram on the compass rose and came up with an estimate of true wind direction and speed. In another vector diagram using this information and some assumptions based on previous experience he was able to estimate what speed we would be making and what would be the best course we could expect to make.

He figured that when we got out in the open we would be hard on the wind with about 11 knots of apparent wind steering about 120°M, not being able to get up to our desired course of 109°M. This would take us south of Southeast Breaker, unless the wind backed. I thought that it would at some point during the day and that if we were lucky we might not even have to take a tack to get up to our mark.

The genoa cars on the 8° track were in the moderate air position for the #1. Had there been less wind, I would have moved them forward one position and if we had had drifting conditions I would have wanted the blocks outside the lifelines with the sheet eased to put the patch 10 inches off the spreaders. This would have made the sail fuller, the helmsman would have sailed a bit lower but we would have picked up enough speed through the water to give us an overall gain. I decided, however, that we would have enough wind

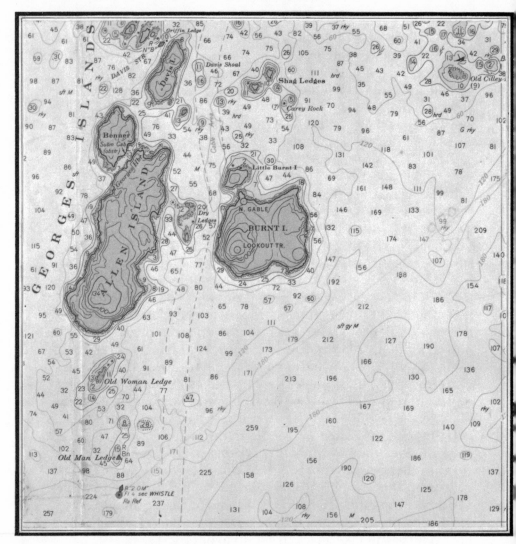

Allen Island to Matinicus (I)

and calm enough water to trim to the 8° line with the patch
4 inches off the spreader end and the foot touching at the
chains. The main would need about two thirds of the flattening reef and enough cunningham to give us 15 percent depth
with the draft at 47 percent. Idlers would be encouraged to
sit forward and to leeward to give us a little weather helm.
When the lookout tower came abeam we eased *Dancing Girl*

up to a course hard on the wind as we brought the clew of the genny in to the 8° line. The foot of the sail was just against the base of the shrouds and we eased the sheet enough to get the patch 4 inches off the end of the spreader. As the head of the genoa seemed a little deep we pumped the backstay tension up to 3,500 pounds and then we eased the strain on

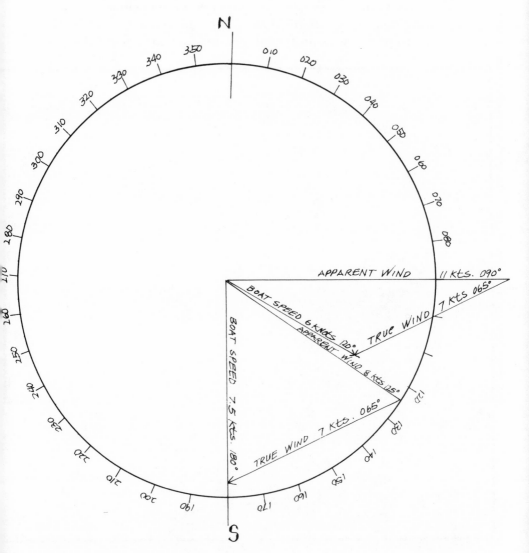

Vector Diagram for True Wind Speed and Direction

the jib halyard enough to put the deepest part of the draft
47 percent back from the luff. The hash mark on the speed
stripe on the sail is at 45 percent and makes a valuable reference point for this kind of adjustment. The leeward telltales on the luff were flowing nicely. The weather woolies
were lifting lightly and the boat's speed climbed up to 6.3
knots as the apparent wind steadied at 12 knots.

We tightened the flattening reef enough to eliminate some
of the fullness in the lower part of the main. Then we
retrimmed the mainsheet to get the top batten parallel to the

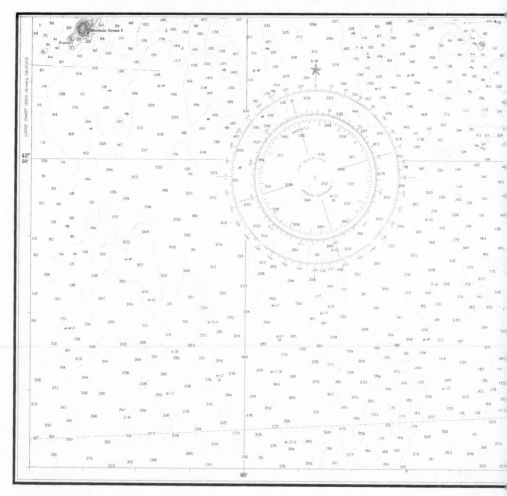

Vector Diagram—Course and Speed

boom. The traveler put the boom on the centerline as we could see by sighting along the boom to the backstay. The helm was using about 4° of rudder. We were in the groove but we could not sail higher than 122° without pinching. It

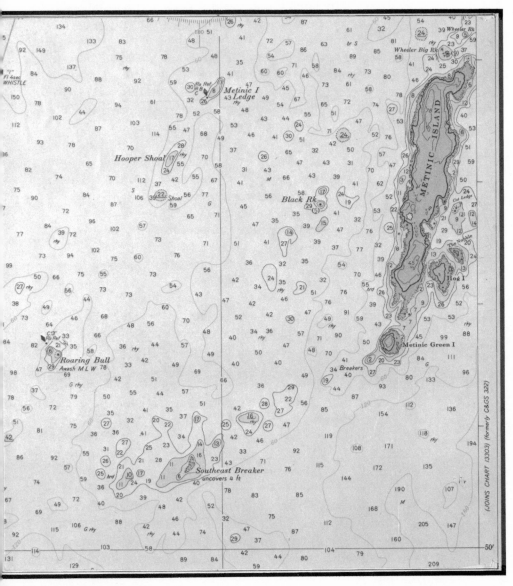

llen Island to Matinicus (II)

was 1045 and a sparkling day. The coast and the islands to
the north of us glistened, displaying their brightest colors in
the clear air and summer sunlight. A porpoise suddenly
materialized in the calm waters and played just outside our
bow wave to starboard.

Half an hour later the apparent wind had backed so that
we were sailing 118°. The velocity was up to 17 knots and our
speed had come up to 6.5. I brought the backstay tension up
to 3,800 and hauled in 3 inches on the genoa sheet. This left
the patch 3 inches off the spreader. We hauled in the last bit
of the flattening reef and put in enough cunningham to control the lower fullness along the luff. We trimmed the main
to balance its shape with that of the genoa. The wind was
continuing to back and strengthen but it was not going to lift
us enough to pass to the north of Southeast Breaker. On my
recommendation, we eased the sheets and came right 10° so
that we would not go into waters shallower than 20 feet. This
was enough to bring our speed up to 6.7 knots. Tactically, I
expected the wind to continue to back for the remainder of
the day due to the center of the cyclonic system which I felt
was passing slightly to the south of us. I thought the seas
when they came up on the 10-foot shoal would become sufficiently turbulent to reduce our pointing efficiency to the
point that we would have to ease our sheets and head off at
least 10°. I thought the turbulence would cost us more than
we could possibly gain by holding up. As we passed the edge
of the shoal-induced turbulence our speed dropped to 6.2
knots. I eased the backstay to 3,000 pounds and the main
and genoa sheets another 6 inches and came off another 5°.
It being half tide, the depth finder went down only to 25 feet
but I thought we might have done a little better if we had
passed 100 yards further south and avoided every bit of the
turbulence.

The wind was definitely getting stronger and *Dancing Girl*
was lying over 27°, further than would produce maximum
speed. She felt logy. I gave the mainsheet a quick release and
let the main flog. Our speed did not decrease, a sure sign
that a reef was indicated. I said, "We'll reef the main. David,
you handle the mast and Ann can take care of things in the
cockpit."

David went forward and freed the main halyard and the reefing line for the first reef and checked to see that everything was in readiness. Ann had the mainsheet clear and was positioned to work fast. She shouted, "Ready."

A moment later David was set and did likewise.

"Go ahead," I called.

David lowered the main halyard to the first mark and cleated it, as Ann eased the main sheet so that there was no strain in it. He then hooked the grommet over the reefing hook and hauled the halyard tight. He grabbed the reef line and with his feet well braced hauled it, without the winch, tight enough for me to shout "Okay." David ran to the cockpit and helped Ann trim the main. Then Ann went forward and tidied up around the mast. After watching a few moments, David went forward and used the winch to take in another 2 inches on the reefing line, flattening the foot to optimum shape. The traveler was four holes to weather, putting the boom on the centerline. By feathering up in the puffs I was able to keep the boat moving well without lying over or using too much rudder.

The boat had been originally rigged with roller reefing and the boom still had this capability although the blocks and cam cleats of the jiffy system were mounted on it. In addition to making the reefing lines internal the Old Man was thinking about rigging a wire pennant with a hook on the end of it that could be hung in the reefing tack grommet to speed up the reefing at the tack. When the time came to reef the reef tack grommet could be winched down and the halyard would not have to be over-slacked as the present system required to make it possible to hang the grommet on the hook. The hooks would be eliminated. We were discussing the possibility of having a Wichard snap in each reefing tack grommet, the idea being that with a ring mounted at the gooseneck the snap in each successive reef grommet could be snapped in the ring before the wire pennant was released to take care of the next reef. We all agreed that *Girl* was not big enough to have room for all the reefing lines led back to the cockpit, but we were also agreed the the future was going to see more improvements in the system.

At 1150 we were heeling 25° and the wind was at 22 over

the deck. If it went any higher the 3.7 was in danger of suffering damage with no gain in speed for the boat. We bent on the Solent under the #1, securing it to the lifeline in readiness for when the wind came up more. Our speed was just over 6.7 but I was feathering up more and more of the time to avoid being overpowered. The navigator's noon fix told us that with the help of the tide we had made 100° for the past half hour but that we needed to go 10° higher still if we were to make our buoy. I was steering 100° and with the current all looked possible if we avoided making too much leeway. It was time for the jib change.

The Old Man took the wheel. Big Ann, being the lightest, went forward with a couple of long sailstops around her waist. She sat in the pulpit facing aft straddling the headstay. David, also with a couple of stops, freed up the jib halyard and stood by. When each of us shouted "Ready" he let go the halyard with a run and grabbing the genny's skirt hauled it inside the lifeline as it came down. Ann unclipped the #1 as fast as she could reach the hanks. David got one stop around the sail and stepped back to the mast checking to see that the sheets for the #3 which went to blocks on the 9° track were clear of the sheets for the number one which were at the 8° track. Ann shifted the halyard to the head of the #3 and shouted "Ready" as she secured the luff of the #1 to the pulpit with a stop. I had released the sheet as soon as the halyard was let go and shifted the new sheets to the main winch on each side. David hoisted the #3 and as soon as it was two-blocked, I hauled in the sheet and winched it in so that its foot was pressing in on the forward lower. Ann clipped the #1 back on the headstay and furled the big sail to the lower life line using the three stops to hold it. As *Dancing Girl* has two tack snaps on the stem head there is no need to change the tacks of the sails when changing sails. I shifted the weather genoa car to match the position of the leeward car. The apparent wind was 24 knots and we were heeling 19° making just under 6.7. The Old Man had David shake out the first reef but left the full flattening reef. Our speed went up to 6.8 and although we were heeling 23° we were only using 4° of rudder.

David made us grilled Gruyère sandwiches with a slice of onion in each. The butter in the pan made the bread on each side crisp as it melted the cheese and cooked the onion to perfection. We were having too much fun sailing to want to go below to eat. During lunch the wind had continued to rise and back. As the seas were building slowly, we hauled the halyard tight enough to move the draft forward to 43 percent. Ann cranked the sheet in very tight. The position of the block was well forward to give the necessary control to this tall, skinny sail. The vertical lifting load put a huge strain on the track but fortunately it was well backed to a sturdily constructed deck. We came to 21° of heel without any loss of speed and the Old Man reported that he now only needed 3° of rudder. The Solent is a favorite sail with all who have come to know it during its 9 years of existence. Lean as the wing of a glider, it is the essence of high lift and low drag.

We passed just north of Pigeon Ground at 1243 and expected to be off Bell 5MI before 1330. Because of the building slop, we kept tightening the halyards to keep the draft of both main and jib at 43 percent to prevent our groove from getting narrower than we could stay in. As the day progressed, we were fighting for every inch we could get to weather without reducing our velocity made good toward the mark. We were grateful for the tide's northerly push which made our course over the ground lay the mark even though we were not pointing up to it at any time.

By the time we were inside all was secure and we were ready for the demands of the harbor. We asked a fisherman in a big lobsterman where we could spend the night without being in the way and he suggested that we nest with him as he was not going anywhere until he got his alternator back from being rewound on the mainland.

As soon as we were close enough, Ann jumped over to the other boat with the midships after spring and secured it to a cleat just forward of the counter and then ran forward to take the midships' forward spring and secure it to the mooring bitts on our host's foredeck. While she was there she took the bow breast and secured it to the same bitts and ran aft in time to receive the after breast as the Old Man swung our stern in, swinging on the forward after spring.

The lobsterman said, "Looks like you've done that before. My God! You're a girl!"

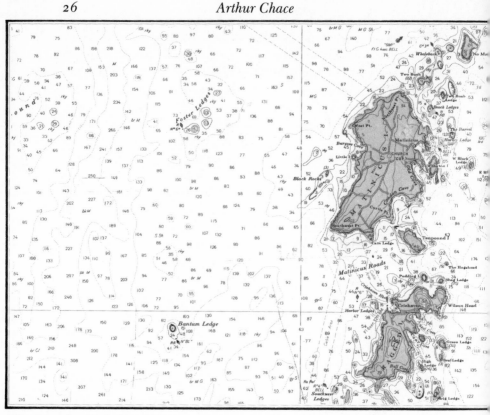

Allen Island to Matinicus (III)

Ann replied, "Yes, but I was never pretty enough not to have to do my share of the work."

While Ann, David and I made everything secure and ship-shape, the Old Man did the preliminary navigation for the next day. Then, with the assurances of the lobsterman that there was nothing we could do to help him and that he would not be inconvenienced if we left the boat unmanned, we inflated the dinghy and went ashore for a walk. The island lives up to its description in *A Cruising Guide to the New England Coast*. The sense of being offshore, far from the land comes from everything you see and hear. In spite of the little changes that time brings, when I am here, I still return every time to the boat with an increased sense of being a mariner in a world dominated by the sea.

When we returned to *Dancing Girl*, our friend was just finishing up on the lobsterman. He did not accept our invitation to join us for a drink or a beer pointing out that he had a wife and two kids waiting for him at home. He thanked us and, standing in his little skiff, sculled off to the stone pier that everyone uses. David gave each of us a mug with a lump of ice in it and passed up the rum bottle and several cans of Coke, cool from the bilges.

"You know," said David, "this is the first cruising we have done with *Dancing Girl* since you put the degree marks on the wheel, and I have to admit I am impressed how well they work with the inclinometer in telling us when and how to adjust sail trim or when to change jibs or reef. I was keeping a casual eye on the angle of heel but quite often the Professor was able to call for a change and make an improvement in our speed toward the next mark before I could read it in the inclinometer."

"I still go a lot by the way the boat feels." I broke in to say, "The new techniques help a lot and we now pretty much know what we are looking for, but I still feel the wallowing motion when our sails are pushing us over too far and we are making leeway instead of headway. By the same token I depend a lot on the way the boat feels when we are pinching, that dead, hobby-horse motion that means we are not moving as we should."

"Perhaps due to better instrumentation," David came back, "I get the feeling that today we are much more aware of what are the factors that affect a boat's speed both through the water and speed to the next mark. In the old days the really good sailors could feel not only if they were pinching but also if they were sailing too fast or too high for the conditions. Thinking of the mainsail as a rudder has made a lot of difference for me. With the telltales streaming from the leech, we know that aerodynamically speaking it is not stalled. With the top batten parallel to the boom we know that we are not over- or under-trimming the main. With adjustable backstay tension, adjustable halyard tension, flattening reef and a cunningham to put tension on the luff we can do a lot to assist the mainsheet in controlling sail shape. Now, when we have set the sail shape according to the conditions, we can, by moving the traveler, be sure that we are getting all the drive the boat can use and, at the same time, make sure that we are not holding it back with too much rudder. In the old days there was a lot of folklore to help verbalize what good sailors felt through the soles of their feet or the seat of their pants. I was very much impressed today to see how much you could accomplish by not wasting any opportunity to move us faster in the direction we wanted to go.

"Just a few years ago there was a joke about a boat that was suddenly beating boats that were thought to have been designed faster because the skipper had taken all the cleats off the boat. Now I get the feeling that that is merely an exaggeration. Good sailors today know and understand the speed-producing factors. They change the sheets and halyards because they know enough to be precise, and they eliminate a lot of unnecessary work by being right the first time. A boat that is always moving at optimum speed is exhilarating, but is somewhat demanding compared to the old-fashioned cruiser rolling along with ill-fitting sails trimmed and cleated in what is thought to be approximately the correct position, but for me, I choose the excitement every time. It is not as tiring if you know what you are trying to do and don't have to resort to trial-and-error. I love to be on a well-driven boat and am bored stiff with lazy cruising. I don't like to play tennis on a court without lines or a net.

"I think that the answer is short days, 20 to 30 miles, sailed aggressively and then the rest of the day spent ashore, reading or just plain puttering around. Sloppy boat-handling is not my idea of fun."

Big Ann came in with, "In the days before I discovered that business is so much fun, I spent a lot of energy trying to become more proficient in the art of sailing but now it is the science that intrigues me. Art is still important but mastery of the science comes first. I feel that although you must be flexible to take care of varying conditions you also need an orderliness about mainsail trim. For example, I think that when conditions provide more resistance to forward progress than the available wind can overcome, you have the sail as full as you can get and still maintain the airflow over the leeward side of the sail and bring the boom as close to the centerline as possible without slowing the boat's progress.

"As the wind comes up, the boom comes up to the center-line. I noticed that the Professor brings the traveler on *Dancing Girl* 6 inches to windward when the apparent wind is 6 knots and then increases backstay and halyard tension to increase weatherliness and speed," Ann went on. At 12 knots on the anemometer the shelf is eliminated and there is just enough twist in the upper part of the sail to take advantage of the stronger air at the masthead. I noticed that backstay tension was increased to correct sail shape when the increasing wind caused the sail to be fuller than ideal. Halyard and flattening reef and cunningham also performed this function. Once further blading of the main could not prevent a rudder angle over 6°, the traveler was moved down to leeward and after that the sheet was eased until half of the main was back winded. It was at this point that the main was reefed to reduce its tendency to turn the boat to windward against the rudder. It is certainly significant to see that up to this point the main provides little and increasingly less of the drive. It provides some valuable slot effect with the genoa and some essential pressure on the boat to come up closer to the wind."

"You observe very well, and what you say is absolutely correct," I interrupted to say, "but I was also using the flattening reef and downhaul to make the draft more shallow and to move it gradually from 47 percent to 43 percent to make the sail more forgiving as the wind and sea came up."

"The data in *Dancing Girl*'s 'Bills and Systems' are a very good start, and it's all right for the Professor and the Old Man to keep the schedule of these sail adjustments in their computer-like brains," said Ann, "but it would really help me, who comes sailing much too infrequently, to have this wisdom reduced to digits that I could read when I come aboard. I am thinking of a much more complete table."

The Old Man replied, "As usual, Ann, I agree with you. It would be good discipline for us to make such a schedule and I would appreciate it very much if you would dig this information from your shipmate's resisting brains and reduce it to tabular form for us to furnish to those who join our happy company in the future. But I'm afraid that there are so many

variables and so much need for art and judgment that we
could not write up an outline that would work. You can try
it though. I always expect you to do the impossible."

Ann grinned and said, "All right. I know when I am being
maneuvered but to show you that I have a heart of gold I
will not only do the mainsail but I will also collect and organize the existing wisdom pertaining to the jibs."

The Old Man beamed and said, "Big Ann, if you ever decide
to marry and settle down, I hope you will put me at the head
of the list of supplicants. 'Til that time, let me see if I can be
precise enough to assist you with your project. I am afraid I
sense rather than reason about jibs, or other sails, too, for
that matter. Let me try.

"In Force Zero winds when the water is an undulating mirror, I think we should use the Solent, our #3 which is masthead and 91 percent. It should be hoisted just tight enough
to remove all wrinkles. I would guess that 1,000 pounds on
the backstay would make it look about right. It should be
sheeted to the fourth hole on the 9° track and sheeted loosely,
say about to the 12° line. Here the goal is to catch and utilize
every breath of air that moves. The jib should be the first sail
to exert forward pressure on the boat, the first to give it any
motion. The sails should be used as much as possible, rather
than the rudder, to steer the boat. The helmsman and the jib
tender by working closely together can avoid a lot of rudder
drag that would otherwise keep the boat from moving. The
boat will pick up enough to make some of its apparent wind
with its forward motion and the Solent is key to this because
it is quick to trim to the wind. As soon as the wind comes up
to a steady 2 knots and is strong enough to take the wrinkles
out of the sail, the 3.7 #1 would be my choice. Remember
this is a heavy-air 165 percent sail and and we have no light-
air #1. Usually, though, it requires 3 to 4 knots to get the
steadiness to make it superior to the Solent. In this range it
is best trimmed outside the lifeline with the block in position
11. The patch should be about 10 inches off the spreader
and the foot 4 inches off the base of the shrouds. The draft
should be well forward and deep. The backstay pressure at
1,000 should make the shape look right."

The conversation then was directed at building a table that would present in concise form how *Dancing Girl's* sails should be trimmed. Most of the facts were stored in the Old Man's memory, but all of us participated in the discussions.

David, who had been listening, grinned and added, "Ann, I assume that when you get all the data analyzed you will provide a nomograph to cover Boyle's Law and absolute humidity."

"David, why do you always try to destroy the orderliness of my life? I operate on the theory that man is an intellectual animal in an orderly world and you keep demonstrating to me that I am in a most disorderly world and at times a most emotional creature. I am convinced that all problems can be reduced to mathematical formulae and you keep pleading for art and judgment. Well, I am right and it is possible to put into our computer a factor to recognize the effect of the weight of the air on the impact a wind of a given velocity will have on sails of given area, and, as you so sagely and destructively suggest, the temperature of the air affects its volume and so the weight of a given volume. I could also compute the weight of the water carried in air at a specific temperature and relative humidity. In fact, as I think about it, I can see a program to take readings of wet and dry bulb temperature and wind velocity and apply this to input from an expensive analysis of sail shape versus resistance of hull due to the bottom not being perfectly smooth and to each type of wave measured as to height and steepness. What you have implied is absolutely true. Precise tabulations without inclusion of all contributing factors are deceiving. The data for the program are no better than the observations used. And, if I may state your position more precisely for you, I would say that while tabulations of sail trim under varied conditions gives reference points for reaching optimum trim with minimum of false moves, in the final analysis, the art of the sailor will be the determining factor in the time it takes to reach a given point and perhaps in the pleasure of the passage."

David said, "One of the reasons I love you is because you are so polysyllabic. Another is because I like to watch your mind at work."

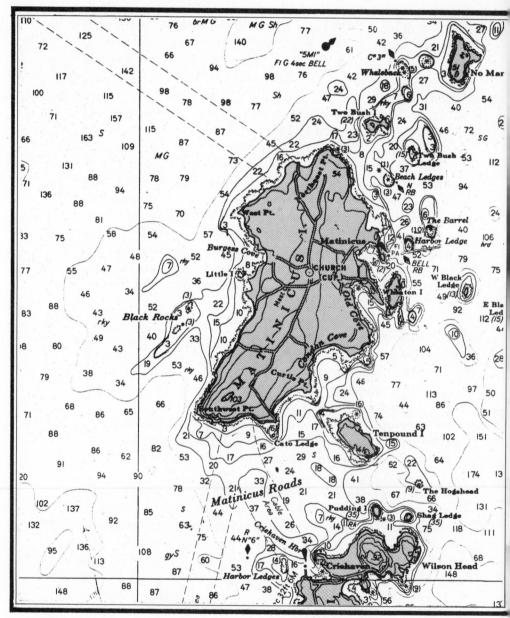

Matinicus

The Old Man interjected, "Aside from your philosophic discussion, I believe that what Big Ann has offered to tabulate may not be reducible to tabular form, but the discussion of the factors involved will always be a big help in clarifying our thinking and improving our art."

III

~~~~~~~~

Spinnakers

When we woke the wind was from the south, Force 2 and the weather report projected that it would veer and increase as the day went on. The temperature was expected to get into the 80s. The Old Man suggested that it would be a nice run to Burnt Coat Harbor and that it would be a good day for a fresh water swim in the quarry there. As it was the middle of the week the crowd would not be able to get there and we might even have it all to ourselves. The forecast was for fog tomorrow.

It looked like about a 30-mile run for the day, longer than usual and possibly less wind than we would like for a lot of the time. In other words we had better plan 6 hours under way and if we wanted to get that swim we better hit the track. We agreed that the time to go was right away. Get out and get going and clean up and have breakfast underway.

The #3 jib was bent on and hoisted and the main unfurled and ready to go. The mooring lines were cleared so that they would run freely and could be released from *Dancing Girl*. Lines 1, 2, and 4 were taken in. The jib was trimmed, the bow was pushed off, and we took a strain on line 3 to start us moving ahead. Ann held a fender aft to keep us from rubbing against the lobster boat. Once we started to move clear, line 3 was taken in, the main was hoisted and trimmed and we were on our way out of Matinicus Harbor at 0815. The mooring lines were all hanked and placed in the mooring line mesh bag which went back to its place in the port locker.

The Old Man gave me the wheel and took over the navigation while Ann and David handled the sails. From Matinicus Harbor Bell the course was 082 M to Whistle 10RB 12.1 miles away. When Can 5 was abeam we came to 096° to allow for the current. The wind made this a broad reach on starboard tack. Our speed was 3 knots. It was time for a change. With my okay, Ann ran forward and rigged the reaching strut and hung the starboard spinnaker guy in it. David went below and passed the spinnaker in its bag up to her through the forward hatch. She tied the bag on deck and rigged the pole, clipped on the fore guy which David slacked so that it would let the pole rise above the pulpit, rigged the topping lift and hauled it taut. The spinnaker was in its worm with its zipper forward. It was easy to bend on the halyard to weather of the jib, snap in the guy and take the sheet from the ring in the pulpit and attach it to the clew in front of the headstay. She then two-blocked the spinnaker while David trimmed the guy so that the pole was undertrimmed by about 30° but well clear of the headstay. The worm's zipper was forward and she secured the tie down tape to the mooring cleat.

Ann shouted, "Ready," David did the same and when I called "Break it out" Ann pulled the slide off the bottom of the zipper. As David trimmed the sheet the zipper fell open. When it had opened completely Ann gave the worm a tug to free the Velcro tape at the top and skillfully gathered the worm in her arms as it fell. She bundled it up and stuffed it in the bag which she then threw down the hatch. She then pressed the hatch shut. She lowered the Solent and secured it with one stop to the lower life line. She coiled the loose end of the spinnaker halyard and hung it from its cleat and came aft to tidy the lines in the cockpit as David trimmed the pole perpendicular to the wind. He went forward and adjusted the pole height so that the luff would break evenly along its length as I came up a little to test it.

The true wind had increased to Force 3 and our speed through the water had come up to 5.5 knots. The anemometer was still reading about 4 knots. The upper and lower luff telltales were streaming nicely. At David's suggestion Ann took over the cockpit and he went below to get breakfast started for all hands. The Old Man had been punching keys and figuring and now reported that the electronics were running a plot to second guess his dead reckoning position. The lobster pots around West Black Ledge and Mackerel Ledge suggested that we would probably have about 1.5 knots of northerly set on this leg and a quick sketch on the compass rose resulted in a change of course to 087°. Ann trimmed the sheet to get the luff on the verge of curling and then went forward to adjust the pole height to make the luff curl evenly over its length. The anemometer showed no change in apparent wind velocity but the speedometer came up to 5.7, on the average.

Ann was forward where she could see the chute easily and was tending the sheet by hand with two turns around the winch. She called to me, "Professor, please give me another turn on the winch. This wind is freshening.'"

The Old Man came up to join us in the cockpit and to enjoy the sparkling summer morning. At this point David gave each of us a large glass of freshly squeezed orange juice, remarking that this would be the only time we would live this high on the hog but he felt like using up the oranges while they were still store fresh. He then passed up a plate for each with two fried eggs, two pieces of bacon, and two pieces of toast which had been cooked in reverse order in one Silverstone fry pan. This was followed by a mug of coffee for each with utensils and paper napkins, butter and raspberry jam. He took the wheel to let me eat and Ann cleated the sheet so that she could enjoy her repast, David was sailing by the spinnaker, keeping the luff on the edge of the curl. The boat speed was staying around 5.7 and the anemometer was reading about the same. We were in the groove and the living was easy.

Ann finished eating first and took the wheel to let David get his breakfast and as soon as I finished I went below to wash the dishes and clean up in the galley. When I finished the chores I went on deck only to find that the wind had veered and we were having to steer 112° to stay at our best speed. I took the wheel while Big Ann trimmed the guy and eased the sheet so that we could go more down wind. When she had the pole back against the lower she eased the sheet while David went forward and adjusted the pole height to get the clews level. He then adjusted the topping lift while Ann handled the foreguy to make the pole perpendicular to the mast. By turning downwind we had reduced the relative wind to 5.4 and boat speed to 5.0. While Ann and David made the final adjustments on the spinnaker the wind backed and I adjusted our course to give us maximum VMG (Velocity made good to the next mark). The final result was that we were steering 088° with apparent wind and boat speed both at 5.5. There was nothing we could do to make the main more effective as it was already pushing against the spreader with the shelf fully extended and the vang as tight as the sail needed to make the leech stand well.

At 0900 when we had been underway 45 minutes, the Old Man took a fix with the hockey puck using the left tangent of Seal Island, Matinicus Rock Light, and the right tangent of No Man's Land. The depth finder could not touch bottom. Seal Island was coming up abeam to starboard but we would be about a mile closer to it than our intended track. We had made just short of 5.5 knots good during this time, the new course for Roaring Bull was 081° allowing for an estimated 1.5-knot current from the south and an average speed of 5.5 knots. We would get there faster by steering our optimum course of 088° to keep the sails working, jibing later when we were close to where we wanted to go. Actually the weather report promised that the winds would veer and strengthen as the day progressed which seemed to promise us a chance to jibe and possibly to go into some of the other downwind or reaching rigs.

The rule of thumb is that when going downwind the helmsman should head high enough to keep a steady strain on the sheet. To sail lower than that means that your spinnaker is ineffective. Using the compass rose it is easy to make a diagram showing the increase in speed necessary to justify a given number of degrees off course. It is easy when sailing to leeward once the sheet is developing a steady strain to come up a little bit at a time until the speed gained is not enough to justify sailing further off course.

Once this analysis has been made it is easy to sail the optimum course on each tack while tacking downwind to avoid

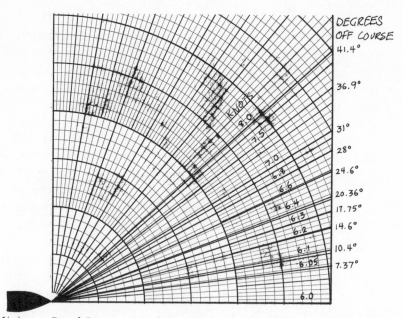

Minimum Speed Increase Needed to Maintain Speed Toward Goal with Various Degrees Off Course

getting too far off the mean course to destination. Today we were going to stay on starboard tack until port was the better for the buoy and then jibe.

For the moment there would be little to do. The sails were set in their optimum conformation and it was simply a case of the helmsman sailing the boat as far to port as possible with dropping the boat speed below the apparent wind velocity. The rest of the ship's company had only to stay out of the helmsman's line of vision to his gauges and to be available on short notice should a squall or other unexpected problem arise.

The Old Man said that as it was such a fine day it was sinful not to take advantage of it to air bedding. Ann and David volunteered and shook out each sleeping bag and clipped it to the lifeline. Then Ann got all the towels and washcloths and between them they pinned all of them to the lifeline.

David turned to me and grinned, "Let me know when you are thinking of broaching and I will get all my own stuff below while it is still dry."

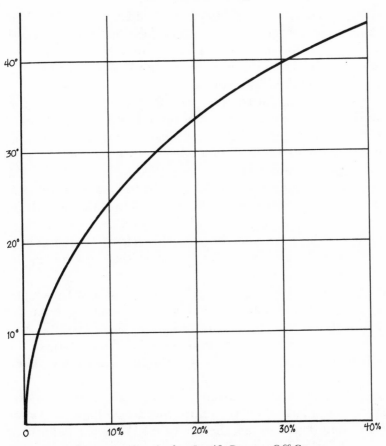

Percent Speed Increase Required to Justify Degrees Off Course

During the next hour the wind continued to veer and by 1000 when the Old Man cut us in again we were having to sail 108° in order to maintain the efficiency of the sails. The wind over the deck was 5.6 and the boat speed was about the same. The Old Man stuck his head up from the navigator's desk and said that our course was now 070° which meant that we had to jibe. "We will be able to make that I think on port tack."

He told me to keep the wheel; he would handle the cockpit. Ann and David ran forward. David raised the base of the pole to the mark on the mast that indicated the pole end would be able to swing back and forth freely without catching on the headstay or the jib. He then lowered the topping

lift to let the pole pass under the headstay. The Old Man
hauled the foreguy taut to keep the pole under control.
Dancing Girl does not use a lazy sheet or lazy guy because we
all seem to feel that the extra lines complicate more than they
help in the limited space on our foredeck.

Ann shouted, "Slack the guy," and the pole swung forward. She released the guy from the pole and shouted "Clear."
The Old Man trimmed the new sheet as Ann swung the pole
across and clipped in the old sheet which became the guy.
The new guy was trimmed. I shouted, "Jibe-Oh," and the
Old Man swung around and trimmed the main flat as I put
the wheel over. He then let the sheet out till the sail was on
the spreader but not on the spreader end, and went back to
adjusting the sheet and the guy while David set the pole at
the proper height. We never lost more than .2 knots in the
course of the maneuver.

"You know, Old Man," I said, "when you and I do a jibe
with just two of us aboard I am not sure it is that much harder
than with four the way we just did it. As I analyze it, Big Ann
is not tall enough or strong enough to handle the base of the
pole on the mast, because the word slide is a misnomer when
the pole is under any kind of compression. The tackle does
not give any mechanical advantage so the slide is hard to move.
David could have done the entire foredeck job just as you or
I do when there are just the two of us. When the helmsman
has to handle the spinnaker sheets and the main sheet and
the jib he is pretty busy and it is my recollection that more
often than not the foredeck man has to run aft to take care
of the last part of the trimming of each sheet before taking
care of the pole height.

"Looking at today's jibe I would like to suggest that next
time we jibe the chute David take care of the entire foredeck
and Ann come back and help in the cockpit where I thought
there was room for improvement. I have never seen a spinnaker jibe that I did not think could be made safer and more
efficient by more speed and precision. To me any spinnaker
that is not full and drawing always looks like an accident up
in stops. Once the pole height is adjusted both at the inboard
and outboard ends then the foredeck job calls for one fast
strong person to move the pole from one guy to the other.

Once that has been done the key action is in the cockpit getting the sheets adjusted and the main jibed."

The others talked about their own jobs briefly but all agreed that we should try the proposed system on the next jibe. Big Ann added, "The trouble with most spinnaker work on cruising boats and a lot of racing boats, too, is that the crew waddles around like they were at an old folks picnic. There are very few foul-ups and disasters that could not have been prevented by more precise crew work."

David muttered, "Slavedriver! But unfortunately you are right."

At 1015 the Old Man sighted the 10RB whistle buoy bearing 068°, slightly on our port bow. As usual, the fact that his eyes were not as good as they had been in earlier days was more than offset by the fact that his eyes had had so much practice looking for navigational aids he could find marks well before those with younger and better vision.

Five minutes later it was still 068°, but the wind was veering and we were having to adjust our sails in order to get better performance on our course. The bearing continued steady, and as the true wind continued to veer the apparent wind increased to 6 knots and our speed did the same. The telltales on the spinnaker were steadying down now and streaming making it easier for Ann and David to maintain ideal sail shape. The halyard was two-blocked for we had finally decided a year ago that we really did not gain any appreciable speed by easing it out to put the head of the sail out where it would avoid some of the main's backwind. That was a good theory but it did not work for us and it did create a problem by oscillating first to one side and then the other making the boat hard to steer and more anxious to broach.

At 1035 the buoy came alongside and we could see that the current was between 1 and 1.5 knots, not a full 1.5 The navigator told me to come left to 053° to head for buoy 2A off Colt Ledge remarking that it was about 5.3 miles and that he was counting on about a knot of current behind us. Our apparent wind came forward to 330° M, but the true wind was 290° M. The guy was trimmed to put the pole 015° M 322 relative.

The spinnaker sheet was under the boom to give more

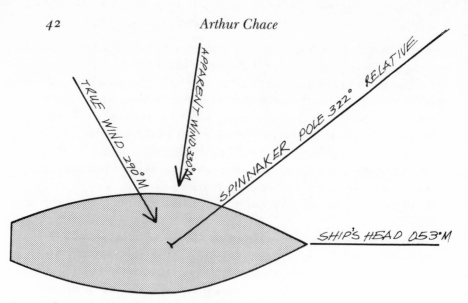

True and Apparent Wind When Reaching

fullness and power and the pole was lowered to make sure the upper and lower luff telltales were lifting evenly. The main had to come in a little to get its telltales streaming and now was off the spreader. The vang tension had been adjusted so that the top batten was kicked slightly to windward of the boom. Until the flow can definitely be established on the lee side of of the main it is best to try for a slightly closed leech. When sailing off the wind drag is not the enemy that it is upwind. *Dancing Girl* worked her speed up and the apparent wind moved forward. The luff of the chute was on the edge of a curl. David was hand tending the sheet with three turns on the winch. Ann was on the winch handle to give him support when the sheet had to come in. The speedometer showed 6.7. The apparent wind was 15 knots from 80° relative. The pole was 20° over square. I was using about 4° of rudder.

David gave the sheet to the Old Man and went to the mast and assisted by a sudden short slacking of the sheet was able to move the base of the pole a foot and a half up the slide on the mast. He trimmed the topping lift as the foreguy was eased by Ann until the pole and the clews were level and the luff was perfect. The main had to come in a little more and the vang eased to keep the telltale on the top batten stream-

ing. Ann called, "6.8. Let's get 6.9!" I was still using only 5°
of rudder and the feeling of graceful power began to domi-
nate the boat.

Ann said she wished she had a staysail and the Old Man
told her that if the wind came forward a little more we would
be able to set the Solent and get a tenth or two extra speed.
He went on, "I used to carry a staysail because I really enjoyed
fooling with the sail as much as I enjoyed the extra tenth of
a knot it gave me, but I got to figuring how many times we
had to throw that bagged sail around and how infrequently
the wind would permit us to use it. I decided not to bring it
this cruise. At this moment my thinking is that although I
would not buy a staysail for a cruising boat, I will carry it next
year seeing that I already have it. Once several years ago on
a reach we were able to carry both the Solent and the staysail
under the spinnaker in fairly light air and by so doing we
were able to drive over a 45 footer that just had a simple
spinnaker and mainsail rig. Remembering an incident like
that gives me pleasure over a fairly long period of time. I like
to see *Dancing Girl* do her best. Now that we can rig an inner
forestay and set the storm jib on it, we also have the capability
of setting a working staysail there which is a great rig for
mooring, anchoring and maneuvering in close quarters."

At 1100 with Bell #2 at Roaring Bull Ledge abeam to port
about a mile and a half away, the Old Man cut us in using
the left tangent of Western Ear, and the right tangents of
Eastern Ear and Great Spoon Island. We were on course with
2.4 miles to the nun at Colt Ledge. The apparent wind backed
about 10° and the pole had to be brought back 5°. The velocity had been dropping and was at 11 knots with the speedometer reading 6.0. By 1115 the apparent wind had moved
forward to 070° relative and the pole had had to come forward 10°. The wind velocity was averaging about 9.2 and the
pole had been brought down about 8 inches. Although the
water was a little calmer our speed through the water was
down to 5.6 knots.

At 1132 the buoy was abeam and on instructions from the
navigator we came to 047° to take us between Cod Ledge and
the Lower Head of Marshall Island. The wind angle was about
065° relative. The pole was brought to within 5 inches of the

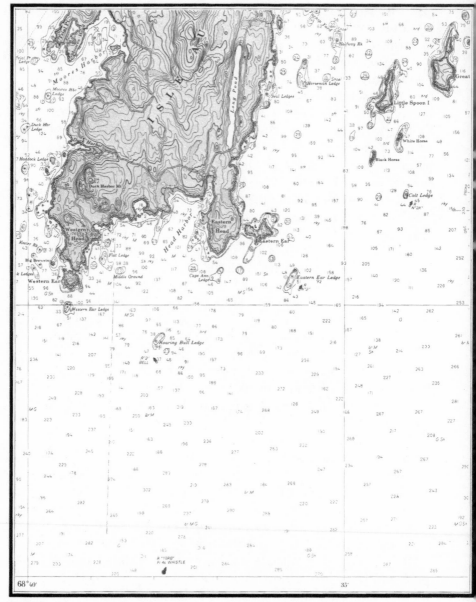

Middle Portion of Run from Matinicus to Burnt Coat Harbor

forestay and down to within 18 inches of the pulpit, setting the tack about 3 inches below the clew. The mainsheet and vang were adjusted to give a nice flow of air over the main's windward and leeward telltales with maximum fullness and

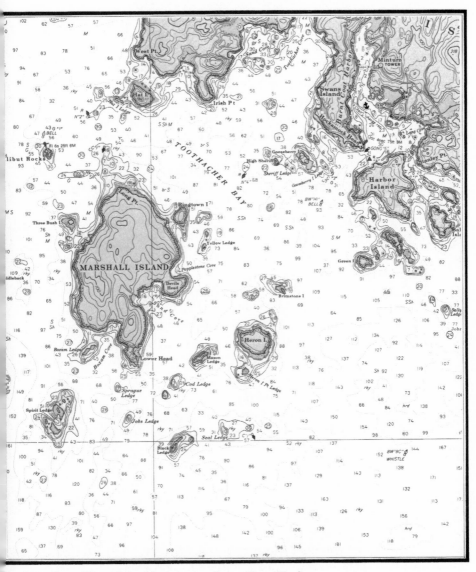

inal Portion of Run from Matinicus to Burnt Coat Harbor

about 5° of rudder. With the Old Man's permission Big Ann ran forward, took the stop off the Solent and hoisted it while David trimmed the sheet. I watched the speedometer and after everything had settled down reported that we have gained 0.15 knots.

The wind had become quite variable. Ann rigged a twing

on the spinnaker sheet using a block hooked to the stanchion base at the chains. She sat in the cockpit with her feet braced so that she could haul down the sheet whenever the chute became unstable. The jib sheet had to be eased to give the chute all available air at the same time. Ann and David worked together like clockwork, maintaining perfect sail shape. The wind became increasingly weak and variable so that for more and more of the time the jib was hurting more than it was helping.

David spoke up, "Captain, I've never seen your new pole-less spinnaker in use. Is it true that we can carry it about with the wind 10° further forward than the spinnaker?"

The Old Man nodded.

David said, "Lets try it."

"Sure. Go ahead. I love the challenge of making a spinnaker work well, but because we do a lot of sailing with only two aboard, there are occasions when the poleless makes sense even for a traditionalist. There is also the fact that in sloppy conditions this sail is a lot more controllable and more forgiving than a true spinnaker. I think you will find it interesting. Go ahead."

"If you will handle the cockpit, Captain, Ann and I will go forward and make the change."

"Great! Let's go," said Ann, starting toward the bow.

David went below as Ann cleared the spinnaker halyard and the take-down line. The new sail in its bag came up the forward hatch followed by David's head. He handed the sail to Ann and she handed him the takedown line and took the sail in its bag and clipped it to the lifeline. She went to the mast and uncleated the spinnaker halyard and after making sure the sheet stopper was closed to hold the halyard, took the turns off the winch and shouted, "Ready." The Old Man and David shouted in unison, "Ready," and I shouted, "Drop it." Ann opened the stopper, releasing the halyard, and David brought in the belly line and the spinnaker with flailing arms, stuffing all down the hatch in front of him.

When all free sail was safe in the cabin out of the breeze the Old Man eased the sheet and guy. Ann removed them from the chute and clipped them together as she stuffed the chute below. The Old Man centered the sheets at the forestay by trimming the former guy and easing the sheet. David came up the hatch with the halyard which he handed to Ann who clipped it, outside the Solent, to the head of the new sail, which was rigged in its sock. David then went to the spinnaker halyard and hoisted as Ann took the foreguy behind the jib and attached it to the new sail's tack. She went to the cockpit and rigged the foreguy to put the tack 4 feet above the stem. She unclipped the two spinnaker sheets and clipped the weather one to the bullnose ring and the leeward to the clew of the Gennaker. David dropped the jib as Ann hoisted the Snuffer up off the Gennaker. The Old Man trimmed the sheet as fast as the sail emerged from its sock.

While David tidied up the lines at the base of the mast, Ann stopped the jib to the lower lifeline and then watched how the sail was drawing. "David," she said, "in these conditions I think this sail would be more forgiving and pull a better if we moved the draft forward a little bit. Why don't you ease the halyard about a foot and then come up here and see if we can get the foot about 12 inches lower without having to let the sail luff. When we do it I want to put the upper tackline snap on the headstay to keep the sail from sagging off the leeward. Sag increases weather helm and gives more side force relative to forward force."

David agreed and by applying their joint strength effectively, they were able to get the tack snapped to the headstay just about 3 feet off the deck. David then winched the halyard taut enough to move the draft to what we agreed was 40 percent. The Old Man tried various positions for the sheet block on the tow rail and finally settled for having the genoa car on the tow rail about 6 inches forward of the heel blocks.

We were using about 5° of rudder and the apparent wind was 60° off the port bow averaging about 8 knots. The speedometer was running around 4.8. The main had the full shelf and was being trimmed to keep the telltales streaming on both sides of the sail. The draft was at 50 percent. I asked if any one else would like a turn at the wheel and Big Ann lept at the chance.

When she relieved me I eased the vang about 3 inches to further ease the leech and Ann reported that the wheel could keep us on course with 6° of rudder. To get the precise setting we eased the boom off to leeward until there was a slight bubble of backwind at the luff and then retrimmed just enough to remove it. By using more vang we were able to get the main further to leeward without having it backwinded. Although more helm is acceptable when reaching than beating, it is amazing to me that experienced cruising people who are good seamen will happily bob along with their mainsail acting as a big aerial rudder set to give them a lot of unnecessary weather helm which the rudder has to offset, knocking 20 percent off their boat's natural speed in the process. You do not have to be racing to enjoy getting into port an hour earlier or increasing your cruising radius by 5 miles or so without increasing your time under way. Besides steering the boat is a lot more pleasant when you are not having to fight an unnecessary weather helm. With a modern tall masthead rig so much of the propulsion comes from the headsails that the main is sort of a chameleon—first of all it is a rudder, then it increases the efficiency of the headsail slot and only then does it contribute to the boat's drive and speed through the water.

Dancing Girl was sliding along extracting every bit of propulsion available in the wind. The helmsman was beaming as she guided us through the wind shifts. The sails were trimmed as well as we could do it and it was more efficient to change our heading slightly back and forth to meet conditions and average our course than to be constantly fiddling with the sails in hopes of maintaining optimum speed while staying exactly on course.

A day like this provides daydreams to carry you through the winter. The fir-covered islands and islets, the rocks and ledges, like great dozing sea animals awash and seeming to rise and fall in the swell, the blue summer sky accented with clouds, all provided the setting for *Dancing Girl*'s graceful progress. We silently soaked up the scene.

At 1220 the navigator noted that we were sailing up the range created by the right tangents of Devil's Head and Lower Head. The depth finder confirmed that we were coming up between Spirit Ledge and Black Ledge, pretty groupings of rocks and islets which could be the jaws of death in a fog or storm. At 1234 Job's Ledge, barely disturbing the pattern of the waves today, passed 200 yards to leeward. The navigator called for a course change to 062° stating that this would have us heading for the entrance to Burnt Coat and requesting that as soon as we could identify the abandoned lighthouse on Hockamock Head to let him know. He planned to have us steer for it if the bearing was right. We eased the traveler and took in the vang so that sail shape would not change as the boom went out. We eased the Gennaker sheet and moved the block forward a foot to eliminate twist as we came to the new course.

David ducked below to get lunch. In a few minutes he sent up three bowls of jellied madrilene, a screw-top plastic box full of crisp saltines, a pitcher of iced tea, plates, utensils, and a bowl of shrimp salad. Stating that he had eaten his soup so that it would not melt, he relieved Big Ann on the wheel. It is my theory that the first and most important sign of civilization is when people have come to the point where they eat their meals indoors. I consider it barbarous to eat in the open air with the wind blowing the food off your plate, but this time it was pleasant to enjoy our surroundings while we ate. As usual Ann was the first to finish and relieved David to eat. I was next and went below to clean up. Because we were out in open water I was able to use the salt water pump to rinse everything before washing and by the time David had finished eating, the galley was picked up and clean except for the dishwashing which only took a moment with hot soapy water and a rinse in fresh. Everything was left to dry in the rack.

At 1250 Ann reported sighting the old lighthouse 5° on the port bow and the navigator, mumbling how damnedly unpredictable the currents are in these waters, told her to steer for it and then touched up the sail trim as she did. A few minutes later she reported she was being set to weather and came to starboard until she got the bearing steady. Trim was again adjusted to the apparent wind. The Old Man kept cutting us in, hoping to build up in his log some understanding of the currents in this area to be of assistance some foggy day in the future. At 1300 the navigator sighted the black and white bell, "HI," 3° on the starboard bow and told the helm to steer for it. David touched the sheets but there was not much he could do to improve our trim.

At 1316 the buoy was abeam and we headed for Gong 3 at the mouth of the harbor. Old Man said we would anchor so David brought the two Danforths up and made them ready to let go. When we were two boat lengths from the gong David and I ran forward. While he freed the jib halyard I took the stop off the the #3. I grabbed the snuffer line, freed the Gennaker tack and hauled down the Snuffer over the sail. He raised the jib. Old Man slacked the Gennaker sheet as I got my hand on it and I brought the sail in its sock inside the jib. He had trimmed the jib as soon as David had it two-blocked. David let go the spinnaker halyard and the Gennaker came down. I unclipped the halyard and secured it to its ring in the pulpit. I unclipped the spinnaker starboard sheet and took it forward under the jib, and clipped it and the port sheet to the ring in the pulpit. I stuffed the Snuffer in its bag and dropped it through the forward hatch. I followed it through and neated up the sail stowage in the forward compartment.

David was tidying up around the mast and we both returned to the cockpit at the same time. The Old Man had trimmed the traveler one position below centerline and had brought the Solent in so that it had practically no twist. David had hoisted it so that the draft was about 43 percent. I hauled down the cunningham to keep the main at about 50 percent. The apparent wind was 5 knots. Our speed was just under 3 knots. David went forward to tend to the anchors. The Old Man took the wheel and Ann went forward to take care of the halyards at the mast. I was ready to handle the sheets in the cockpit. We were hard on the wind now standing up the channel but the wind was soft and fluky. The captain found an uncrowded spot to the right side of the channel. I was watching the depth finder which was swung into the companionway so that the Old Man could see it. He tacked and, as planned, came around 20° too far. The starboard anchor was let go and after we had run a boat length the boat was brought up hard on the wind. The depth finder had indicated we would have 8 feet at low water and David paid out rode. When 80 feet was out he cleated it and the anchor grabbed, spinning the boat about onto port tack. We let go the port anchor. Again we came 20° past our desired course to get the rode clear of the hull and then headed back to the first anchor. David was taking in the starboard rode fast enough to keep it from getting slack and Ann helped him keep the port rode running free.

When 80 feet were veered to port, Ann cleated that rode and the boat snapped around into the wind. David cleated the starboard rode. Ann dropped the jib and the main which David and I furled. After the boat had settled down we eased the anchor rodes so that they formed an angle of 60° with each other and secured them. The navigator then took a round of bearings and logged them and read the depthfinder and converted the reading to maximum ebb and logged it also. We took all possible halyards and clipped their hoist ends to stanchion bases so they could not slap the mast. We then rigged gilguys to hold the other ends off the mast and did the same with the flag halyards, giving some assurance that a change of wind during the night would not start our mast ringing like New Year's in Italy. A check around the boat showed that all was shipshape for the night and we were ready for our drink to set the anchor.

IV

~~~~~~~~~~~~~~~

First Team

We had spent the night anchored in Stickland Cove in Roti Bay on the south coast of Newfoundland. We all had a before-breakfast swim in the 55-degree water and felt very worthy and somewhat exhilarated. David felt inspired and produced Bakeapple berries with *Crème super sterilisé* (heavy cream, which we had obtained in Saint Pierre, sealed in regular cartons but sterilized at high pressure and high temperature so that it will keep for months without refrigeration if it remains sealed) and stacks of french toast, dusted with cinnamon, with real maple syrup and lots of slow-fried bacon.

There were only a few scattered high cirrus clouds and the wind was on the light side so we spent the morning airing bedding, doing laundry in buckets, and having a general field day below. We agreed on an early lunch and David was able to make a salad based on the small amount of fresh salmon left over from the poached grilse we had had for the previous night's dinner. When he presented it with a dressing of mayonnaise with chopped chives and dill garnished with sliced hard-boiled eggs it earned him enthusiastic praise from us all. Iced tea with fresh mint was the beverage and we consumed a lot of it.

"The weather charts look pretty good for the next three days," said the Old Man. "I think we can see some pretty

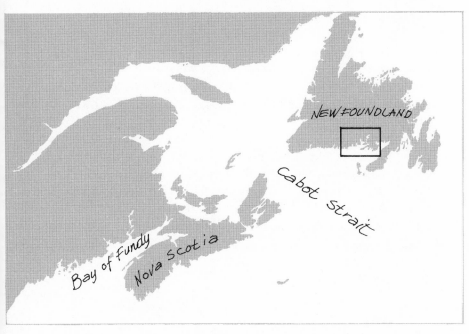

exciting scenery if we go through Lampidoes Passage to Pushthrough today and then do some of those bays to the west of here in the next few days. The wind will be on the nose today but we will be in sheltered waters. I think we will have some fun with the 3.7 #1. After all we have the first team aboard. You might all like to to take a look at the chart. I have plotted the courses."

It *was* going to be fun, but we should do it well. We bent on the #1 and rigged the foreguy as a tacking line. We ran the sheets inside the lifelines to blocks in the #2 position on the 8° track and then stopped the sail to the upper life line out of the way of the anchors. We put the flattening reef in the main, bent on the halyard and hooked it under the spare jib halyard winch. We put 3,800 pounds on the backstay. All the idle sails were stowed in their places in the forward cabin and the anchor mats were ready on the forward bunks.

When the bunks and locker tops were all bolted in and the necessary seacocks closed for sea the Old Man took the wheel. I was ready in the cockpit. When Ann and David were ready forward the Old Man said, "Let's hoist the main."

It practically shot up. While Ann secured the halyard David went forward saying, "Which anchor first?"

The Old Man said, "Port. I will want to get off on starboard tack to get out of here."

As we swung over to port tack David uncleated the port anchor rode, I trimmed the sheet, David brought in the rode as fast as he could, actually pulling the boat ahead. Ann eased the starboard rode just enough to keep strain off it. We were going 2 knots when we went over the port anchor which David had up and down and cleated. David sang out "Up and down. . . . Broken ground. . . . In sight. Dirty." He gave it a couple of quick shakes and then took the starboard rode from Ann who had been gathering it in as the Old Man headed for it. She took over the cleaning of the port. David had caught up and had the starboard up and down, cleated, as *Dancing Girl* passed over it.

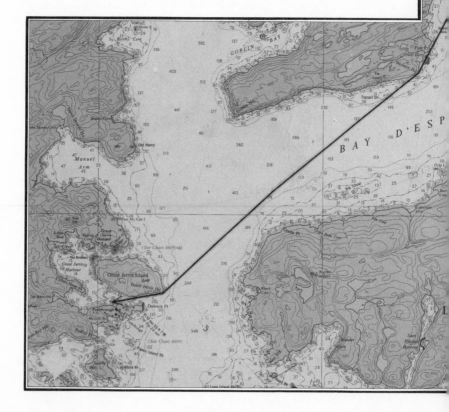

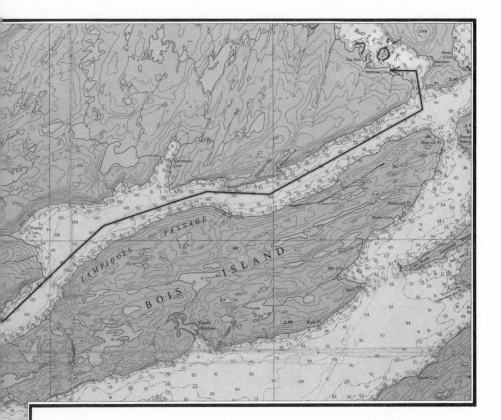

"Broken ground," shouted David, turning to finish washing off the port anchor, while Ann worked on the starboard. Her small size made her less effective than David at this phase of the anchor detail. His next shout was "On deck." I eased the sheet to keep our speed below 2 knots as he shook and swung the other anchor to get the mud off. "On deck," he shouted and I trimmed in the main. He pulled the stop from the jib and went to the mast as Ann stowed the anchor rodes in their bags.

"Ready for the jib?"

"Ready!" replied the Old Man.

"Going up! . . . Two-blocked," sang out David as he put the winch handle in for the last 3 inches of adjustment. Ann tailed for him, cleating the halyard at the middle mark.

He ran aft to the cockpit while Ann finished making up the anchor rodes in their bags, stowed all ground tackle below on their pads and then tidied up the foredeck and mast area. David ground while I tailed as we got the genoa in 4 inches off the spreader end. The new 4-inch marks on the spreader ends did make it easier to judge that distance. With the block on the 8° track the jib looked perfect when the sheet was trimmed this way.

"Ann!" the Old Man shouted. "Ease the jib halyard an inch. The water is calm enough to let us have the draft at 47 percent. On your way aft ease the main halyard a couple of inches. The draft is a little farther forward than we will need. Then take in the flattening reef all the way. I think we can use a pretty precise sail shape today. David move the traveler up another 2 inches and ease the main if you have to to get the boom on the center line. I would like the backstay at 3,800 for now. Check to see that the top batten is parallel to the boom.

"When you all are ready," he went on, "I would like to try a couple of tacks to see how it goes. We are going to be beating through the passage and the wind will be a bit stronger in there, perhaps 16 knots. I'll sail the boat and Professor, will you navigate? Navigation will be mostly depth finder, so I think you'll be busy with that and calling boat speed.

"David, you grind and I think that you will be able to release the old sheet and handle the tacking line also. Ann, you will move the traveler across, take in the new sheet until David is through with the tacking line, and tail and call the jib. Let's try it that way and see how it works. We can change if someone has a better idea. I will try to steer and watch the gauges but will depend on Ann to call the jib. Coordination between the tailer, grinder, and the helm will be the answer to keeping the speed up. I think we all know each other and the boat well enough to make this a first-class operation."

Ann thought for a couple of moments and said, "Captain,

as I see it, the Professor will be working his magic and watching the depth finder. At the crucial moment he will shout, 'Time to tack!' and by your plan stand by to ease the jib sheet as you come down 10° to get that extra speed going into the tack. I am in position to handle the sheet more easily than he. You will shout 'Ready about!' when you come down and 'Hard alee!' when you are up to speed. The man who releases the old sheet should winch it in enough as we come up to keep it drawing as long as possible and then let it go, cleared to run, when it starts to luff. I think I should be that man rather than the Professor because I can do it and stay out of the way of the big muscles and then swing facing aft and move the traveler over as soon as it is unloaded and be in position to take in the slack on the new jib sheet as it is available. My powerful friend, David, can bring the tacking line in fast enough to avoid any wear on the sail and swing around, grab the winch handle and start grinding as I start to slow down bringing the sheet in. I can call the jib as David gets it in and I think I can give the speed a look when the foot is 2 inches off the shrouds and call our speed and again when the sail is 6 inches off the spreader end. I will try to call the speed for everyone to hear and the jib for David as the Old Man eases her up into the groove. If we work together we can trim so we produce maximum acceleration as the speed increases and we get hard on the wind."

We all agreed that that sounded more complicated than it was and the Old Man said, "Let's try it Ann's way. Professor, get down in your hole and make out you're reading the tea leaves. The rest of you get set up the way we would be beating in close quarters. Is everybody set? Okay. Let's go!"

I started calling the depths as I would be doing closing a shore fast. After a moment I came up and stood in the companionway shouting, "Time to tack."

"Ready about!" shouted the helm.

"Six-four. Ready!" from Big Ann. The others called "Ready."

"Six-four, 6.5, 6.5, 6.5," intoned Ann.

"Hard alee!"

David only needed to take one full turn at high speed on the winch before Ann called, "Five-eight, stop trimming, 6.0, trim, 6.4, we are coming up now. Trim! trim! Another inch,

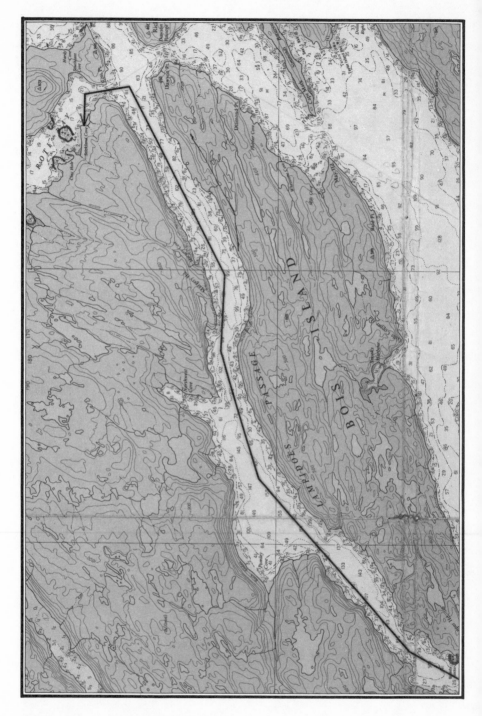

Stickland Cove and Lampidoes Passage

David. Six-five, 6.4, 6.4. Beautiful. Skipper, it would be hard to beat that helmsmanship."

"I thought it went well. Let's get back on starboard and see how it goes."

It went equally well and although the wind had turned to follow the channel into Roti Bay we were going to make it on starboard tack. As we beat our way into Lampedoes Passage the wind veered and we kept working up. With a delicate touch on the helm we were staying in the narrow groove making just over 6 knots with *Dancing Girl* really clawing up to weather. The wind was varying but the O. M. was staying with it and the water was calm. The apparent wind velocity was over 19 more often than not. After we passed Roti Point we were making 217° magnetic most of the time.

The Old Man and I agreed that although the chart showed good water up to the cliffs we would tack at 10 fathoms. There were occasional lifts and headers but we were making 220° when we approached the South Bank. I called time to tack at 15 fathoms the first time because the bank seemed awful close and there was a spot with 9 feet on the chart right against the cliff. This was pretty lonely country for taking a chance of hanging up on any rock, charted or not. Our speed did not drop below 5.8 in the tack and when we were back on the wind we were making 290°. We had almost a mile to go on this tack and and we were headed for a place where the bank went almost straight up to 500 feet, a circumstance that seemed to shorten the distance to it dramatically. This time I was timid and called for the tack at 20 fathoms and I noticed that the Old Man was quick to call, "Hard alee."

After we were squared away on the new tack Ann was equally quick to point out that our speed had dropped to 5.4 because we had not gotten all the extra speed we should have going into the tack. "It is better to tack early enough so that we can do it right," was her point. This was a short leg and we were somewhat headed to boot. We could do no better than 212° on this leg but if this direction held, after our next tack we would be able to go for four miles on 282° before we had to tack to stay off the wall. The wind was not steady and Ann and David were hand-tending the jib sheet and traveler to keep perfect trim as the helm tried to keep us in the groove.

The apparent wind velocity was climbing to 21 knots in the gusts and the Old Man was feathering up to keep our speed up without letting us be overpowered.

We were nevertheless headed and when the depth was down to 15 fathoms the old man said, "That land looks too damned close when I look at it under the boom. Ready about!" We shouted ready almost in unison and the tack went well. Our speed did not go below 5.8. Once we were squared away on starboard tack, I urged everyone to take a look at the dramatic headland that had forced us about. I pointed out that there was a pond on top of it to which I hoped to climb some day. "Maybe there are some trout in that pond waiting for me," I said.

Starboard was a short leg and we had to tack over to port in 2 minutes to stay out of the hard water. This time we would be able to go for 2½ miles before we ran out of water. Ann and David acknowledged that they would not be unhappy at having better than 20 minutes to rest and look around. Handling the boat was good exercise and great fun, but at times it seemed a shame that we had so little time to soak up the scenery. The geology in the passage was dramatic and it was interesting to try to imagine what the earth looked like while that cut was being formed. I noted silently that we had never had the courage to go all the way in to 10 fathoms as we had planned, but we had been close enough to toss a potato on the bank any time we tacked.

We went well into Pomley Cove headed for the dramatic rockslide area, but I worried that perhaps some recent slide might have fouled the shore since the last survey. I called for the tack at 15 fathoms and then we had 11 minutes before we would be forced back to port tack. After that it was a series of quick tacks, the longest being a 5-minute run on port into Poole Cove. There were a number of occasions when by the time we were squared away I returned to my chart just in time to call, "Time to tack." Once the Old Man suggested I not take us in so close to a rock pile. *Dancing Girl* was beautiful, racing like a greyhound in an open field and we were all having a lot of having a lot of fun and excitement with our exercise.

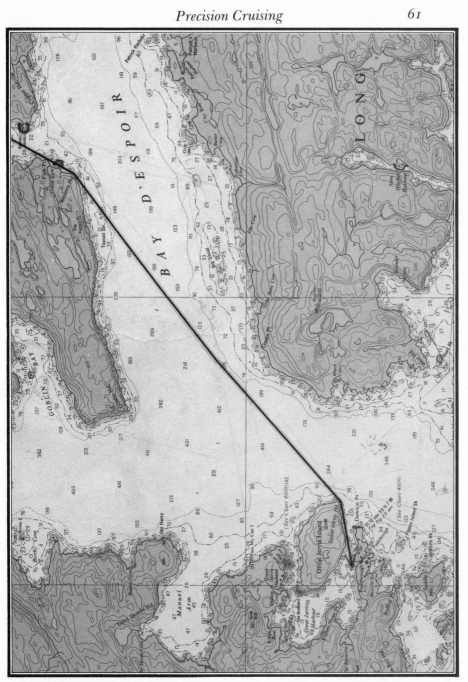

Western Head to Great Jervis Harbour

When we finally reached the open waters of Bay Despoir, however, no one was sorry.

The wind was playing around 21 knots and the Old Man reminded us that the 3.7 had to come down at 22. Ann volunteered and went below and brought the Solent up through the forward hatch. She rigged the sheets on the 9° track and hanked it on the headstay below the #1. She stopped it to the lower lifeline along the starboard bow where it would be ready, but out of the wind. After a quick check we single reefed the main and although we still carried quite a luff in it our speed went up a tenth of a knot. Careful feathering in the puffs kept the angle of heel about 23°. The helmsman was using 4° of rudder most of the time. The wind never got to 22 but the outcome was in doubt for the next hour as though the wind was maliciously keeping us in suspense.

Starboard tack took 20 minutes and then we beat for 45 minutes toward Pass My Can Island. We never go there though because there was no point in going so far that a wind shift could force us to ease our sheets to clear Great Jervis Head. As we headed south of Great Jervis Island for Pushthrough the apparent wind softened to 17 knots. We shook out the reef and we moved the draft of the jib to 47 percent. As we got in the lee of the land the last sailing was in light air. We eased halyards and sheets to maintain sail shape and finally released the cunningham and the flattening reef. Toward the last the wind was so soft that we had to move the traveler 4 inches to leeward and ease sheets to get enough power to maintain optimum speed.

The tide was an hour short of dead low when we rounded up off the remains of the Government Wharf at Pushthrough. We started the engine secured the mainsheet amidships and trimmed the starboard jib sheet tight. Ann let go both halyards and I kept the jib on deck and out of the water. David folded the main as it dropped and starting at the clew put five long stops around it making almost as small a bundle as an old-fashioned harbor furl. I quoted to David the old lines of unknown origin, "My Daddy told me if you made a furl tight enough you wouldn't need stops to hold it. Never saw him do it, though."

I folded the #1 in its sausage. It is soft enough to furl and we did furl it when the occasion demanded. Folding puts a lot fewer creases in the sail and is a lot easier on these modern sails with their coatings and laminations. It really does not take that much longer. With the hanks we could leave it bent on the headstay and under control as we bagged it. When the sail was secure and the sausage zipped up over it, we used the halyard to hoist the after end of the package up the headstay out of the way.

Ann was in the pulpit with Polaroid glasses because we had considerable doubt as to the chart's accuracy. She had a leadline in its sack on the bow where she could get it if needed, but the water was so clear that eyes were better. I had the depth finder running and a hockey puck around my neck in case there was any need to take a bearing on anything. The skipper said we would be going alongside the wrecked dock port side to, headed out. We hung the fender board on two fenders amidships and got the big fender out to be ready if needed. We rigged the bow and stern lines ready to go over as breasts and ran a forward- and an after-spring out through the eye on the forward genoa car which was pinned amidships. Although the wharf's concrete surface was canted at a slight angle the pilings all seemed to be in place though somewhat out of plumb. We came in slowly at an angle and at the last moment the skipper gave it right full rudder and backed it down hard. As the boat stopped he gave it a hard jounce ahead with full engine and then backed again. *Dancing Girl* twisted up against the dock, putting the fender board against two pilings. No need to use the after spring to warp in this time. David got over with the lines and arranged so that each went around a bollard or cleat or through a ring and back to the boat. Now we could tend each from on board and if we wanted to get out in a hurry we would be able to do so.

Ann and David went ashore for a short walk and returned with a hatful of raspberries for supper and a report that there was little trace of the once active outport that had justified the government building what must have been a rather impressive wharf, suggesting an active fishing operation. David set a batch of brownies baking in a covered frying pan on top of the stove using a Flametamer to prevent burning them on the bottom. The Old Man had lit the charcoal in the cabin stove and the cabin lamps were lit. The bottle of 151-proof rum from Saint Pierre appeared on the table with the last of the smoked salmon and a very sharp knife, capers, a pepper grinder, and half a lemon. Making melba toast was beyond the limited capacity of our stove but we had a box of Devonshire melba toast which served quite well. While we entranced ourselves with light chitchat and increasingly brilliant conversation, the cabin became redolent with the curried shrimp David was cooking for dinner. A really great day was going to end with an appropriately great meal.

V

Duo

Dancing Girl had arrived at Handy Boat Service in Falmouth Foreside, Maine, in the early afternoon in time for the departing crew to get a taxi and catch their plane and for the Old Man to arrange for the resident electronic swami to come aboard to check out and correct some excessive noisiness in the VHF. I had phoned for a taxi, picked up a great wad of mail waiting for us at General Delivery at the post office and had gone to Shaw's Supermarket and purchased all the provisions we would need for the next five days. While I was shopping O. M. had filled us up on water, ice, diesel, and stove alcohol and had had the yard do the 50-hour lube oil change which had just come due. We had all the necessary equipment but it is a lot easier to let some flexible young man squeeze himself in alongside the engine and make the filter change.

We were assigned a mooring for the night and at supper feasted on a salad featuring Shaw's justly famous fresh crabmeat washed down with a nice little Chablis I had picked up on my shopping trip. Fresh french bread and the first Concord grapes of the season completed the meal and afterward we sat at the table with brandy and coffee contemplating the unmitigated hardships of the sailor's life. The next crew was not due for four days and the two of us planned to spend the

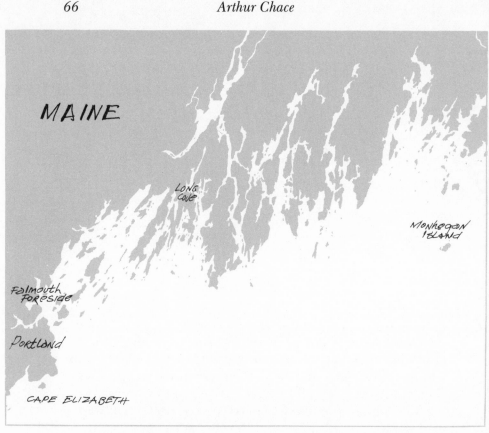

time catching up on reading and paper work in Long Cove on Orr's Island. A study of Chart 315 suggested that it would be a pleasant sail to pass between N"18" and Littlejohn Island, go around Chebeague Point and then between Haskell and Little Mark Islands into Mericoneag and Harpswell Sounds, finally rounding Dog's Head and feeling our way into the cove. Neither of us had been there but the chart looked as though it might be attractive and it received favorable mention in the *Cruising Guide to the New England Coast*.

In the morning the barometer was 29.91 rising slowly, the wet bulb temperature 53 and the dry 63, indicating a dew point of 45. As the water temperature was 56 there seemed little risk of fog. It was a beautiful clear sparkling day and the NOAA weather announcer was almost poetic in his praises and lyric in his optimism for the next few days. The water

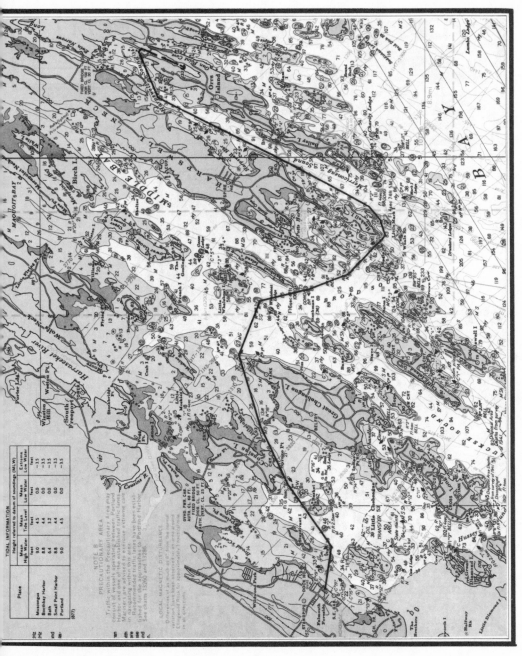

asco Bay—Falmouth Foreside to Long Cove

was calm and the wind light and variable with promise of pleasant breezes for the day.

O. M. turned on the loran and set its computer's time by the chronometer and did the same for the comparing watch on the bulkhead and the Ship's Bell Chelsea. With so little wind the water was so calm that he was able to get a pinpoint visual fix which he used to put an ASF correction in the loran to reduce local error for the day. This would mean that should the fog close in we could rely more heavily on what the loran told us. He then entered the following waypoints:

> Sturdivant Ledges C"1"
> Spruce Point "5"
> Littlejohn Island N"18"
> Chebeague Point C"3"
> RB N marking 3 foot shoal
> Haddock Rock C"3"N"4" South of Haskell Island
> 4342.7 7001.7
> Interval Shoal C"3"
> 4347.7 6957.9

Although he was at ease utilizing loran's miraculous powers he was well aware of its limitations and of the need to be prepared at all times for the moment that some manifestation of Murphy's Law would leave us without access to its wisdom. We were both made nervous by those who, entranced by its convenience, ignored its limitations. On *Dancing Girl* loran is considered to be a miraculous back-up for dead reckoning or celestial navigation. When conditions are difficult for piloting it can also give you a good approximate position.

The Old Man plotted the courses and distances on the chart and let me study it for a while. It was agreed that I would have the wheel except during sail changes when the skipper would take over so that he could watch our position and not get too far away from the instruments and chart while I was buried in sails. We agreed that the Solent was the jib to use for several reasons. The area was thick with lobster pots demanding that we take frequent evasive action. The wind would at times be too light and variable to fill a larger sail. If we should use a spinnaker the Solent would be the proper sail to provide a takedown blanket. It was possible that at times the channel would be sufficiently narrow to require us to quick tack through, which with our #1 would require a stronger and more vigorous winch man than either of us.

We checked over the engine to see that all was in order and when we were satisfied we started it to be sure that it was ready to start quickly and run well. We then secured it. When everything was checked out and ready we hoisted the main. The wind was at 120° magnetic registering 5 knots on the anemometer. When we swung over to port tack the Old Man took the wheel I ran forward, hoisted the jib, cast off the mooring to weather of us, gave the jib a quick back to push us onto a close reach, ran aft and took over trimming the sheets from the Old Man so that he could concentrate on getting steerageway and avoiding the many lobster pots. The base course for our first leg was 089° but we were having to go as much as 20° above and below it to get through the obstacle course. When all was shipshape I relieved the wheel.

Although it was the clearest of days or perhaps because conditions were so perfect O. M. was using the loran to navigate, but he was also taking visual bearings and plotting them as though he were dependent on them. At times, although he worked with great skill, there was not time to get every detail in the log but most of it was recorded, enough so that we could have kept informed of our position using either system alone. The recorded visual data taken from the log where we recorded it is enough to tell the story and follow our progress on the chart reproduced here.

1213 R&G CAP 707.35 c 089 (Red and Green Buoy close aboard to port Continuous Log reading 707.35 steering course 089.) Starboard tack 1218 C"1" (Can "1") CAP 707.60 cc 078 (Changed course to 078)

1239 Upper Basket Ledge AS 26 feet (Abeam to starboard. Depth 26 feet)709.08

1307 N"18" CAS (Nun "18" Close aboard to Starboard) S 3.11 (Our speed 3.11) wind 3.7 cc 083 Wind light and variable

1316 S 6.13 wind 11

1320 cc 095

1327 C "3" CAS 712.50 cc 158

1422 RB N (Red and Black nun) CAP 715.90 cc 160

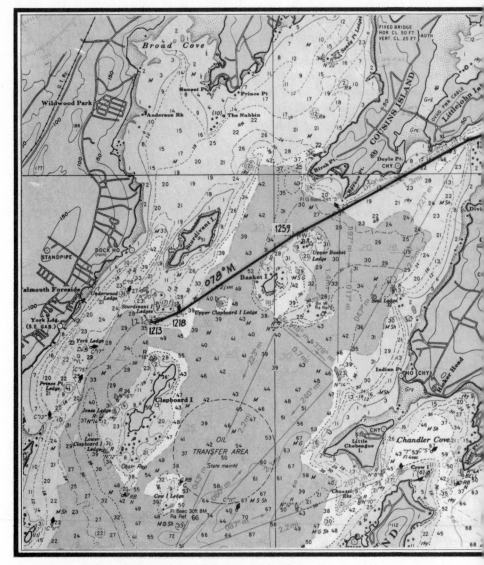

Casco Bay—Falmouth Foreside to Little Mark Island

1430"3" CAS 716.94 cc 158
1435 Mark Island Monument AS tacked to starboard
717.48 set triradial down Solent cc070

That last entry sounds easy. What happened was that
O. M. relieved me on the wheel. I shifted the port jib sheet

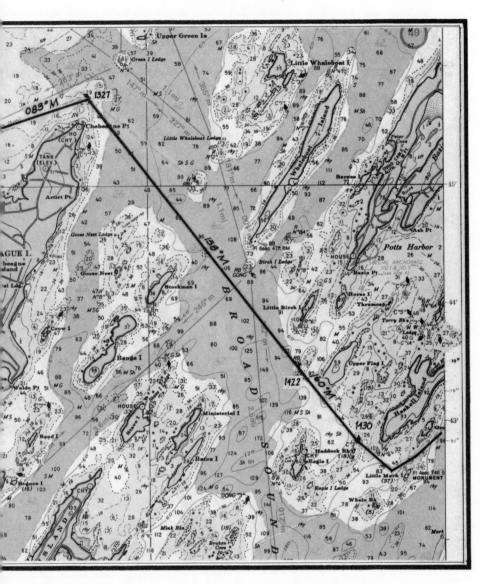

to the secondary winch and put the port spinnaker sheet on the port primary winch, cleating it with 6 inches of slack and moved the starboard spinnaker sheet up by the starboard primary winch with 2 feet of slack in it arranged so that we were ready to make a similar change when we tacked. I then

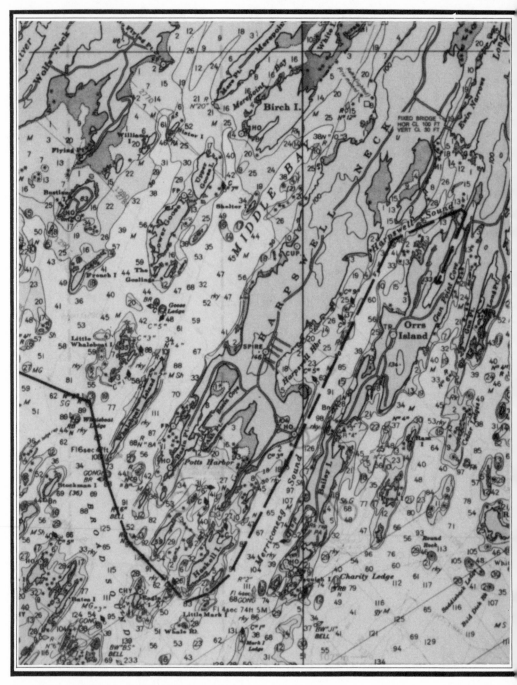

Casco Bay—Little Mark Island to Long Cove

slacked the foreguy 4 feet and recleated it. I went below and came up the forward hatch with the triradial, which was in its worm in its bag, which I secured by the lanyard on its bottom to the port stanchion base.

I raised the spinnaker pole eye on the mast to the clearing mark and secured uphaul and downhaul, clipped the fore-guy to the pole and raised its base and clipped it to the eye on the mast with the clip opening up. I clipped the topping lift to the pole end and raised it above the top of the pulpit to starboard of the headstay. I took a bight of the starboard guy, clipped it in the pole end but left the snap attached to the bullnose in the pulpit. I took the halyard from the bull-nose and bent it onto the head of the spinnaker in its worm. I arranged the worm so that its zipper would be forward and clipped the guy and sheet to the tack and clew. I secured the worm's retrieval tape to the mooring cleat.

I untied the reaching strut and rigged it abaft the forward lower to its padeye on the mast, clipped in its topping lift, clipped the guy lines to the base of the stanchion forward and aft of the shrouds respectively and hoisted the topping lift to make the strut perpendicular to the mast and took the guy and placed it in the strut. With the helmsman's okay I two-blocked the worm, ran aft and handled the sheets as the helmsman brought us over to starboard tack.

I then trimmed the guy to get the pole 3 feet off the fore-stay and went forward, checking to see that there were no foul leads, that the jib sheets were over the pole and all was in order. I shouted "Ready!" The helmsman replied "Break it out!"

I pulled the slide down off the zipper which fell open all the way to the top. With a jerk to clear the Velcro at the top it was free. (You must never free the top Velcro until the zipper has opened all the way to the top and given the swivel time to remove any twists that may have gotten into the chute. The worm dropped on deck without getting wet. The Old Man shouted, "Third time in a row, dry worm." I gave a quick but appropriate bow to acknowledge the applause, gathered the worm into the bag which I stuffed down the hatch. I lowered the pole base to the point that would make the pole level when the clews were level. I again ran aft and

adjusted the sheet, guy and foreguy to what looked like optimum levels and went back forward, dropped the Solent and
stopped it to the lower lifeline with a single stop, tidied up
the halyard ends and after checking that all was in proper
order went aft and relieved the Old Man who was itching to
get in a little navigation. He said, "You put on a good show,
son." I replied, "Thank you, oh most revered Captain." With
a younger person we would have rigged to have the chute
break out as we tacked but that would have involved more
bending of my arthritic back.

> 1437 CC 070 717.80
> 1444 CC 040 718.71
> 1455 C "3"CAP 720.1 CC 046
> 1517 Approaching High Head 50 feet 722.5 Up Solent
> Down triradial

Again the Old Man relieved the wheel. He was better than
I on the foredeck but he felt that as navigator he should not
allow himself to be distracted. I moved the spinnaker sheet
to the secondary winch and put the Solent on the primary. I
went forward, took the stop off the sail, cleared the jib halyard and freed the spinnaker halyard so that it was held by
the stopper alone, slacked the pole topping lift so that I could
easily reach the pole end, and shouted "Ready!" The helm
answered "Hoist away!"

I two-blocked the Solent and went aft and trimmed it, put
a twing on the spinnaker sheet to facilitate its retrieval, let
the guy run forward until the pole was just off the headstay.
I hauled the topping lift taut. I took a heavy strain on the
foreguy to make sure there was no slack in the system. Then
I ran forward and grabbed the lanyard that releases the
snapshackle and, standing well clear of the pole so it could
not club me when it was freed of the sail, shouted "Ready!"
When the helm shouted, "Let go!" I yanked the snap-shackle
open freeing the spinnaker tack, released the spinnaker halyard stopper, and with that line in my right hand ran aft to
sit on leeward side of the deck house gathering in the sheet
with both hands.

The spinnaker was pulled into a rope in the lee of the main
and as soon as it was under control, I eased the halyard as

fast as the chute could be gathered in with full-arm swings. Holding the balled sail between my knees I unclipped the halyard and clipped it to the lifeline. Conditions were not too difficult so the sheet was also released and clipped to the lifeline and the sail thrown down the companionway under tight control. I passed the foreguy to the helmsman so he could trim it for me, went forward and raised the pole butt up the mast to the clearing point, shouted, "Trim the foreguy!" and slacked the topping lift. I released the pole butt from the mast and placed the pole in its chocks, unclipped the foreguy, clipped it to the lifeline and took the guy from the pole and clipped it in the bullnose. I brought the topping lift to its place on the mast bale and secured it, got the halyard and sheet and brought them forward under and outside the jib and clipped them in the bullnose.

As a matter of interest the Old Man and I differ as to the best system for a one man spinnaker douse. He likes to stand in the forward hatch with the halyard in one hand and do a belly line takedown. I admit it does work well but if the halyard jams or catches, it's hard to straighten things out.

When the foredeck was secure I unrigged the reaching strut and returned it to its housing and tidied up around the mast. As there was still time I got the two anchors on deck and rigged them ready to let go, hanging from the lifeline outboard on each side where they would not be fouled when the jib came down. The bags containing the anchor rodes were each tied to the lifelines, open so that the warp would run freely when the anchor was let go.

I relieved the wheel and the Old Man dove below to study the chart and correlate it with the scenery around us which although beautiful suggested many hazardous bits of geology and few objects usable as navigational aids. It was obviously going to be a matter of depth finder and eyeball used with caution. The winds provided us with 2 to 3 knots through the water and the opportunity to tack frequently as we worked our way against the wind coming at us from the head of the cove. We had a break from the tide for it was 2 hours past dead low and we had another 6 feet of water on its way to float us off should we goof. Using tangents on the two little islands and the point we could have a rough idea of our location and watching the depth finder for any sign of shoaling we could be tacking whenever we had any doubts about the water ahead stay in areas with minimum risk of grounding.

We put 3,000 on the backstay to allow for some power and were using enough flattening reef to leave us with two thirds of the shelf. The traveler was on the center line and the jib had the draft at 45 percent. The telltales told a happy story. The Old Man came up the companionway and said, "Time to tack!" I said, "Ready about hard alee!" O. M. cast off the old jib sheet and I came over slowly enough so that he could trim for the new tack without need for a winch. The navigator went back below to his chart and instruments and I combined an effort to go as close to windward as possible with a striving to see what lay beneath the surface of the water. The shoal coming out from the west came farther than I remembered the chart to show and the point extended farther south. I was glad the Old Man was doing the navigation. We were standing in quite far to the west and I could tell that we were trying to get past the narrows with as few tacks as possible and avoid having to tack in the extreme narrows.

Again we tacked at what seemed to me the last minute and again the teamwork between wheel and sheet was near perfect. No need for a winch and no great loss of headway. "With a little luck," Old Man said, "the pressure will be off after this next tack. Tack now, fast!"

This time the winch was needed and I tailed as the Old Man ground. "The bottom suddenly started up too fast to suit me that time," he explained. "I doubt if we had 6 inches to spare under our keel. You spun her just right. At that point maintaining headway was not one of my major desires." I came up slowly giving her time to regain lost steerageway.

"The rest of the way in is simple and I have it memorized. I will relieve you and continue to run the navigation. Keep a lookout though, when you can," said the Old Man.

"The wind varies quite a bit in strength and direction. I am making about 145° on this tack and we are tacking in about 85° degrees. Our speed goes from 2.5 to 3.5," I told him as he took the wheel, thanking me.

"We will secure the jib on the next tack," the skipper said and I went forward wrapping three stops around my waist.

I cleared the jib halyard to run and checked to see that I

had the anchors arranged not to interfere or be interfered with.

"Ready about!"

"Ready!"

"Hard alee!"

I cast off the jib halyard, pulled down the jib as it crossed the wind and furled it tightly with three stops to the upper starboard lifeline, out of the way of the anchors.

"We will be anchoring after the next tack, starboard anchor first, with 8 feet at dead low and 6 feet to go till high water," the skipper said. I faked out 100 feet of rode on deck for the starboard anchor and the same for the port, cleating each to its mooring cleat at the stated length. At "Ready about" I lowered the starboard anchor to the water with my right hand, holding the rode loosely in my left. The Old Man tacked and ordered "Let go" as he came to 080°. I let the rode run through my hands holding it up to permit the helm to see that it was clear. After a boat length we came up to 100° and as soon as the line could be seen running out in the clear on the starboard quarter I dropped it in the water, and merely watched to see that it was being laid out straight with no bunches or fouls. I picked up the port anchor and hung it at the water's edge. We were going 3 knots when the starboard rode came up on the cleat, the water squeezed out of the line, and we had a good set. The skipper tacked around to 270° and I let go the port anchor. I started taking in the slack on the starboard rode as I watched to see that the port was running out properly. When we reached the cleated length we were again going 3 knots and there was no doubt about our set. I cleated the starboard rode after removing the the previously made turns from the cleat.

After we lowered and furled the main I went back and adjusted the rodes so that there was 60° between them. We locked the wheel and, after admiring the beauty of our surroundings and arranging our halyards so they would not slap against the mast, went below for our anchor-setting drink. Mentally I gave our day an A+ —beautiful scenery, lovely weather, some precise maneuvers well carried out, and enough exercise to keep us in shape. I was tired and happy. The rum had fresh lime squeezed in it and the Old Man was going to cook fresh swordfish and corn on the cob for dinner.

VI

~~~~~~~~~~~~~~~~~~~~~~

Stormy

Before leaving Gibraltar the Old Man had visited the weather office at the air base. The incumbent wise man promised us three days of good weather and fair winds but pointed out that there was some bad weather in the western Atlantic which might bring us some misery before we reached Las Palmas. We got under way at 1000 on the engine in light fluky winds but soon had the sails filled and the engine secured. It was a beautiful and sunny first of March as we passed the Pillars of Hercules driving on starboard tack with the triradial, main, and staysail pulling like a team of Clydesdales. I thought back to ancient times when this was as far as the prudent Mediterranean mariner would go, for beyond, where we were headed, lay all the terror of the vast unknown. This also was the gate to the Mediterranean where the Allies in World War II used underwater nets and big flying boats carrying magnetic detectors and patrolling in lazy figure eights to make certain that few Axis submarines passed in or out undetected. Over the years a great many warships knew these waters well, but I was glad that on this trip we were sailing in comparative peace.

The Old Man was navigator as usual on this trip and I was cook to give me a chance to study my shipmates and to savor the entire voyage. David was the starboard watch captain and

Big Ann, because she was a week younger, was the port watch captain. The twins, Tyler and Ryan, were the starboard and port watch standers. Having graduated from college at 21, they were taking a year to seek wisdom in an unstructured environment before going to work. Sailing with their uncle was to be the marine part of their program. It was a big part.

Dancing Girl stands watches four on and four off, dogged, which we feel gives people a chance to make the best use of their time. By having each watch stand a 2-hour watch at supper time they change schedules each day and only have to stand the mid watch every other night. This works out so that the 1600 to 1800 and the 1800 to 2000 watch standers have their dinner after and before their watches respectively. We feel that this schedule permits the crew to settle into the routine and stay more rested than any other and to get an equal share of the good and the bad duty.

Our noon fix on March second showed that our young people had driven us 167 miles noon to noon. The second day, in spite of aggressive sail trimming and changing, our run was down to 163. At noon we had the 165 percent #1 up and were 42° off the wind making 6.7 knots. More important, though, there was a definite swell with very long rollers coming in from the west. At lunch the Old Man, pointing these out, reminded us that there was a storm off there and suggested that we use the next few hours to do everything we could to be sure we were ready for it. I took the wheel so that all the watch standers could eat together. Big Ann read *Dancing Girl*'s "Bill for Preparing for Heavy Weather" out loud and we had the steps carried out within 15 minutes of finishing lunch. When I relieved I readied three cans, each containing a freeze-dried one-dish meal for six people that is prepared by just adding boiling water. I believe I can boil water safely in most heavy weather on the Seaswing stove and use it to keep full each of two one-quart thermoses when the water in either is used to prepare a meal. I also got out a can of each of the crew's favorite snacks, the lurps (a mixture of nuts, raisins, and M & Ms) and the banana chips.

We logged the wind direction every hour but we were definitely not in the weather system we feared. The barometer stayed steady at 29.85. We wanted to stay outside Morocco's 200-mile limit to minimize the risk of piracy reported to be common closer to shore. We were on the Great Circle course for Las Palmas and were now hoping that the storm would pass well to the north of us because if it did not we were in the path of the dangerous semicircle with no place to hide. In the northern hemisphere cyclonic storms rotate in a counterclockwise direction and advance usually on a course somewhere from east to north at between 10 to 30 knots. It is obvious that south of the center the speed of advance is added to the wind speed, whereas north of the storm the speed of advance is subtracted from it. Think for a moment of a storm with 50-knot winds advancing at 20 knots. South of the center a ship will find itself buffeted by winds of 70 knots (20 knots speed of advance plus 50), while a ship to the north of the center will only have to contend with 30 (20 knot speed of advance deducted from the storm's 50).

The next day at noon the wind had veered so we could carry the triradial with the wind just forward of the beam. We were really driving, never dropping below 7.5 and occasionally holding 2 knots faster for 2 minutes at a time. The previous day's run had only been 158 miles but now the horse was headed for the barn. Each helmsman in turn was crouched like a wrestler circling an opponent ready to counter every move before it got started. *Dancing Girl* seemed eager to run ever faster but with a wild, scarcely predictable, determination to escape the helm's control, by force or by stealth. She was a controlled runaway, and the helmsmen were finding that 20-minute tricks were all they could handle. It seemed to me that Big Ann, in spite of her small size, and because of her sea sense and quickness, was slightly better than the others, but I admit prejudice. They were all magnificent.

During the first dog watch the Old Man stuck his head up the hatch and said that the inclinometer had not been below 22° for 10 minutes and that Ann had had over 8° of rudder too much of the time. We should at least put in a flattening reef and might find that the first reef was even faster.

"I'll handle the sheet, Ryan, if you'll handle the line." When Ryan shouted, "Ready!" the Old Man shouted, "Letting go!" Ryan hauled in the flattening reef hand over hand. Ann shouted, "That's well!" and the Old Man hauled the sheet back in before Ryan could get back to help him. The flattening reef was in.

Ryan relieved the wheel and Ann, watching the boat speed, wind speed, and inclinometer tried to put the final touch to our sails. "I may have picked up 0.1 knots, but I'm not sure. Ryan, I am going to dump the main and see what happens to our speed."

"Okay."

A quick easing of the sheet told her what we wanted to know. "Captain," she called. "That first reef will help. I will take the wheel. If you will handle the halyard and the Professor the sheet, Ryan can put the reef in."

I told Ann I was frying chicken and cooking peas and needed a minute to secure the stove. She said, "Never mind. I can release the sheet and if you will lend me a hand getting it in we will be okay and will not delay dinner." I thanked her

and Ryan and the Old Man went forward, clipped on. The
O. M. cleared the halyard and shouted "Ready!" as did Ann
and Ryan. It was now Ryan's exercise.

"Ease the halyard!" he shouted.

"Down!" called the Old Man as the mark on the halyard
was on the line.

Ryan hooked the grommet over the pigtail and called,
"Hooked on, hoist."

The Old Man called, "Two-blocked!"

Ann called, "Sheet is slack!"

Ryan shouted, "Hauling!"

Ann called, "That's well." I grabbed the mainsheet and
between us we hauled it in to the right trim.

"We may be reefing more later," said Ryan. "I will put in
the lacing line. Might as well be tidy. It may be a long war."

"We gained 0.3 by that and we were sitting up straighter
and using about 2° less rudder," reported Ann 5 minutes
later.

We were able to eat dinner at the table fairly successfully
by using wet paper towels for place mats to keep the plates
from sliding and by putting the fiddle boards up on the table.
The crew liked my cooking and used bread to wipe up all the
juice in the pans and on the plates, not only to help me, but
it did make the dishwashing much easier. They also applauded
my wisdom in making double the recommended amount of
chocolate pudding. I cleaned up quickly and dove into my
sack, suspecting it might be a busy night. I noticed the watch
standers were sleeping in their oilies and safety harnesses but
I planned to get as much sleep as possible before I had to
sleep in harness. I had all my gear carefully arranged and
rolled up under my pillow, ready for instant donning when
the call came.

I was up at 2330 to call the oncoming watch and set out
milk and cookies for them. I got quickly back into my sack
but was aware that the four of them at the time of relieving
the watch had changed from the chute to the Solent jib. At
0330 I was again up for the watch change and offered them
hot water for instant cocoa, coffee, or bouillon cubes. I made
a peanut and butter jelly sandwich for each. They put in the
second reef while they were all on deck for the watch change.

At about 0440 I awoke to the shout of "All hands on deck!" accompanied by pounding feet and flogging sails. I quickly climbed into my oilies and safety harness and rushed on deck to find that both watches, working together, had brought a semblance of order to the chaos I was expecting to see. I felt guilty for if I had slept fully dressed I could have helped. A quick glance at the wind speed indicator showed we were being favored with about 55 knots of wind. Ryan had been on the wheel when the wind veered 90° and doubled its velocity. The spreader must have been nearly in the water as Ann had clawed her way forward and dropped the main and the jib. She had gotten a stop around the jib to hold it to the lower life line and a couple of stops around the main. Ryan had run off to ease the chaos. I was glad to note that the watch captains had been sailing with the drop boards in place and the companionway closed tight since the first reef had gone in.

Dancing Girl behaves well under bare poles, and with the apparent wind 130° off the port bow she was now running through confused seas at about 3 knots for Las Palmas. The forestay and, of course the running backstays, had been set up during David's watch and he was now bending the storm jib onto the forestay while Tyler and Ann bagged the Solent and got it below via the companionway. The forward hatch had been tightly dogged since the first reef had gone in. The Old Man and I put five more stops on the main, giving it a tight furl, rigged the boom crutch, and secured the boom in it. We hauled down tight on the mainsheet, cleated it, and then using the free end of the sheet put tight half hitches around the furl every 9 inches.

The wind was roaring in our ears and there was so much spume that you could not tell if it was raining. The seas were confused and the boat was lurching about, trying to throw us into the seething sea. Our movement about the deck was limited by the need to be clipped on at all times.

I suggested to the Old Man that he and I could help Ann's watch tidy up and that David and Tyler could resume their interrupted slumbers. We proposed this to Ann who sent the starboard watch gratefully below. We bent halyards on the storm jib and the trysail. We taped the snap-shackle on the jib halyard and moused the screw-in shackle on the main. We put a stop around the luff of each. We set the trysail tack and rove the sheets through the properly placed blocks so that the sails could be set as quickly as possible. The Old Man went below to his chart table, but I stayed in the cockpit to savor the miserable weather.

After a few minutes Ann was called below and asked Ryan to take over and to call her if anything started to happen. Through the Lucite drop board I watched the captain and the watch captain conferring over the chart in the red night-vision light. It was a short time before she was back on deck, announcing in a voice loud enough to be heard over the storm, "The wind is from 120. That means the storm's center bears 220, farther south than expected. Las Palmas is about 200. We're assuming the storm center is advancing on a course of 010 at 20 knots and that we can't get over to the north of it where the winds will be 40 knots less. Let's come to a course of 100 and set our storm sails. We'll let them fill, probably on a course of about 050. Once they're drawing we may be able to sail 070. We want to get as far off the storm's track as we can. But we don't want to destroy ourselves in the process.

"Ryan, you must be dying for a turn on the pointy end and those weight-lifter's muscles will make the halyards work faster. The less time we have our sails flogging the better. Professor, we need your calm wisdom on the wheel. I'll handle the winches and keep an eye on the gauges."

I shifted my safety harness to where it would not interfere with the wheel and relieved Ryan, who went forward and clipped on the starboard jackline. He then had me unclip him from the helmsman's jackline. He and I reported ready, and Ann called down to the captain, "We're about to set the sails and come to 050."

The captain acknowledged. She shouted, "Ryan, free the port storm jib halyard as you go by. Check for fouls. Then cleat it, go forward, and while you lie on the jib to control it take the stop off the jib and put it around your waist. When you're set, jump up and hoist the sail tight. The Professor will try to steer a course to minimize flogging without making hoisting too hard. As soon as the jib is up, hoist the trysail. Be sure the halyards are secure before you come aft."

Big Ann continued: "I'll be trimming both sails as fast as I can. I'll need help for the final foot or two. The plan is to get the sails up and drawing before they flog themselves to bits. I want to get away from the storm's tracks fast. Professor, you'll make a big difference by steering the best course."

"Is everybody happy?" Ryan and I each waved a hand, visible in the binnacle's red glow. "All right, let's go."

I swung our head to the right to wear around to 100°, hoping to pick up some extra steerageway. Ryan moved with the grace and power of a tiger getting Sunday dinner, and Ann, seeming to be in no hurry, made the winches and lines snap to do her will. *Dancing Girl* was like a skier in the first gates of a slalom. I could see the seas in the dim light well enough to avoid the bad ones but it was going to be a real run.

When Ryan was back in the cockpit, puffing slightly, Ann slapped him on the shoulder shouting above the wind, "You are great, kid."

"Thanks, Grandma, it was fun."

Sailing the boat was fun, too, and I was sorry when Ann said she was ready to relieve me. "We're sailing 050 swinging as much as 15° to either side for the best path through. The captain wants to sail as high as 070 if we can make it but I'm not sure it wouldn't give us too much of a beating. We're logging the wind direction and speed every hour. We expect it to veer and hope it won't increase. Tell the captain of any changes."

"I relieve you, sir," said Ann.

"Thank you, sir. Please call me at seven, I am thinking of giving you kidney stew and kippers for breakfast."

"Around the reeking wreck the wretched retchers ran," said Ann as I dove below having checked to see that there was no wave about to try to join me in the cabin.

I stuffed my sleeping bag in its sack to use as a pillow and lay down fully dressed, boots and all. I started to muse about the joys of sailing and the excitement of operating as a team under difficult conditions. Before I could organize my thoughts much or reach any brilliant conclusions I was asleep.

When Big Ann sent Ryan to call me at seven I woke up rested but with no sense of how much time had elapsed. It was rough and it was a little surprising to see how much much twisting and turning motion a rigid hull could achieve. Ryan told me we were now steering 070° and the wind had veered to 145° and was now blowing a steady 65 with higher gusts. Ann had had him furl the trysail about half an hour before because the boat was over-canvased. Down in the troughs we were almost out of wind but when we got on top of a wave we were being knocked on our ear.

I took advantage of being first in line for the head and while I was there I took a precautionary Dramamine and decided to postpone shaving until a time when I would not have to lie in the sink to keep my face steady enough. I got out three cans of roast beef hash and temporarily stowed them in the sink, where I also set three grapefruit. I tried heating a kettle of water in the Seaswing and decided that our hold-down spring was up to the task as long as I was close enough to dampen wild gyrations when they occurred. I wore the lobsterman's apron and was securely in the cook's belt which left my hands free. At 0720 I lit the stove and put some butter in the pan and set it on the burner. I opened two cans of hash and pressed the contents down in the pan as thin and even as possible and put the cover on. At 0730 I set the pan in the sink where it could not spill, turned the burner down very low and woke David. I offered him a Dramamine, a glass of water, and a Saltine. He threw all three down and headed for the head. When I called Tyler he was dubious but finally took all three.

I returned to the galley, clipped the belt into its two pad eyes, put the pan back on the stove, and turned the burner up. I decided I would feel safer with one hand ready to grab the handle. I made David and Tyler's coffee, stirring in the sugar they both took and set the mugs in the sink to cool. They were dressed and ready to go on watch with their bedding secured when they arrived for breakfast at 0739. As each braced himself on the leeward bunk I gave him half a grapefruit and a spoon. I also gave each a paper towel for a napkin and offered them coffee, for which both wanted to wait. As each finished his fruit I was ready with a good serving of hash alongside which I had placed a dollop of ketchup. Neither wanted seconds but Tyler accepted a strawberry jam sandwich to have with his coffee. After reading the log, David went up on deck, clipped on and went around the boat looking everywhere to see how every part was standing the gaff. He looked for signs of chafe or fatigue or for any cotter pins or nuts coming loose. He also checked all shackles to see that they were either moused or taped. I put the third can of hash in the pan, for it looked as if we would need it.

Ryan was the first to be relieved and came down and went directly to the head. Ann was down by 0757 and wrote up the log immediately. When Ryan emerged they both ate, but as each planned to sleep fully dressed, as I had, neither unrigged for the meal. I woke the Old Man and asked him if he wanted to eat. He did and got up, and although I remained standing in the harness where I could watch the stove, we had breakfast together. He was pretty sure the center was going north of us and that from now on the winds would veer and decline. It was his plan that as the wind changed we would keep changing course until we were within 50° of the course for Las Palmas at that time and then would start to increase sail as fast as the weather permitted. There was no need to beat ourselves down unnecessarily clawing to wind-ward, but when we could head for the barn there was no point in dilly-dallying along the way.

We got the trysail on just before lunch and, although we had to eat from bowls in our laps, everyone had seconds and the twins had thirds of the freeze-dried Tuna Neptune which I prepared by merely adding boiling water. By dinner time the barometer was climbing and we were using the triradial and the single-reefed main. I gave them butterflied leg of lamb which I had told the butcher in Gibraltar how to pre-pare by cutting out the bone and flattening the meat to make a steak-like slab. I had carefully inserted pieces of garlic clove all through the meat and roasted it in a covered pan. The aroma was powerful but everyone stuffed on it. Ryan did say, though, that a gull that flew too close to leeward of us dropped stone dead in the sea.

This storm had blown its best, but now the wrestling match was over and we were going to win this one in due course if we made no mistakes. The watch captains were pouring on the coal as fast as *Dancing Girl* could use it. One mark of a good crew is that after a storm they get the speed back up as fast as conditions improve. I was happy to see that these kids were aggressive. They never had us over-canvased, but we were never the least bit under-canvased either.

VII

~~~~~~~~~~~~~~~~~~

Heavy Weather

Dancing Girl was dancing around her assigned mooring at the Royal Irish Yacht Club at Dun Laoghaire (pronounced Dun Leary) in winds frequently gusting to 35 knots. The dinghy racing continued, apparently without concern, but the kids knew what they were doing for we only saw one capsize. As far as we could see they all thought they were having a good time and were happy operating in a constant deluge of spray which we had found quite chilling earlier in the day, sailing over from Arklow 28 miles away. During that sail several squalls had come through at over 55 knots and we had been on storm jib and trysail most of the way, reaching at better than 8 knots a lot of the time. David said steering made him think of Ben Hur at the races. The seas were not difficult to handle, however, and I had found it an exhilarating day in spite of the heavy rain that beat on us from time to time through most of the morning.

In these waters the weather often threatens, and the BBC weather forecasters always take the threats seriously. This time they had been right to do so. We were glad that the winds had permitted us to sail our course without being any closer to the wind than a close reach. We had been making very good time but we knew we had been working when we arrived. There were five of us abroad, for David had by chance

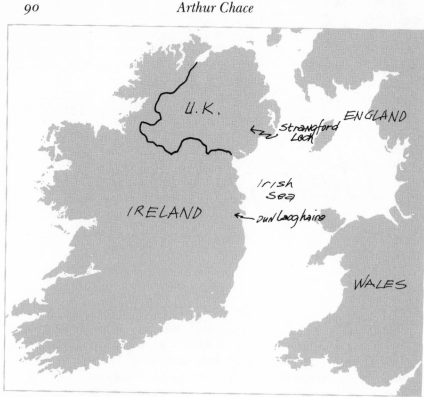

The handwritten labels on the map read: U.K., ENGLAND, Strangford Loch, Irish Sea, IRELAND, Dun Laoghaire, WALES

The Irish Sea

encountered Roger Reeves who was in Ireland on business, in Arklow with two days to kill.

Roger had played guard to David's tackle for two years at school and all four years at college. They had lost touch after graduation but were genuinely pleased to see each other. It seemed logical that Roger spend his two days with us even though he had in his background little sailing except in sheltered fresh water. Luckily he turned out to have a cast-iron stomach and was entranced by the constant struggles of our first day at sea together.

It had been a day of safety harnesses and heavy spray coming over the foredeck, and in borrowed oilies Roger had been out there in the thick of it, his strength and native intelligence making him an asset. The day brought out many warnings about going overboard, green seas coming down hatches left open too long, lines breaking and releasing lethal amounts of stored energy, unpremeditated jibes and unnoticed other vessels on steady bearings. Roger accepted it all as being like football where if you were not aggressive and self-protective at the same time you might suffer damage. The Old Man was concerned that Roger was not sufficiently impressed with the need for planning ahead to avoid the hazards lying in wait for the unwary and made an extra effort to paint the picture in strong colors.

Now that we were riding a mooring in the comparative safety of the harbor the Old Man was trying for instant completion of Roger's education. "I know I sound as though going sailing is a hazardous business but in actual fact the greatest danger in going sailing is that it seems so idyllic and there are such long periods in which there is not the slightest shadow of a problem that we get lulled into a sense of security that is unjustified anywhere on this globe. In New York City everyone is aware that danger is everywhere. Did you ever notice the real New Yorkers always look both ways before crossing a one-way street? The real city dweller lives defensively, constantly evaluating each situation as to potential hazards, and taking defensive steps automatically. Being at sea is far safer but that does not mean the one can abandon all caution. Common sense is all that is necessary.

"When you are cruising you are more likely to be on your own than when you are racing and you are less likely to have a full crew of vigorous young experts to snatch you from the jaws of disaster if you get careless. It is therefore more important that the cruiser plan ahead as to how potential disasters will be handled. Being prepared is usually good prevention." The Old Man, as usual, was getting a little carried away by one of his major concerns and the instruction of Roger began to take second place to the exchange of ideas between the four experienced members of the group.

David came in. "As an impecunious drudge with few obligations and constrictions, I sail often on other people's boats and the sailors I respect seem to do a lot of preparation before they set sail. The storm jib has its own stowage and is in it. The piston hanks are freshly lubricated and none are frozen. If the trysail is not bent on its own track on the mast it is at least in its own stowage with the sheets and tack lines neatly coiled and spliced into the clew and tack respectively. Somehow the skipper seems to have everyone aware as to where, how, and when these sails will be set. The tack points and the blocks to be used are known long before there is any chance of a mad scramble to work out some way to get the sails set.

"A well-found ship is prepared at all times to take a knockdown without anything coming adrift. Although it takes a moment longer to get into the icebox it is good to know that the cover is bolted so that even a 360° roll is not going to fill the cabin with blocks of ice and the flying top to the box. The same thinking applies to the batteries and the lockers and sliding bunks. I think I can tell a lot about the skipper just by seeing if there are enough buckets for a bucket brigade, up-to-date fire extinguishers, wooden plugs, spare standing and running rigging, rivet gun and rivets, wire and clamps, a collision mat and tools and so on."

"I agree with what you say," I said. "But also I like to see that the skipper has been thinking about safety of personnel should heavy weather be encountered. Coast Guard requirements are a fine start although in some cases they do not go far enough to handle the problems of the kind of boats we take to sea. I like to see well-maintained safety harnesses and provisions for running proper jack lines fore and aft. I like to see good strong bunk cloths to keep sleepers in their bunks. I like to know that if a storm comes up all reasonable precautions will be taken to keep all hands aboard and should disaster strike and someone go over the side we will have the best possible chance of getting him back alive."

"In my opinion proper preparation is essential, but plans and procedures must be written up, reviewed regularly and disseminated to all hands." Ann added, "When the action starts is not the time to reveal the plans. I know that every few years there are storms or hurricanes in the softest crusing areas, and I like to know that the skipper has thought about the problem and is prepared to handle it. We all know of cases where sailboats in what are usually sheltered waters have suffered significant storm damage. I like to see that there has been enough thought on the subject so that there are wooden plates to put over ports if they get bashed in by the sea and to see enough canvas and battens to restore workable water-tight integrity after storm damage to the hull or cabin."

"I agree with you both about the steps to be taken before setting sail," said the Old Man, "but there is a lot to be done after we get to sea before we find ourselves in a storm. Take weather reports, for example. In every area the situation is different and it is up to the skipper to find out from HO, 117A, *Radio Aids to Navigation,* and informed people in the area what are the best available sources of weather information. There is often good information available using single-side-band radio. In many areas a facsimile receiver can bring you up-to-date weather charts several times a day. At sea, I have on occasion gotten very good meteorological information from passing ships. The ship's barometer should be read and logged regularly at intervals determined by the area and the conditions. The barograph should be consulted at least once each watch, more frequently if there is any significant change taking place. Swells rolling in from distant storms can often be your first indication that trouble is brewing. Study the clouds for they can give you warning as much as a day ahead.

"Once you suspect that you may be about to be involved in a tropical disturbance start logging in the wind direction and velocity every hour. Remembering that when you face the wind in such a system the center is 10° behind your right shoulder in the Northern Hemisphere. If you know or can guess the speed of the storm's advance a plot of bearing changes plus this information will give you a rough estimate of the distance off. If possible you should head to get out of the storm's path, remembering that in the Northern Hemisphere the winds rotate in a counterclockwise direction."

"As soon as it looks as though you may be getting into bad weather," I said, "everyone should start making preparations to minimize the ill effects. Everyone should put on clean, dry, warm clothes. Boots, foul weather gear, with a towel around the neck to keep the water out, gloves and anything else you may need should be donned or stowed in a secure place, easily available. I like to see flotation vests go on to increase the rather poor chances of getting picked up if you go overboard. Then get into your safety harness and start clipping on to see that you stay aboard. Arrange your hood so that you can turn your head without it covering your eyes or scooping any transient spray or green sea.

"I like to prepare. Thermoses of hot soup and of coffee to eliminate the need for heating them when the going is rough. It's also smart to plan meals that can be eaten from a bowl and cooked in one pot with minimum risk of spilling. The cook's safety harness should be clipped to its pad eyes ready to put on. The companionway curtain should be rigged to keep the navigation area as dry as possible."

"Professor," broke in the Old Man, "you are right about the crew's health and welfare, but remember that the boat comes first. Without the boat the crew's welfare is minimal. A careful check should be made of everything topsides to see that there is nothing left exposed that could be stowed below. Burgee and ensign should be secured before they are reduced to fringed hoists.

"Oars, boathook, fender board, swabs, dodger and everything else that does not need to be on deck goes below into secure stowage. Presumably at this time the boat is reaching to get as far as possible from the storm's track before being compelled to shift to the storm sails. Everything is made ready for a quick change when the wind's velocity reaches the level where the stormsails are faster. The forestay and the running backstays are rigged and the storm jib is brought up on deck and bent on the forestay with sheets and blocks in place and the trysail is made ready to hoist.

"When the moment arrives, the Solent, presumably reefed by this time, is struck below and the storm jib hoisted. Then finally when the triple reefed main is demanding too much rudder to keep us on course it too is brought down and furled as the trysail is hoisted and trimmed. The boom is lodged in the boom crutch and the sheet hauled tight enough to insure that it stays there. I like to take the tail of the mainsheet and use it to put a series of half hitches, one every 9 inches, around the main and hauled very tight.

"Putting distance between the vessel and the storm's track is the objective as long as possible, but it is also necessary to get sea room and this can be an awkward conflict. In the final analysis seamen know that rocks can grind a boat and its crew to little pieces in a blow but a well-found vessel should be able to survive all but the ultimate storm at sea. We also know that beating into a storm is a very hard way to live and that the faster you are moving the more violently the boat reacts to the waves. On several occasions at sea when the crew was getting over-tired, I have hove to or lain ahull while all hands had a chance to eat a good meal in comparative comfort. The contrast is great, but before we decide that we will heave to or lie ahull in every storm there are a number of other factors to consider.

"Years ago one of my friends told me a story about heaving to in a schooner in a gale off the mouth of Placentia Bay in Newfoundland. The yacht rode like a duck and seemed to making no more than a knot on a southwesterly course. The vessel's motion was easy and they all went below delighted at their seamanlike solution to the blow. Five days later when things calmed down a bit, they were able to take some sun sights which showed that they were at the head of the bay, having threaded their way between a number of hazards such as rocks and islands. I do not want to bet that my luck will be as good as theirs. Another friend of mine told me of dropping a destroyer off the flat-sided back of a 50-foot wave in a North Atlantic storm. I want to do everything in my power

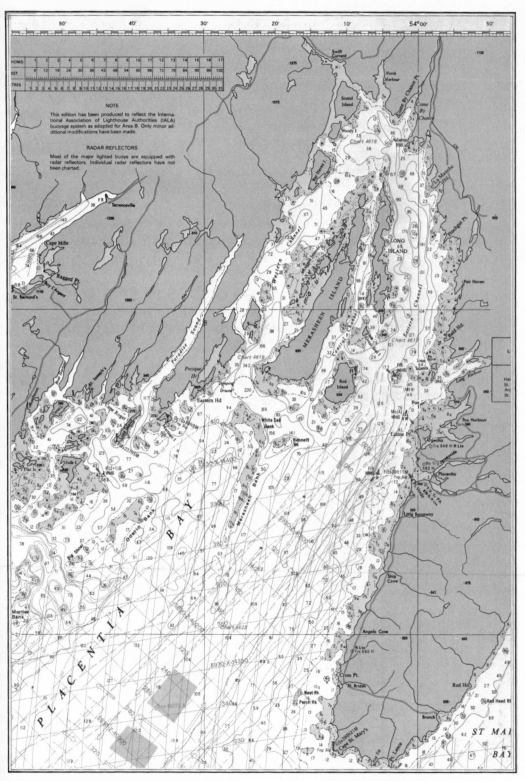

Placentia Bay

to avoid seeing how *Dancing Girl* would handle such an experience. I have seen flat-sided waves and really do not want to even run into one.

"I have been at anchor in 120 knots of wind and hope I never have to handle it at sea in this or any other ship. If I do, though, our wheel will be manned and we are going to have steerage way and we are going to try to pick the safest course through the turbulence.

"As a card-carrying worry wart, in spite of all the reassuring statistics, I do not want at any time to be at sea in a boat with no one on the helm and without steerageway. The calm courage of the many solo voyagers has me in awe. I know the ocean is infinitely large. Once I had twenty-six icebergs in sight at the same time and sailed right through the midst of them without having to change course once or come close to any one of them, but I still like to think that I and my shipmates can avoid the breaking wave that will roll us, the big ship with the seasick radar operator, or the derelict awash and ready to allow us to break our bow in on it. I want to have steerageway."

"I agree with you, Old Man," I came in. "I know you remember that lovely soft night in 1975 off the southern end of San Salvador in the Bahamas when we were hove to under main alone with the wheel locked. We were planning to ride that way till morning light made it practical to run up the west coast and pick our way through the narrow entrance into the dredged snug, little harbor of the Riding Rock Marina. All our information had convinced us that we would be enjoying balmy winds, no greater than 6 knots from the northeast. The only change we expected was that the wind might veer during the night but not enough to cause any problems. We planned to have two people on watch, standing four-hour tricks and keeping each other company. Because it was such a soft hazard-free evening all four of us were below eating a candle-light feast based on three very big langosta we had purchased from a diver we had encountered off Rum Cay earlier in the day, when we had thought there was enough wind to get us into port well before dark.

"Dinner was suddenly interrupted when it started to rain and the wind became very squally from the general direction

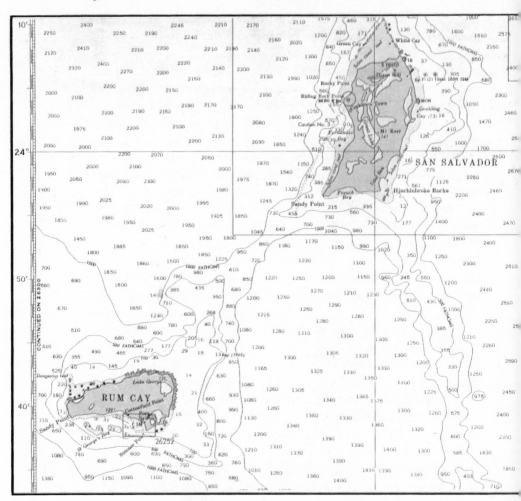

of the northwest. We grabbed for our oilies but changed our minds when we were knocked on our beam ends by winds that were gusting to 70. I let go the main sheet and the boat came up a little with the flogging of the main adding to the roar of the wind and rain. We got the drop boards from their stowage by the companionway, seated them, and slammed the hatch shut. Getting the main furled tested our seamanship and soaked us through and through. As soon as we could spare a hand we sent people below one at a time to get into their oilies and safety harnesses while the rest of us went cautiously around the ship lashing down everything we could not get below.

"When I was a young man the concept of safety harnesses had not been applied to boats and we went around the roughest decks, remembering 'one hand for the ship and one for yourself,' knowing that if we forgot our retrieval would be unlikely. We did not lose too many people but today, when we are used to wearing the harness, I think most of us feel very insecure in a blow without one. I know we were all hanging on for dear life that night and felt surprisingly freed when we were at last clipped on.

"As I recollect in the old days we were struggling for our lives in conditions that we today consider merely stressful. Just because I have a safety harness clipped to the jackline does not mean that hanging by it in the water would not be traumatic, but it does mean that I am not betting my life on not making a false move. Nevertheless when the wind pipes up the stresses build on us and our equipment and any failure is increasingly liable to be spectacularly dangerous. Remember that there is a lot of energy stored in an overloaded line and when it parts it can give a human leg standing next to it a deep groove filled with hamburger.

"As the weather turns bad it becomes increasingly important to plan ahead and not take any chances that things can foul up. Remember, Roger, how when any of us went forward today to do any work on the foredeck we were not only clipped on but also lying down and braced even when we were not holding down a sail. Remember also how we talked through every exercise before undertaking it. When the sea seems to be trying to get you it's like fighting a fire on an oil rig. You cannot take any chances or leave anything to luck."

VIII

~~~~~~~~~~~~~~

Voyage Plans

We were swinging easily at a mooring at the Portland Yacht Club, enjoying the long daylight of an early June evening. We had arrived after dark the night before after an easy twelve-day trip from Saint Martin. We lay on a mooring, flying our Q flag, and went into the float after breakfast. It had been a reach most of the way with staysail and spinnaker and sparkling seas and sunny skies, as though the authorities were trying to make up to us for all the rough trips we had suffered in all the various waters of the world. The facsimile weather chart had looked so idyllic that we had eliminated a planned stop in Bermuda feeling that when things are too good to be true, the wise do not waste them. The miracle of SSB (single-side-band long-range radio) had produced the phone call that brought the new crew to the dock at 1630 this afternoon and they were settled in and beginning to feel that they had never been away. The SSB had also enabled us to notify customs the day before that we would be arriving at 2000 and to be instructed to call them on the telephone as soon as we were up this morning. When the Old Man called he was authorized to clear by mail and let our ocean crew go on their way.

There was surprisingly little to do. As usual, water use on the trip had been a little less than the planned rate of one half gallon per person per day. The 30 gallons in our six emergency jugs had covered our needs and they were now empty and stowed. The 70 gallons in our installed tanks would take care of our cruising requirements. Because we had only used the engine for battery charging, we still had more fuel in jugs than we needed for gunkholing our way east. All we did want was to wash down with fresh water below and on deck, put 150 pounds of ice in the box, and load provisions for the cruise ahead.

Although I was not to be the cook on the next leg, I had prepared a shopping list covering food, condiments, paper goods, liquor, candles for the table, stove alcohol, charcoal, etc., and went off in a taxi to the local supermarket. My chauvinism and patriotism always get a boost when I visit a stateside supermarket after a period of being dependent on foreign imitations and today was no exception. On our cruise just finished, we had had to make some concessions to conditions beyond our control. In spite of creative and ingenious shopping, the Caribbean markets had required a number of compromises both in fresh and in canned foods. South of the Gulf Stream, the water temperature made it impossible to keep ice more than 8 days even with the strictest controls on who could open the ice box. We had planned that if we decided to by-pass Bermuda, we could go into our freeze-dried emergency stores and this had proved highly successful. We had carried a couple of extra jugs of water for this purpose and considered ourselves to be eating like kings, not only with reconstituted steaks and chops and hamburger, but also with the one dish meals that are far better than most of the canned attempts to achieve the same goal. *Dancing Girl* values her reputation as a "Good Feeder" and this trip had done nothing to harm that.

The twins and their wives were packed and ready to go when the Old Man, returned from talking to customs and a quick visit to the telephone, produced reservations on the next plane out and a taxi to take them to it. I took off in another taxi to do my provisioning and the Old Man did the icing and washing and then stowed the charts and books for the areas we had put behind us and got out those for the area ahead. When I returned, I unloaded every case and box on the dock and checked every item to make sure we were not putting roaches or other wildlife aboard. We stowed frozen things first, then things requiring refrigeration, then items not improved by sitting in the hot sun, and, finally, the things requiring no special care. We took *Dancing Girl* out to our assigned mooring and finished readying the forward cabin for the new crew as the club launch came alongside to deliver David and Big Ann. With all the sails bagged and secure to the life line on the port side of the foredeck, it was easy for the new arrivals to sling their gear down the forward hatch and unpack and stow it. Oilies and boots went into the foul weather locker by the companionway after traveling clothes were hung in the hanging locker in their waterproof dress bags.

After cooking for two weeks, this was to be my last meal before David took over and I had readied a fillet of beef to be pan roasted with garlic and red wine, accompanied by fiddlehead greens and snow peas. For desert there would be heavy cream with some of the first raspberries of the year, but first it was time to loll around the cockpit and sip restorative potions.

I proposed a toast to "We four together again, and again." The Old Man said that he was delighted but surprised that both of them could advance their vacations 5 days on such short notice. Big Ann explained that the timing was perfect. David's new television promotion was not only better than any had hoped, but it had also caught the public's fickle eye and he could do no wrong. She was also getting a lot of credit, not entirely undeserved, for selling her major client on a new program to start in a month that would double her consulting fees from this source in the next year. "There is no need for either of us to think about business 'til we get back to the city. I must admit, though, that I am impressed at the way you can come in from two weeks at sea and five months out of the country and be ready to go cruising after one day in port."

The Old Man pointed out, "It's no particular stunt to do what we are doing if you keep up with the boat's maintenance and are going into familiar waters. On a gunkhole cruise with the prospect of being able to get provisions and boatyard support within a couple of days at any time, the problem is not much greater than that involved in getting in the family car and driving to Boston. Simply stated, it is my belief that, if you can get crew, a well-maintained yacht should be able to depart for any port in the farthest reaches of its cruising area with a week's notice.

"For the normal sailors, with no compulsion to test themselves by seeing how far they can go by being tough and modifying their normal way of life, their boat's cruising range is limited by the number of days' stores it can carry for a normal crew. Boats sailing for twenty-four hours a day can use and accommodate crew for one more watch than those that anchor or moor each night. Although my wife and I sailed many miles with just the two of us aboard, we usually cruised along the shore with four so that all our energies would not be consumed by the need to handle the boat. With four we can man the boat and drive it at its enjoyable maximum and yet arrive with chores and maintenance pretty well up to date. By the same token, off shore, six persons give us the capability of having two fully manned watches plus a navigator and a cook, each of whom is available should an extra hand be needed. Such a complement means that, regardless of the length of the voyage, the vessel should arrive with all maintenance done and the crew as fresh as when they started.

"For offshore voyages, without mechanical refrigeration, we can carry foods dependent on ice for up to 11 days, some fresh foods like carrots and cabbages will still be good after 30 days. In planning, we provide for a conservative ETA, allowing for 50 percent more time than we expect a slow trip to require. One hundred miles a day has worked out pretty well for us over the years. We have never gone slower. To this, depending on the area, we add up to 40 days to take care of such untoward happenings as dismasting or loss of rudder.

"Because we are no more anxious to be killed close to shore than the middle of an ocean, we try to maintain our boat's ability to handle the storms that occur close to land as well as those far offshore. In my opinion, getting hit with the top of the ice box, a floor board, or any other projectile is highly undesirable regardless of the boat's location. Flying back-

wards out of an upper bunk can put just as much blood in a
sailor's urine off Greenwich, Connecticut, as in the middle of
the North Atlantic. Losing the mast because of a failed turnbuckle is unacceptable in any waters. To sum up what I preach
is that the proper cruiser should at all times be 'in all respects
ready for sea' and the skipper should know it well enough to
know its needs in all situations.

"Let me set up an imaginary situation. It is Thursday evening, April 26, and we have just returned from two weeks'
easy cruising, just tuning the boat and visiting friends and
favorite harbors around Long Island Sound. I am at home
in beautiful Fairfield, Connecticut, and *Dancing Girl* is seven
minutes away in Southport. The phone rings and it is old
Tom, my college roommate, calling from Trinidad to ask if
we can meet him with the boat in Tobago on May 24. My
twin nephews and their wives are available for the next three
months. A quick look at the globe says about 2,200 miles. A
look at the pilot chart for last May which I happen to have in
my navigator's desk says less than 1 percent of vessels reported
gales along this route and that, once we are past Bermuda,
hurricanes are most unlikely. Tobago has far less risk of hurricanes than New England. In fact my recollection of the his-
tory of storms is that there has never been a hurricane in
those waters. I remember that some years ago my insurance
company insisted that I not leave Bermuda for the north later
than June 10th or 12th. That means that if we are to have
the boat in northern waters for the summer, we will have to
do a fast turnaround and do a non-stop back. An alternative
would be to make this the year of our long-dreamed cruise
south to be in Rio for Carnival. Everything looks feasible, we
can get there and get out, so I say, 'Sure', and arrange phone
numbers to call in Trinidad and Tobago in case we have any
need to communicate. I promise to call him on the radio when
we are two or three days off Tobago and can give a solid
ETA. As it is his nickel, I reluctantly admit there is nothing
more to say and hang up. Using a pair of dividers instead of
my fingers to estimate the distance on the globe comes up
with a distance of a little less than 2,000 miles. That means
for rough figuring we can use 20 days rather than the 22 that
I had in mind when I agreed to make the trip.

The pilot chart for May shows that an average trip over this route will run into about 2 percent flat calm and average winds along the way have run between Force 3 and 4 or between 7 and 16 knots, mostly in the higher ranges. The further along the way we go, the less likely that the wind will force us to beat.

"Battery charging takes one half gallon of fuel a day, 10 gallons for the trip. We carry 33 gallons which means, with 23 gallons for propulsion at 0.8 gallons an hour, that means 28.75 hours of steaming at 6 knots, 172.5 miles under power. I decide we might as well carry an extra 20 gallons in jugs to give us an extra 150 miles under power in case we get into trouble. We have the jugs in the boat or in an attic ashore. We will not figure in the 5 gallons of fuel we can make in an emergency out of the lube oil and lamp kerosene supply we always carry.

"A careful look at the chart decides me that nowhere on the trip will we need more than 20 days to reach port after a dismasting or other disaster. Add to this the 20 conservative days for the trip gives us 40 days at half a gallon of water per day for each of six people or a total of 120 gallons. The boat's tanks hold 70 gallons of water. We can freeze 20 gallons in soft jugs in place in the ice box using dry ice. Using more dry ice as the food is packed, I plan to have the ice box frozen solid on the day we depart and use other food the first 36 hours so that it need not be opened until the third day. Another 15 gallons of water in jugs will be stowed in the bottom of the port locker. The remaining 15 will be stowed on top of the deck house and will be emptied into the water tank we are using at the rate of a jug every two days. Unless this comes close to filling the tank we will know that water consumption is more than allotted and can take prompt corrective action.

"This evening we start making lists of things not to be forgotten and arranging for someone to baby-sit the house and the dogs. There are usually some delicacies in the freezer that will deteriorate if not included in our provisions for the trip, a side of smoked salmon, a dozen quail, and six eider duck steaks. The rest of the fresh meat will have to be brought tomorrow so the butcher will have time to freeze it for us.

There is always a short list of appointments to be cancelled and people to be notified of our change in plans.

"My secretary has become very efficient at providing a shore-based backup for my wanderings. Not only does she pay the bills and generally keep track of things like expiring licenses, but she also acts as a message center and clearing house. We arrange a frequency to be guarded, usually at 1000 for an hour each day, so that she can call me with any problems that occur and she can instruct others who want to talk directly as to how to use the marine operator. As we have a hard time getting away from the phone, it is more efficient for them to call me at the pre-arranged time than for me to run up a lot of charges because they cannot get to the phone when I call.

"I do not believe that people who go to sea have the right to expect others to incur a lot of expense trying to get them out of a hole that they themselves have dug. I try to be prepared to jury rig and get ashore safely from most of the accidents that can occur at sea. On the other hand, I try to maintain a well-prepared life raft and to carry on EPIRB (emergency radio beacon) with the thought that, if my position is fixed accurately, I would hope that there might be someone within range who might effect a rescue. My secretary keeps track of our plans and ETAs so that, if we turn up missing, a rescue might appear practical. She is prepared to notify the Coast Guard when it appears certain that something has gone wrong. Morally, it seems to me that no sailor is entitled to outside assistance until he has taken all reasonable steps to be independent and stay out of trouble. I am not as pure in my philosophy as those who go to sea with no radio and no provision for asking for help. They are right but I am willing to fudge a little with my secretary being prepared to alert others when I am missing.

"The next morning starts with a phone call to the Cruising Information Center in Salem, Massachusetts, to see what they know about Tobago and to authorize them to do any work for our account that they can complete before we sail. I would expect that they will be able to tell me the charts I will need and the various government publications that might be of assistance. They usually can suggest which of the available guides have been found valuable by other cruisers, and sometimes they can relay reports from other people who have cruised the waters in which I am interested. This is a volunteer organization set up by the Cruising Club of America and the Peabody Museum to facilitate the passing of information from cruising people to cruising people. It is supported largely by tax-free donations and its charges are moderate. They have always been of great help to me when I have called them.

"Armed with the information and advice obtained, I can now go to the telephone and call the various chandlers and suppliers who might have what I need and on occasion may be able to add valuable information to what I have already accumulated. With telephone orders, I try to get a shipping number to permit tracing the shipment from my end and to make sure that the goods ordered are in truth in stock. In some cases, you will be foolish not to pay extra to be sure that the shipment arrives before you depart.

"We have set Thursday, May 3, at 1000 for our ETD in order to ride the flood in to Hellgate and catch the ebb out through the Narrows. *Eldridge Tide and Pilot Book* makes figuring this quick and easy. I want to have sufficient information aboard so that we can, without difficulty, get into alternative ports along the way—chart kits for The Virgin Islands, The Bahamas, Florida East Coast, Norfolk to Jacksonville, and Cape May to Norfolk have to be purchased. We have Caribbean charts. We already have the coverage for Block Island to Cape May. Most food we will get locally, but we may have to shop around for freeze-dried and other dry stores. Banana chips are quite popular. To prevent monotony we also carry dried pineapple, peaches, and apple chips. The convenience of freeze-dried one-dish meals, which are prepared by merely adding boiled water, dictates that we carry a few cans, but you must be sure that you have enough water aboard to meet the needs of reconstitution. The same applies to their steaks and chops which can be completely reconstituted. They are more convenient and provide more varied and interesting meals than heating up canned stew when the going is rough. The dried foods are easier to stow because they are light enough to go in the ends of the ship if necessary.

"We check out the markets where really fresh vegetables

are sold, being sure to learn when they receive new deliver-
ies, making a careful mental estimate of the life expectancy
of each and make plans to carry as much as we can stow and
use. We do not plan complete meals but do try to have a
choice available to the cook so that meals can be tailored to
conditions.

"Bilges and under bunk areas are packed with canned food,
including modest amounts of crabmeat, shad roe, and other
specials for use when morale building is in order. A canned
whole capon or two permits the cook to gain accolades when
refrigeration is just a memory. If you are able to stock enough
specials, even the usual staples will seem like treats. Be sure
you know what the food in a can is going to taste like when
you open it. Some breads keep longer than others, there are
some canned breads, but I like to have fresh baked bread
even though it means extra alcohol for the stove. It gives the
cabin a lovely smell and the crew seems to eat it as fast as the
cook can make it.

"While laying on these stores, the cook should keep a tally
of how many meals are coming aboard, for in the final analysis, we want to be able to feed six people for 40 days. That is
240 breakfasts, lunches, and dinners, plus snacks. Any food
not consumed can be used later. The stores you lay on for a
tropical destination will be quite different than those you will
want for a run down to Labrador. The principles are the
same but to live well you must plan for the conditions you
expect. It is possible to have a standard list and try to load
the same stores for all 40-day periods, but, depending on
where you must shop, there can be a great variation in what
is available.

"As they become available, canned goods, charts, publications and clothes for the trip should be packed. A book or
other inventory control system should be used so that we know
what we have and where to find it. The ice box is to be frozen
on Monday morning with ice and dry ice and on Tuesday
most of the frozen food plus more dry ice should be packed.
On Wednesday May 2, all is to be repacked with the last of
the frozen food and more dry ice. Wednesday night the box
is to be sealed, not to be opened until Saturday. We hope
that, if all goes well, we will still be on refrigerated food on

the 13th. This depends on how lucky the cook is in getting frozen foods to fill every nook in the box.

"On Wednesday fresh bread and fresh produce, except for that which we can get fresh on Thursday before 0930, is to come aboard and be stowed. All hands will check over their own gear and areas of responsibility and be set by evening so that they can be aboard ready the next morning for last minute stowage and to get the boat underway as four bells strike. We have sailed enough together to know that we will cast off the last line at 1000 and that each of us can depend on the others so that there will be no last minute rush to take care of some neglected bit of essential work."

There was a pause with David came in with, "You know provisioning for a long voyage from the States as you describe is a science, requiring more art the farther you are removed from home base. When we are cruising along the shore the goal is to try to get 10 days' supply into the ice box with enough ice to hold it for those 10 days. Sometimes it is not easy and sometimes it is impossible, but I love the challenge, particularly when it is possible to fill out the menu with fresh local vegetables that do not require ice. Some of these can be pretty exotic, but they add zest to the shopping. I remember some really hilarious shopping in Greece, France, and Spain where my command of the local tongue would fill the market with laughter, but also the desire to help. Everywhere I have been, the women in the markets seem to respond to a poor helpless male pleading for help and cooking instructions.

"I figure that, if the natives eat it, so can we, if we cook it the same way they do. Squid, goat, octopus and most of the sausages and cheeses have been successful, but I shy away from the idea of eating things uncooked. When I make a shopping run, I usually come back feeling that I have really gotten to know the people.

"This kind of shopping requires that you keep running track of how many meals of each type you have acquired. There are some items I will always grab, tough-skinned, peelable fruit, garlic, 8 oz. jars of Hellman's mayonnaise (each enough for one meal but not requiring refrigeration until opened), ultra-sterilized milk (requires no refrigeration until opened but inspires the crew to drink every drop at the first

opportunity), pickles, and preserves. In countries where it is
safe, native lettuce seems to fill a basic yearning in most shipmates. Fresh fish and lobsters bought from the fisherman,
like mussels picked from the rocks, make my mouth water
just to think about them."

"You are right about every port being different," I added.
"In Europe, I was impressed with the wide assortments of
tinned foods, unknown in the markets home but permitting
an acceptable standard of living in areas where refrigeration
is not the way of life. On the other hand, in Labrador, we
had to make do with 'mystery meat' cut in cubes, apparently
with a chain saw and sold by a very helpful man whose dialect
was incomprehensible to me and mine to him. Pointing, ges-
turing, and smiling obtained for the cook the makings of a
challenging meal. 'Courage and Creativity' should have been
blazoned on the cook's banner when provisioning in the out-
ports in earlier days."

"I do not agree with your oversimplification, Professor,"
said the Old Man. "You and David, in emphasizing the art,
neglect the science. The definition of any problem is the key
to its solution. I would put 'Define and Digitize' on my banner. How many days and what margin of error in what conditions can help you decide how much bacon, how much
sausage, how much scrapple, how many cod-fish cakes and
so on through pancake mix, oatmeal, grits, Shredded Wheat,
fresh fruit, frozen orange juice, Tang, dried apricots, and
freeze-dried apple to make apple sauce. On this basic struc-
ture of need you can, using the screen of available to eliminate the impossible, build an inventory of the practical. At
this point creative flexibility can produce gracious living. We
all try to make *Dancing Girl* the best feeder afloat and because
we are pretty good at it, we live pretty well."

I went below and put water on to boil and got the dinner
set up to cook. It took me about two minutes to put on the
clean tablecloth and the napkins, candles, pepper and salt,
and silver and then I was back at the foot of the companionway able to be part of the conversation.

"A new boat is different but the principles are the same,"
the Old Man was saying. "Check to see that the nuts are tight
on all through bolts, including stanchion bases and particu-

larly winches. (I once found winches to be screwed to the winch islands which were not connected to the deck at all.) Do a careful survey of all standing and running rigging to be sure it can stand a long life at sea. Check your pumps and scupper and soft wood plugs. Have we a bucket for each member of the crew to bail with? Is the pump suction protected and of ample capacity so that the buckets will not have to be used? Are the fire extinguishers in good working condition and suitable? (I carry one more than the Coast Guard requires.) I have a fog bottle ready by the galley sink so that the cook can go to work on a fire before it gets a start and a canvas bucket on a line by the companionway in case that is not enough. I think through all the things I can imagine that might go wrong and see if we are equipped to handle them without outside help. My book of 'Ships Bills and Instructions' covers all that I have been able to distill from my experience over the years but I keep learning from talking to others, many with far more experience.

I like to think this means I could get any acceptable boat in shape for ocean voyaging in a couple of months and that, once the boat is up to snuff, I will be smart enough to keep it that way, because cruising is most fun when your precise planning prevents unpleasant surprises.

"We used to relabel cans with indelible felt pens, remove the paper labels so that they could not come adrift, and clog the bilge pump suction. Then we would carefully varnish the cans to prevent rusting. Our experience was that this time-consuming effort did not prevent cans from rusting when the varnish rubbed off which it did very quickly when wet. Now we still mark the cans with waterproof ink but instead of removing the labels, we put the can in heavy gauge poly bags which we seal with tape very carefully. The bags do not often wear through before we are ready to use the cans. The only disadvantage of the system is that the bags are not biodegradable and cannot be thrown over the side. This means that our big bag of plastic is a bit bigger when we reach port. In some ports with different standards than ours with regard to pollution, all trash and garbage, biodegradable or not, is dumped into the harbor. As the saying goes, we try but we do not always win.

"Provisioning is time-consuming. There needs to be a simple organization of the stowage and this needs to be precisely recorded in the inventory book. No one should ever take any item out of stowage without immediately recording the fact in the inventory book. Fresh fruits and vegetables will go into the mesh, Pullman-car–type clothes hammocks rigged in each bunk, permitting air to circulate, and again an effort must be made to make sure that no one but the cook ever takes anything from these stowages. With so much coming aboard it is important to be sure that all stowage is made with an 180° roll in mind. An easygoing 'It doesn't really matter if I make this little exception' attitude means a lowering of the boat's standards unacceptably. Our reputation is based on doing things precisely and well.

"During the week we have allotted ourselves, we must make a check of all equipment, spares, running gear, standing rigging, ground tackle, running lights, fog signals, steering gear, damage-control equipment, in fact everything that can be imagined as being important at some point during the projected voyage. This is no time to guess that something is okay. The terrible reality of Murphy's Law must haunt all hands during this crucial week. Precision is essential and any approximation will come back to haunt the boat. Depending on the manpower available, every task must be assigned to one person. Again, a book in which all tasks are listed as thought of, assigned to one person, checked when started, and initialed when completed will cut down on midnight worry sessions when you are helpless to take any action until morning.

"When you are offshore you should have thought out how you will navigate if the power fails. How will you get there if the engine will not start. What will you do for running lights? How will you jury rig a mast? Or a rudder? What will you do if a floating log holes the hull? These questions and many more somewhat similar should be answered before you shove off. Precision preparation is all that it takes to have a happy voyage."

Supper was ready, our discussion seemed to have covered the subject and we went below to what turned out to be a very good dinner.

IX

~~~~~~~~~~~~~~~~~~~~

Anchoring

By previous arrangement, *Polaris* led the way at low tide into
the sand hole that formed the easternmost part of Port Jefferson. She was to anchor and *Dancing Girl* was to lie off close
enough to observe and then come along side to starboard to
raft for the night. *Reprehensible* would then go alongside port
with the thought that *Polaris*'s big anchor, a 66-pound Bruce,
could easily hold the raft throughout the night without any
threat of midnight anchor drills. The schedule then called
for the Old Man, respectfully addressed as Commodore
Mayhew by the juniors, to talk to the group about anchors
and anchoring.

Polaris was under power as it worked its way in slowly but,
when it aproached the 9-foot spot where it intended to put
the hook down, it headed into the wind. The engine was
backed down, the anchor was left hanging at the dip until
headway was lost. It was then lowered into the water to serve
as an indicator when sufficient sternway was achieved. At that
point, the rode was eased out rapidly but not so fast that the
10-foot chain attached to the anchor could fall on top of it.
The nylon was let out fast enough to avoid taking a strain
until 90 feet were in the water. There was enough tension,
however, to be sure the line did not drift over near the prop.
The rode was then cleated and the engine stopped. The nylon

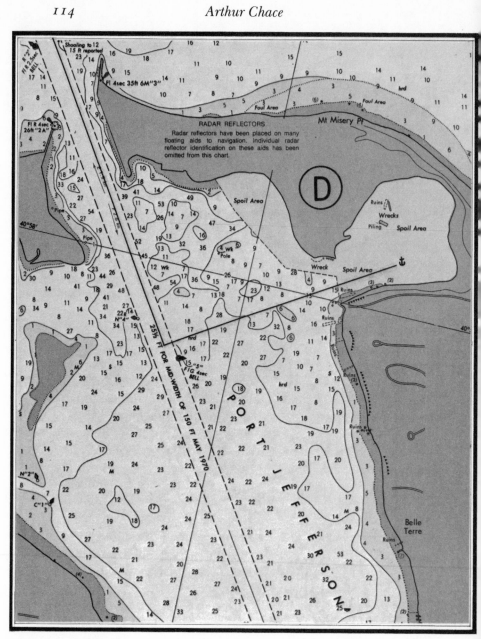

Port Jefferson

came straight and squeezed the water out of it under the strain but the instructor on the foredeck was not satisfied and shouted back, "Skipper, we don't have a good set here. The anchor's moving. I think we'd better try it again."

The kids groaned but hauled the anchor back up out of the water. The trouble was apparent. It had acquired, caught in its flukes, a rather second-grade automobile tire. Although it had been catching at first, the tire served to prevent it from getting a hold. With the aid of a boat hook, a line was passed down through the tire, back on board and the tire freed and brought aboard to be taken later to its final home ashore where it could cause no more trouble to honest seamen.

When all was set, *Polaris* moved slowly forward again, lowered the anchor at the appointed place and backed down. This time, when the anchor rode straightened out, there was no doubt about it having caught. The instructor called back, "Skipper, we have a good set this time. You can secure." *Polaris*'s skipper hoisted the alpha flag to the port spreader to tell *Dancing Girl* that they were ready for it to come alongside.

Girl came in slowly with two big fenders rigged on the starboard side and a junior standing by each of the four mooring lines: bow line, forward after spring, after forward spring, and stern line. The commodore timed his approach so that he was alongside *Polaris* just as it was about to complete its swing to port and the lines were handed over without any need to heave them.

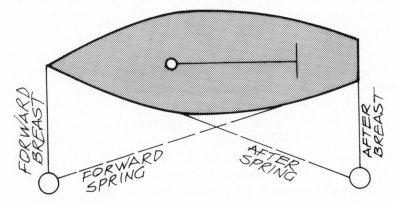

The Docking Lines

This series of sketches illustrates the use of mooring lines when coming alongside another boat to raft with it. Sketch A illustrates lines 1, 2, 3, and 4 ready as Dancing Girl *begins her approach. Two fenders have been rigged to protect the most likely contact points.*

The Old Man had explained the importance of getting the after spring over quickly so that he would have a sure control to prevent running up and locking spreaders should anything happen to the engine. As *Dancing Girl* forged slowly ahead with right full rudder, the spring hauled the boat in alongside *Polaris*. The forward spring went over next and was quickly secured to prevent *Dancing Girl* from dropping back in the breeze. The bow and stern lines were gotten over smartly and adjusted to make the two boats parallel.

The fenders were given their final adjustment to ensure that they shared the load and would permit no contact between the boats. The Old Man then instructed his people to bring the lines, after they had passed around the appropriate cleats and winches, back to *Dancing Girl* so that, if the need arose, it could get underway without too much need for assistance from *Polaris*.

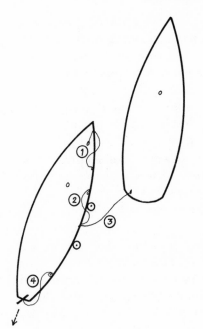

Dancing Girl *is now making her approach and has gotten number 3 over first to make sure that the boat can be prevented from moving forward so far that the spreaders tangle.*

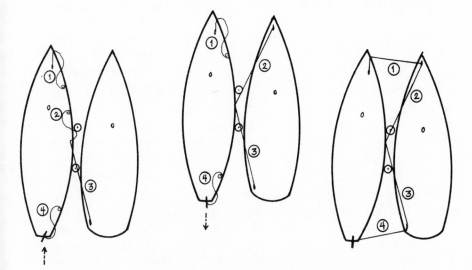

These sketches in #1 show line 3 swinging Dancing Girl *in against* Polaris *and at the same time keeping her from advancing further. In #2 we see that 2 is in place keeping the boat from dropping back. #3 shows 1 and 4 in place to keep both the bow and the stern from swinging out.*

Reprehensible, who had been lying off observing and waiting its turn, started in on the starboard side but its angle was a little off and its timing also with the result that the raft swung away from it just as it was about to put its lines over. Heaving lines were ready and the spring was gotten over quickly. *Reprehensible*'s forward motion resulted in the spring pulling the bow in neatly alongside in the proper place and, by use of full rudder, the stern came in also right on schedule. The other lines were put over and all was secure. By the time the sail covers were on and all was secure, the three-boat raft was swinging easily in the wind.

The Old Man began his talk: "The anchoring had gone well, particularly so because *Polaris* was able to demonstrate so well the importance of really getting a good set before you secure the anchor detail. Some years ago, after a long, hard day, we were going up into Sam Hitches Harbor, on the south coast of Newfoundland. The rain had started to come down, producing miserable, freezing trickles on our skin because we had not had time to get into foul weather gear. I was just about frozen and, when the foredeck honcho told me that he had a good set, I was happy to accept his word and go below.

"After drying off, I even got into my bunk to get warm, only to be awakened a short time later, just before the keel ground on a rock. We all shot up on deck, and after checking to see that there was no line that could get into the screw, started the engine and carefully eased our way back out away from the shore, avoiding the big boulders we could see on the bottom through the crystal water. We had anchored to two anchors, but the story would be even more interesting if we had used only one. The anchors had come together as they had dragged and as we hauled on them, each came in, helping little to assist us in getting out into deep water. They slid in and, when they came up on deck, each was clean except for a slight trace of organic mud that was of such a light consistency that neither could really get a grip on the bottom.

"We cleaned up the anchors and went back to where we had anchored before and, with greater care, checked out what had happened. At first, we put an anchor over and, when we took a strain on it, we realized that what we had thought to be a good set was really a mouthful of sloppy stuff without holding power. The water was too deep for happy anchoring in most of the harbor, in fact in most cases the cliffs seemed to drop down into deep water. I saw one place where there seemed to have been landslides over the years and guessed correctly that there would be a build-up of useful gravel there. That time the anchors set hard and we spent a peaceful night.

"When a hard day is over you hope the tedious details of anchoring and putting the vessel away will pass quickly and without a hitch and you tend to look for reasons to believe the anchor is well set. This is understandable but, if you want to sleep well and not have a lot of problems, you have to be sure that the anchor is not going to come loose and let you drift around. Things are a lot harder to correct in the middle of the night. It does not matter what kind of an anchor you use. You should always have enough scope out at low water to guarantee more than 5-to-1 scope at high tide. I like to use 10-to-1 scope when I am anchoring to give the anchor every chance to get a good set. In areas where the tides are great, where I am not going to be crowded, I put out enough scope to give me as much as 7 to 1 at high tide. I have 10 feet of chain on each anchor, connecting it to the nylon rode, taking some of the abrasion on rocky or coral bottoms. I figure that this just about takes care of the distance from the water's surface and the mooring cleats on deck and eliminates the need to worry about that aspect. Scope is easy to remember; if you are anchoring at low tide in water that is 10 feet deep, 10-to-1 scope is then 100 feet. This gives you a nice, flat angle with the bottom so that, when you put a heavy strain on the anchor, the flukes will dig in and hold, rather than have a tendency to be lifted as often happens when riding to a scope of less than 5 to 1.

"In the accompanying diagram, note the comparative angles of 3-to-1, 5-to-1 and 10-to-1 scopes. Note particularly the difference in the angle of strain on the anchor. There is very little to choose between the 5 and 10 but as you approach 3-to-1 scope you can see that you are suddenly exerting a significant amount of upward lift. You will also note that a boat that is comfortably off a pier at 5-to-1 scope will not get significantly closer at 10-to-1. The difference between 3-to-1 and 5-to-1, however, is something you should keep in mind.

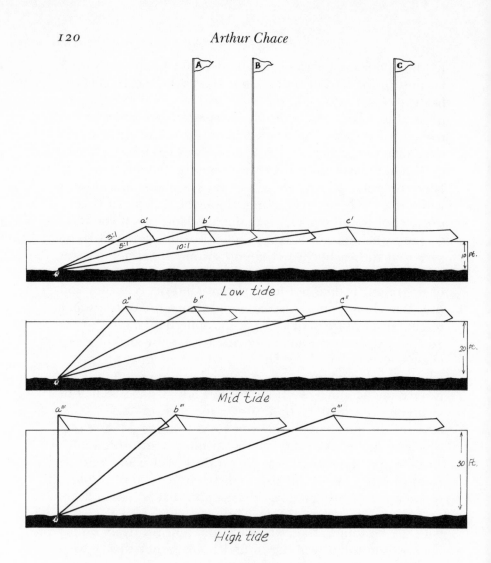

Low tide

Mid tide

High tide

"Once we were anchored off the Pitons in the Caribbean and there was a heavy chop rolling into the bay. The wind, however, was swirling in all directions which meant that, from time to time, we would lie in the trough and roll our ears off and put a heavy load on our anchor. The simple solution was to row a second anchor ashore from the stern and set it by hand on the beach. Remember that, when you are rowing an anchor out, you put the anchor in the boat and coil the rode on top so that you are not dragging the rode through the water but merely laying it in the water. It tows a lot easier in the boat than through water.

"As an alternative to using an anchor, you can put a line around some firm object, such as a bollard or a tree on the beach to hold you off when you are lying in a position too narrow to be controlled in any other way. Ideally, you will not put your anchor rode or your mooring line around a fir tree because of the pitch that may come of the bark, but there are occasions where you will accept this disadvantage. If the line goes out around the object and back to the boat, you can then release one end and bring it in without having to go ashore.

"In many anchorages the boat will pivot on its anchor, either in the wind or the current, so that there will be many turns in the ground tackle by morning. In a situation like this, if you are only using one anchor, there is a considerable risk of your breaking it out when you are applying a load from the direction opposite to the one in which you set the anchor. Last fall, we anchored in Conscience Bay where the current runs about 4 knots as the big, shallow bay drains and fills through the narrows where it is deep enough to anchor. In the morning we had seven turns between our two anchors and I was very glad that I keep my anchor rodes in 100-foot lengths with an eye at each end so that I can shackle lengths together. In this case, there was a shackle not over 15 feet short of the cleats on which the anchor rodes were secured. By opening the shackle on the unloaded rode, I was able to uncleat it and then, holding it in an easy coil, unwrap it from around the working rode and then return it to the cleat. If I had had a very long length, I would then have been able to handle it easily because I keep my anchor rodes in nylon mesh laundry bags which permit me to take the unused line in an easily handled bunch.

"Some years ago, after two stormy days when it was too rough to consider going into the harbor at San Salvador in the Bahamas, we anchored in a cove nearby for the night, hoping that the conditions would be better in the morning. The cove was sheltered from about 300° magnetic clockwise to 180° magnetic and, as the wind was from 350° and the rule in the Bahamas was stated to be that the wind always veered, we thought we were safe for the night. However, as if often the case with these local rules, Murphy's Law applied and the wind backed so that, at one o'clock in the morning, the wind

was blowing straight into the cove and bringing with it a significant sea. The boat was jumping on her working anchor
line like a scared horse on a tether and it was obviously very
close to breaking the anchor loose. In this situation, we had
a lee shore and were in real trouble.

"The obvious solution to that anchoring problem was to
veer the working rode until we were over the lazy anchor and
pick that one up. Then the plan was to start the engine, take
in the loaded anchor and get out to sea where we could be
safe. The boat was bouncing so that the foredeck was not an
easy place to be and, as I recollect it, I had to lie down in
order to work without risk of falling overboard even though
I was in my safety harness and clipped on. The boat was
brought slowly up until it was over the anchor, the anchor
rode was drawn taut and then we powered ahead breaking it
out and were lucky enough to get it on deck and secure before
it banged the hull. We all heaved a great sigh of relief when
we were outside standing off and on under storm jib and
trysail with plenty of maneuvering room. One of the things
to remember about anchoring is that there are times when
you do not want to do it.

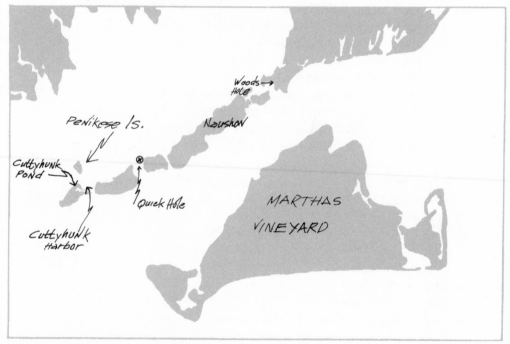

The Elizabeth Islands and Martha's Vineyard

"Another occasion I remember is 10 years ago when, after a pleasant day of picnicking in Quicks Hole, we came around to spend the night in Cuttyhunk Pond. We came in under power and found that, not only was the harbor full of boats, but that almost every one of them had anchored on very short scope, like 3 to 1 or less, in order not to swing into neighbors. We turned 180° and went out and, after checking the weather report, found that the wind was expected to be from a northerly direction all night. We therefore went up and anchored under Penikese Island knowing that, if the wind came around to that we were no longer sheltered, we could up anchor and move down into Cuttyhunk Harbor. The one thing we knew that we would not do is go back into the pond to take part in the demolition derby that was bound to occur if strong winds came up and all those boats on short scope started to move.

"In conclusion, then, it is important to remember that you should always evaluate your ground tackle so you know how much wind and sea you can handle, which anchors to use, and knowing the tide conditions, how much rode should be put out. And, finally, do not forget there are times when being hove to sea is a lot healthier than sitting in an untenable anchorage.

"I almost always use two 12-pound Danforths set far enough apart in a line perpendicular to the wind with at least 5-to-1 scope at high tide to give an angle of 60° between the rodes. If the angle is too much wider the hooks will pull against each other. If the angle is too much narrower when the direction in which the boat rides is changed by the wind or current the working rode will be long enough so that if it gets some slack in it, it can foul the non-working anchor and break it out.

"As I see it, the working anchor can keep the boat close enough so that the lazy rode being held down by its chain will not foul the lazy anchor. You do not have to do a lot of fancy measuring. Just remember that if the distance between the anchors is the same as the scope used you will have an equilateral triangle which will give you your 60° angle. My system works pretty well. Under sail or power I decide where I want to anchor and approach the place for the first hook on a course perpendicular to the wind or current whichever will have more effect on the boat. Just before I get to the spot for the first anchor to go over I turn 20° below the course and holding the rode up to keep it clear of the screw and rudder I ease the anchor into the water and pay out cable just fast enough to prevent tensions. After a boat length I come up 20° and continue until I have paid out the scope I have figured for the anchorage, ideally 10-to-1.

"I try to have the boat going 3 knots and when I take a quick turn around the mooring cleat the hook either misses obviously or catches and spins the boat around as it sets. Regardless, the second anchor goes over immediately and we head back toward the first anchor, taking in the first rode and easing out the second with enough tension to keep it out of the screw. At 100 percent on the second rode we set that hook. If the first anchor is set, we then equalize the scope on each and secure. If the first has not set, we then try again until we have both anchors well set at a proper distance apart and both anchors having their scopes with an equal angle to the bottom.

"Anyone who thinks about it must admit that although a single anchor of any type will hold well if the orientation of its load remains the same as when it was set, trouble is liable to show up when the wind or current swings the boat to produce a load from a different direction. Some anchors run a risk of getting fouled by their own anchor rode, broken out and dragged over the bottom. Others will break easily and have difficulty resetting. I like the tremendous holding power of the Danforth anchor for its weight and by using two, as I do, I like to think I eliminate the problem of it being broken out by a change in the heading on which the boat lies. As with all matters at sea everything we do is a compromise between answers to conflicting problems and all I ask is that the skipper not ignore any possible hazards. A vessel anchored with short scope or ground tackle with inadequate holding power should have an anchor watch set.

"When moored this way the boat rides securely in a much smaller area and a shift of wind or current cannot break out either hook the way it can a single anchor. By this method I can enjoy the light weight and superior holding power of the Danforth without the risk attendant on its difficulty in resetting when broken out. If sufficient stress develops to cause dragging it is easily apparent from the narrowing of the angle between the two warps. To my way of thinking the people who anchor to a single anchor of a type that will not stay set or reset quickly when broken out better set an anchor watch. While lying alongside *Polaris* secured by its single, big Bruce, I relied on its reputation for setting instantly and the fact that *Polaris* draws a foot more than we do and will hold us off the sand if it drifts into shoal water."

The skipper of *Polaris* laughed and said, "You can sleep well, Commodore. I am moved by your trust in me and will call you at the first suspicion that I might be dragging."

The Old Man chuckled. "The penalty for unnecessarily disturbing the fleet commander's rest is keel hauling as I remember it. I will look it up to be sure."

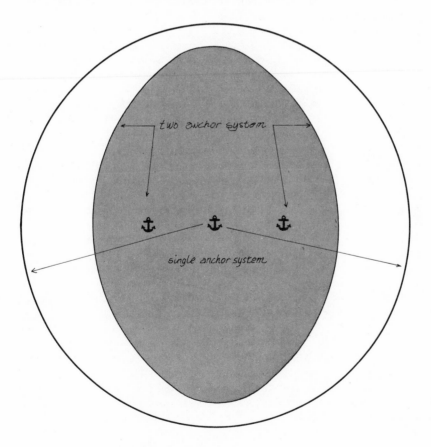

This diagram shows the water through which may pass any part of a 40-foot boat anchored to two anchors in 10 feet of water with 10:1 scope placed 100 feet apart. This sketch assumes that the boat will hang back on its anchor pointing directly into the wind or current and that the stern will be the maximum possible distance from the anchor. In many cases the action of the second anchor will reduce the area that will be needed by the boat were it riding to a single anchor. This sketch also illustrates the area that would be needed by the same boat riding to a single anchor fixed precisely in the bottom and presumed not to move when tide or current shift. This circle should be enlarged to allow for the amount of bottom the anchor will move over while realigning or reset-ting after a wind or current change. In both cases the bow of the boat in question would describe an area 40-feet closer to the loaded anchor or anchors.

X

~~~~~~~~~~~~~~~~~

Navigation

The Old Man had brought us into Hadley Harbor, on Nau-shon Island, to anchor under sail as easily as slipping into the family pew in church. The man on the depthfinder had been calling the feet every 10 seconds, more frequently if there was any change, confirming when it was time to tack. The grinders and tailers felt that he had tacked each time as soon as the sheet was in and were still puffing vigorously. We had anchored with precision and were lying exactly where the Old Man had said we would. Channel 16 blared, *"Sea Dreams* calling Coast Guard, come in, please. We need help. Over to you. Come in, please."

With customary calm and efficiency, the Coast Guard soothed the caller enough to determine that *Sea Dreams,* a white sloop 32 feet long was lost, lonely, and a trifle terrified. It was getting dark and foggy and nothing they could see looked a bit like their Texaco map of the area.

The Old Man exploded, "That flaming idiot, my friends, is the modern boater. He does not have a clue as to where he is. No wonder the Coast Guard is short of funds."

Finally, the Coast Guard told *Sea Dreams* to wait. After about five minutes of silence, they heard a calm female voice "Woods Hole Coast Guard, Woods Hole Coast Guard, this is *Polaris,* over." There was a quick response; they shifted to Channel

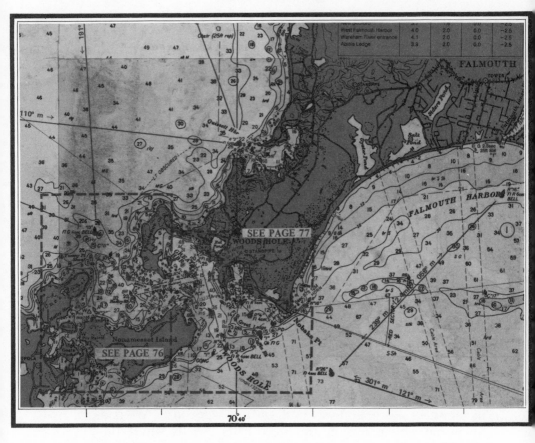

22. "Coast Guard, this is *Polaris*. We are close aboard *Sea Dreams* and are going into Hadley Harbor for the night. They say they will follow us in. We draw six and they say they draw five. We will call you if we need further help. Thank you very much. This is *Polaris* WZQ7393 out."

"*Polaris*. Coast Guard, Roger and thank you. Woods Hole Coast Guard, Out."

The next day had dense fog and no one was sorry that it had been planned as a lay day to permit the crew to go over to Woods Hole to market, attend to business, and to visit the exhibits at the Oceanographic Institute. As one of our group was a relative of the Forbes family, which owned Naushon, and entitled to use the *Charles Olsen,* he was able to take the others with him on the family ferry connecting this lovely

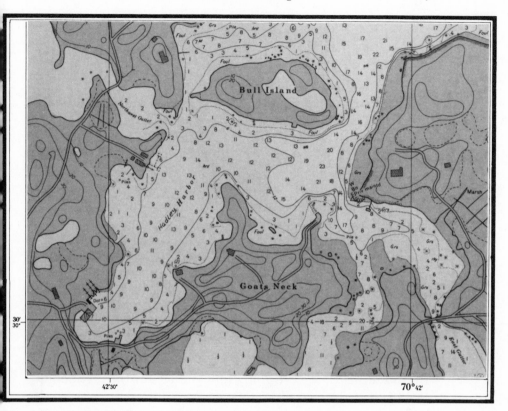

Naushon—Hadley Harbor

family island with the mainland. As the Old Man was rowing back from the ferry dock, checking his hockey puck compass from time to time to see that he was on curse for *Dancing Girl,* a voice came through the fog, "I can see how that big fellow with his radar can go along with a clear picture of what the fog obscures, but I am damned if I can see how you have the courage to go rowing blind through this stuff. I didn't know how fog could be this thick."

The Old Man looked up to see a man in his early forties dressed impeccably in brand new yachting costume from his Greek captain's cap and Breton sweater to his Topsiders. As the boat swung idly around, the name on the transom came into view—*Sea Dreams.* The Old Man explained that before he had gone ashore he had plotted the course on his chart and was using his compass to steer the reciprocal on the way out. The man shook his head and sighed, "You have no idea how much I envy you, sir. This is my first boat and when I bought it this winter, I had no idea how dangerous and difficult it would be to find my way around."

The Old Man felt a twinge of sympathy that surprised him. He heard himself saying, "If you really want to learn learn, climb in my dinghy and I will take you back to my boat and I will show you how we do it. I think that in a couple of hours or so, I can give you a start towards becoming a navigator."

He accepted, stuck his head down the companionway to explain that he would be absent for an unpredictable length of time, and climbed into the dinghy. The Old Man introduced himself (Obadiah Mayhew, called O. M. or Old Man, for obvious reasons) and gathered his visitor's name was Bob and that he had had the most terrifying time of his life the night before. The Old Man admitted he had heard some of the radio transmissions. Bob filled in some details. Responding to a hail, *Polaris* had come close aboard. There were three women aboard about the age of Bob's daughter who was a freshman at college. When they heard *Sea Dream*'s problem they said that they were going into Hadley for the night and would be glad to have him follow.

Bob had been surprised to see how expertly they furled their sails to lead them in under power, but he was fascinated to see them taking bearings on all sort of landmarks that he could not even identify. They seemed to know exactly where they were every minute and later amazed him by saying that none of them had been in Hadley in a couple of years.

As they climbed aboard *Dancing Girl,* the Old Man explained, "Anyone who goes sailing should be expected to at least do that well.

"There are so many clues available to tell you where you are that you should keep a log to record them for possible future use. Just a notebook like this will do. You should have a time piece so that each entry has a time recorded with it— your wristwatch is fine. If you record the date, the record becomes available for use at a later date for comparison. Entering the times of starting and stopping the engine permits you to estimate how much fuel you have taken out of the tank since you last filled it and to compute your fuel consumption per hour with greater accuracy. The competent navigator does not run out of fuel unexpectedly.

"You should log every time you pass a buoy or any other object with a fixed position, including, of course, every time you get a fix. Compass courses steered and your speed through the water help you advance your position with useful accuracy. A guess as to your speed is better than nothing and, with practice, you can become fairly accurate. You soon get a good idea of your best speed, and if you remember that a normal person walks at 3 miles an hour on level ground, you will be delighted at how accurately you can judge the speed of the water going past you. Try guessing your speed this way. You will be surprised at how you can narrow down the area where you might be. If you learn the Beaufort scale you will be pleased at how well you can estimate wind velocity and learn to relate it to boat speed with various relative wind directions and sail combinations.

"Old-time navigators used an hour glass to determine how many knots in a line attached to a chip log, a triangular float, passed through their fingers in a given time after being thrown over the side. A nice, simple system that you can adopt to your own use is throwing a crumpled piece of paper into the water at a mark on the toerail forward and timing to see how long it takes after it hits the water for it to pass another mark on the toerail aft. (If the marks are 30 feet apart, you multiply the elapsed time by 200 to get the number of seconds you need to go a mile—we use the nautical measurement 6,000 feet to the mile.) Remember that it takes 10 minutes to go a mile at 6 knots. Also remember that, at 6 knots, you go a tenth of a mile (200 yards) in a minute. (Run through your head that at six knots you go 5.1 miles in 51 minutes, 2.3 miles in 23 minutes and so on.) Mastery of this concept makes it easy to check the reasonableness of estimates you make for slower or faster speeds for various distances.

"Many cruisers seeking greater accuracy use a patent log (the Walker log is a good example). It is a system of towing a calibrated vaned bronze rotor on a long line which turns the gears behind a calibrated dial which reads miles traveled. By timing fifty rotations you also get an accurate reading from a table that gives knots. As speed through the water is affected by variations in wind and waves, you will probably find that three timings gives you a better average speed.

"So far we have had no need for batteries, but modern man can do so much with electricity that almost everyone uses electronic speed and distance indicators as long as the power lasts. They are wonderful, but accuracy can be affected by the fluctuations in the available power and some are more liable than others to pick up error-producing weeds or other flotsam in the water. Turn them on when you get under way and record your distance run every time you log your position. Thus, you get a pretty reliable clue as to how far you have run from your last known position and you can extrapolate if the electronics stop for any reason. Remember that such instruments give you speed and distance through the water, not over the bottom. If you are in a tidal flow or current, you must correct for that flow.

"Of course, this information is much more valuable if it is used with information from a reliable compass and from helmsmen who know the courses they steer. Compasses should be compensated annually probably by a professional compass adjuster and the resulting deviation table kept where it is handy to the navigator. You should check your compass whenever you can sight over it down a range and even make runs back and forth to check various headings. You may find that a helmsman's knife, key ring, or can of soda is deflecting the compass. *Eldridge Tide and Pilot Book* gives you the sun's declination on any day of the year and its true bearing at any of the latitudes you will be sailing in. You can check your compass bearing of the sun at sunrise or sunset against the true bearing in the table corrected for variation to determine compass error. *Bowditch (American Practical Navigator DMAHTC Pub No. 9)* and *Dutton's Navigation and Piloting* will tell you how to check your compass by taking azimuths at any time the sun is visible. These two books will tell you a lot more and should be a part of any boat's library.

"It is obvious at this point that we are only able to get back to where we started and need charts if we are to know where else we can go. Charts are approximately square or rectangular representations of a small portion of the earth's surface. Large scale charts will have a scale usually 1:20,000 or 1:40,000 which will be stated on the chart. Remember large scale charts cover a small area and small scale charts show a large area. Sometimes these charts have a self-explanatory nomograph on them for solving time-speed-distance problems, but all include a distance reference to permit the navigator to pick off distances with his dividers. These cover areas such as the approaches to a harbor. The next smaller scale charts, usually 1:80,000, cover areas about the size of the eastern half of Long Island Sound. These smaller scale charts are usually available with an overlay of the applicable hyperbolic loran C lines but the loran user should make sure that an old chart has the lines currently in effect.

"On the right and left side of these charts are printed the latitude in degrees, minutes, and tenth of minutes. Because a minute of latitude equals a mile, most navigators take their accurate distances from the sides of the chart when possible. Longitude scale is across the top and bottom of the chart (remember that while the distance between lines of latitude remain constant, the distance between lines of longitude decrease as you move north or south of the equator). U.S. charts also have a compass rose that shows both magnetic and true north at the time the chart was made. Vessels with only magnetic compasses use the magnetic rose which is the inner one. Note how far off you will be if you use the outer. Do not forget to allow for deviation if your adjuster has not been able to eliminate it. The compass rose graphically presents the easterly or westerly variation as applied to the true directions. Easterly or westerly deviation is applied the same way to the magnetic.

"Charts also indicate whether depths are shown in feet, meters, or fathoms. I once talked with a pilot in Saint Pierre about an overconfident German skipper of a freighter loaded with washing machines whose fathometer was set on feet when he thought it was set on fathoms. That year a lot of families had new washing machines that had not come through customs.

"During World War II, there was a story about a 110-foot Subchaser asking a fisherman in Charleston Harbor about the depth. The response was to stick an oar straight down and demonstrate that the answer was about 4.5 feet. The Navy does not view groundings casually and the skipper saw to it that a lead line was swinging the rest of the way in. The modern electronic depth finder is so well developed now that sail-

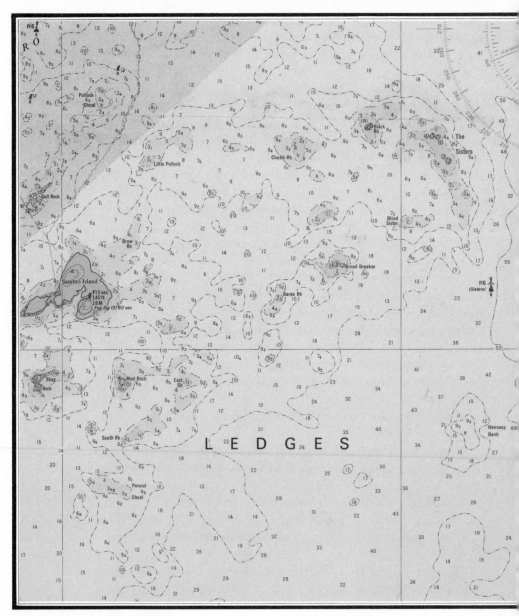

Approaches to Halifax Harbor

ors seldom leave home without one, but they should not forget that the lead line is a very accurate and useful tool, and that the electrical system on a small boat is vulnerable.

"Depth provides a very useful clue and is very reliable except in a few situations where currents keep the bottom moving. Once, during a Halifax Race, we had very thick fog as we approached The Sisters, a buoy that was a mark of the course around which we had to turn on our way to the finish. There was considerable current and our position was crucial. The bottom at the buoy was not distinctive but, by recording the depth every five minutes exactly, for two hours, we were able to get a strip of soundings which we could slide along the chart of the bottom until we got a match. Another illustration was when we were sortieing from Stonington, Connecticut, on our way to Newport in thick fog and a light but steady breeze. A look at the chart showed us that, by following the meanders of the 20-foot line from Napatree Point, we could be led through Watch Hill Passage and always know almost exactly where we were. Remember that the depths shown on the chart are at low water and you may be working at some time between high and low. The tide tables have a section including a well-explained table which permits you to figure exactly what the depth should be at the moment you are there.

"There are a number of very good loran C receivers available today and the state of the art is still advancing rapidly. Changes are coming so fast that, in spite of your normal tendency to ignore reading the instructions until all else fails, it is really worthwhile to study them at once and follow the recommended procedures. The basic principle of this system is the device may, depending on the set, be as much as 1.5 miles off from the charted coordinates, but it will always read the same when it returns to the same geographic position. With a new set or in a new location, you should always record the coordinates that you get at each buoy or other mark or position to which you may want to return. Most sets let you, by pushing the right buttons, store these coordinates for recall at a more convenient time. This feature should certainly be used if someone goes over the side. You can then return to the geographic spot again and again to try to figure out what the current has done with the victim. You can also use the coordinates for the starting point for your search plan if your

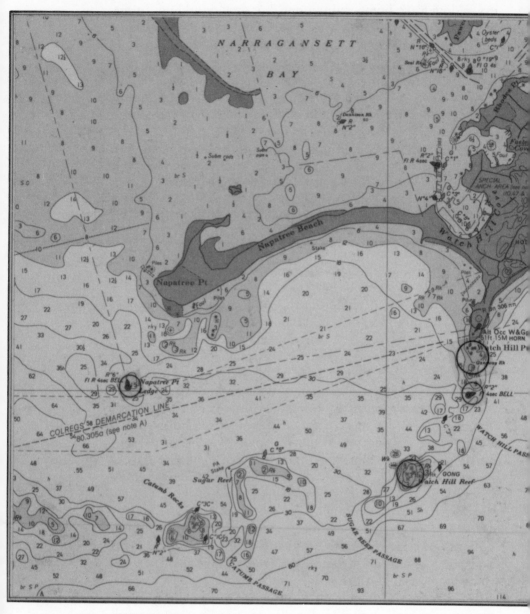

Stonington—Watch Hill Passage

computed position does not produce results.

"At least two of my friends have been involved, in years back, in man overboard situations in difficult visibility where the victim or victims were never seen again. Proper use of loran might have permitted relocation.

"Even if you do not have one of the lorans with a computer, you will often find that there is a line that comes sufficiently close to your intended course so that you can follow it in when foggy conditions makes this desirable. Government charts have a nomograph which permits you, by sliding your dividers along perpendicular to the base line and open to equal the distance between the two nearest lines on the chart to reset your dividers to the exact distance you seek. A better system is to mark the edge of any transparent straight edge with a series of 10 equidistant marks to various scales. You can move this ruler over the chart to your approximate dead reckoning position and then, by canting it get one of these measures to provide on the chart a scale for marking the exact time delays the instrument has given you. By doing this twice, you can define the desired line precisely. Then, for a crossing line, you can slide the ruler along the second pair of lines until the exact point lands on the first line.

"Until you are pretty good at piloting, though I think you should stay away from all the fancy electronic aids. A beginner needs to know the basics when the power fails and he better learn them before he gets into the fancy stuff which will be a lot easier to use once he has the basics. Although the experts say that the crossing of two lines is enough to give a fix, I like to use a third to confirm that Murphy's Law has not applied. An error in mathematics or plotting does not stand out unless you use three lines. A good navigator has a supply of sharpened pencils near his charts table and I like to have a battery operated pencil sharpener nearby. Dull pencils make sloppy plots. A good eraser is essential to keep the chart clean for your current work. I think it worthwhile to get the kneadable ones available in artists' supply stores. A magnifying glass and a good light makes life a lot easier. At night use only red light in the cabin so people coming on deck will require less time to get their night vision.

"Two of the most important tools you need are the parallel

rulers and the dividers. Although a little mysterious to the
neophyte, they are easy to master. The hands of a skilled
navigator are absolutely accurate but the less skilled have a
tendency to let error creep in because they permit slippage.
Moving parallels over a chart, you should always have one of
the two rules solidly fixed to the chart by pressing down on
it with one hand or the other. The same caution applies when
you use dividers—you should be particularly careful to see
that nothing strikes the pointed tips causing them to change
distance before you are ready.

"I believe that the hockey puck hand bearing compass is
the most useful aboard the kind of boats we sail in. In some
cases, however, you'll find that the motion of the sea causes
the card to swing without ever settling down on a particular
bearing. Under these circumstances, the skilled navigator
watches and gets a mental average between the two extremes
of swing and uses this for his bearing. Bearings can be taken
from any fixed object that shows on the chart and, to prevent
error, should always be called in three digit numbers. Thus,
one would say Zero-One-Zero, rather than 10°.

"It's obvious that close objects are better than those farther
away and that lighthouses are better than buoys which can
shift with the current. Before making a trip, the prudent
navigator studies the chart and decides which navigational
aids will be needed on the voyage. For example, on Long
Island Sound there are a number of towers on railroad bridges
that show on the chart, are easy to find and can provide a
bearing when you need a second or third to complete a fix.
Charted church steeples, movie screens, chimneys, and radio
towers all provide excellent points of reference. In coastal
waters, such objects often form a line with another object so
that you can get a range. This permits you to mark a line on
the chart to indicate when, for example, the lighthouse is in
line with the cupola on the court house. If you mark that line
of bearing on the chart and take a depth finding, you have a
useful fix that does not require a compass. Such natural ranges
can greatly facilitate fixing the vessel's position when waters
are rough.

"At night, when you take bearings on lights, be sure to

time them carefully with a stop watch because nothing is more deceiving than a light which is not on the object you expect. During the war, I remember the story going around Charleston Navy Yard about a 173 footer which came into the harbor in the fog and was having trouble identifying a fixed red light. When the light changed to green and automobiles started blowing their horns, the navigator quickly revised his estimate of the solution. Always remember that any entry in your log should include the time at which the observation was taken. It is no good to know that the water is 23 feet deep unless you know at what time you were there.

"Every year the government puts out a tide table for the area in which you are operating and a current table. These two books contain much useful information in addition to the tables and it's well worth spending a day such as this just leafing through and making sure you understand all the information. There are also large charts of an area like Long Island Sound on which you can indicate the time of the current every hour during the cycle. This permits precise computations as long as you keep in mind that these values are average and that heavy winds for a long period of time and heavy rains can make definite changes both in the time and the amount of current you experience.

"When you are trying to compute the effect the current will have on the course you steer, remember to always put on your chart the course steered and the distance run based solely on facts without any addition of judgment. This is called the dead reckoning position and it is indicated by a half circle with a dot at the center. Fixes, which are positions you are sure are correct, such as those obtained by bearings of three lighthouses or a range crossed with a depth, are marked by a circle with a dot in the middle. On the other hand, if you are in an area where current is important, you can come up with an EP, or estimated position, which is indicated by a small square with a dot in the center. Although the EP is, we hope, a more accurate position, the fact that it involves judgments as to the state of the current and the various forces could effect the course you have ordered the helmsman to steer. This means you should always keep your dead reckoning available as the only sure thing you know and then use the EP when you have determined to the best of your ability where you are.

"The easiest way to solve course, speed, and distance problems involving current and other factors is to plot things out on the compass rose. If, for example, you were steering a course of ogo at 6 knots, draw a line from the center through ogo and mark on it '6 miles' obtained from the side of the chart with your dividers. Then look up the tide table and indicate the direction of the current and the speed of the current during that hour. This you put from the end of the line indicating where you've gone. Then, if you close the triangle by drawing a center to the end of the current line, you have an indicate of the actual course made good. It also tells you by its length the speed made good. To decide what course to steer, move the current line in the opposite direction to figure out how much to compensate for the current. Again, the speed is in the distance from the center. If you make it a habit of checking your course and speed compensating for the current in this way, you'll soon be able to tell when you don't need to go to this trouble and when it is absolutely essential.

"Every fix, dead reckoning position, or EP should be appropriately marked at its exact position on the chart showing our time. The course line to reach the point should be indicated by showing the distance below the line in nautical miles, or, if necessary, in yards, and above the line indicating the actual degrees of the bearing from the point of origin. You can also, in addition to the distance, put the speed below the line with an S 6.5, for example. When you are running in thick fog, it is useful to be able to identify quickly all the information on your location. And it is also useful to mark in the conventional way so that anyone can look at your chart and quickly understand what you have done.

"There are a number of good books on navigation and piloting and their use is a matter of choice. I always carry Bowditch because that is the basic bible containing all the facts on the whole subject of navigation and it has many useful tables. I also carry Dutton which is also a complete study of the current system of piloting in contrast with the more detailed and historically complete *Bowditch*. I carry the government tide table and current table and the tidal chart of the area if it is available. Also useful is 117A, the *Radio Aids to Navigation*, which tells you what stations and what frequencies are available to you on your VHF radio and your radio direction finder.

"Coast Guard regulations require that you carry signal flags and the book of signals. A lot of people have, for many years, considered *Eldridge*, which comes out yearly and covers the New England area, generally, as a source of a great deal of very useful piloting and navigational information set up in a way that is easy to understand. *Eldridge* has been increasing its area of operation and the amount of information contained and it is still an outstanding valuable book. A comparatively new entry is *Reeds*, a British publication.

"The more you read, the more you know and the more pleasant will be your hours at sea. I suspect that the woman who brought you in last night will enjoy herself at sea and know where she is under conditions far more rugged than many people now who consider themselves to be good sailors. I would recommend to you that you try to get to be in the class of navigator who has all the tools in his kit. In your special situation, Bob, there is another factor to consider. What would happen if you and your boat were out in the middle of Buzzard's Bay and you stepped on a line, caught your toe and fell, knocking yourself cold on a cleat? I suspect that, if that were to happen today, your wife would feel some alarm and I believe you and she should work out a procedure to handle a situation of this sort.

"It seems to me that the first thing she should do is to heave to. On my boat, that means dropping the jib, pulling the main hard amidships, coming up on the wind and locking the wheel amidships. The boat then eases on and off the wind and moves not faster than a knot. That fixes you in one position. Then, I would hope that your wife would then put a line around you because you are too heavy for her to carry and apply what first aid she can without her having to worry about your rolling over into the water. The next thing for her to do would be to go below, find out where she is on the chart, do the necessary navigation to know where she is, and then decide what kind of a problem she has—is it possible that she will be able to take the boat into a nearby harbor? If so, she should do so probably using the engine rather than going into the difficult problem of single-handed sailing. On the other hand, if the situation is more than she can handle, she is in the position now to call the Coast Guard and this works a lot better if you know which station is nearest you so you can call this station by name and tell them who you are, that is, tell them the name of your boat, description of the boat, your position, which you have gotten from your navigation probably in terms of distance and bearings from well-known objects, her estimate of your condition and, with the Coast Guard, be prepared either to wait for help or to sail for a port at which help is waiting for you.

"In some cases, it is better to sail to a port and then heave to or anchor outside until help can come out to bring her in if she does not feel capable of bringing the boat into the harbor by herself. On the other hand, if time is important, she should be able to take the boat in. Before she starts the engine, however, she should always remember to check to see there is no line in the water because one line wrapped around the screw makes you a sailboat without an engine. The navigator on small vessels such as ours is not only responsible for the position of the boat, but the communication with the outside world and all the various things that we have been talking about today. It is particularly sound planning for you both to know enough to cover what I have discussed with you."

The Old Man then had Bob figure a course and distance back to *Sea Dreams* and had him row the dinghy over there and do the navigation while the Old Man sat in the stern sheets. Everything worked well and the Old Man returned to his vessel with a real sense of accomplishment. He hoped that Bob would learn to be a navigator in the near future.

The Old Man returned to *Dancing Girl* proud of a well-spent morning and decided that he had earned himself a spot of Nelson's Blood before eating. He then had a light lunch of Fall River Allsorts from the icebox and settled back to reading a one-volume edition of Hakluyt's *Voyages* so that he could lose himself in the days when navigators who did not add intuition and luck to the attributes demanded of a navigator nowadays never survived to write reports of their voyages.

XI

~~~~~~~~~~

Emergencies

It had been thick fog for the past three days, but when on the fourth day it increased to dense, we agreed that the thrill of successful navigation in very poor visibility was beginning to wear thing. We were anchored in Cutler, way down east in Maine, but the afternoon before we had crept in using the depth finder and had not even had a glimpse of anything but the loom of the shore. In fact except for the pilings of an occasional weir, either active or abandoned, we had seen nothing but fog in varying shades of gray for the past 84 hours. When the old man proposed a lay day we all concurred enthusiastically. The morning had been spent on chores that could be done below. David, after setting up the folding oven, had baked two loaves of bread and then after letting the stove cool so that he could refill it, he had made two pies with native blueberries that he had put up over a week before when, due to crossed signals, we had bought more than we could eat fresh.

The rest of us had checked over all seldom-used sails and freed and oiled all blocks, snap shackles, piston hanks, vangs, and tackles. Particular attention was given to the storm sails and to the safety harnesses. As it is always surprising to discover how little time it takes for these last items to become unusable, *Dancing Girl*'s routines called for their mainte-

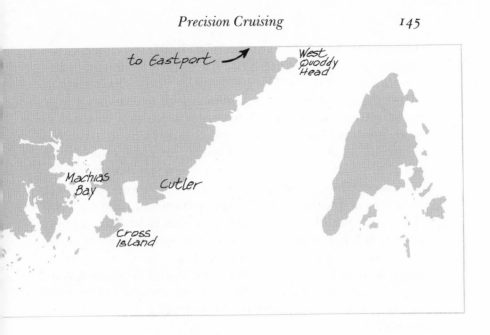

nance on a monthly basis, more frequently if subjected to wet weather.

The Old Man had a story about cruising with a friend many years ago in the Bay of Biscay when they were embayed, almost without warning, in a Force 10 gale on a lee shore. They needed the storm jib and the trysail to get out before they were blown on the rocks. The piston hanks on the storm jib were corroded, half of them to the extent that they were frozen solid. He described vividly the desperate haste with which he had worked to free enough hanks so that the sail would have a straight enough luff to let them work to windward. Finally, after running back and forth across the wind under trysail alone, trying to minimize leeway they, bent on the jib as best they could and slowly worked their way toward searoom and safety.

Then as they were beginning to breathe more easily, one of the strands in the manila sheet controlling the trysail let go. It had rotted while it had been stowed out of sight and out of mind. They were sure that if they had to lower it to be able to bend on a new sheet, the leeway they would have made would put them on the beach. The failing sheet was eased to reduce the strain on it and a new sheet was bent on.

The Old Man said it was an exercise similar to putting a new lead on a bucking horse while someone was playing a fire hose on you. The experience had left him rather religious about regular preventive maintenance of emergency equipment. Of course he had always been a belt and suspenders type any way, but his oft-preached creed was that the less often you used emergency equipment the more important it was that you be sure it would work when you did need it.

Dancing Girl carried safety harnesses for those who might come aboard without their own. A friend of ours had had the experience of having to call up a woman he had met only once to tell her that her husband had been washed over the side and had not been recovered. The Old Man wanted to do all he could to avoid that type of task and he wanted nothing to interfere with the efforts of anyone aboard to avoid putting him in that position. We were glad to comply with his wishes.

David was putting the finishing touches on a most impressive lobster salad for lunch and we had cleaned everything up from our labors. We were spreading the tablecloth and setting the table for lunch when we heard blood-curdling screams from the boat anchored astern of us and barely visible through the fog. There was a great splash, more screaming, and a man's shouts and children crying.

The Old Man listened a moment and said, "There's real trouble over there. David, get the pump and blow up the dinghy hard. Professor, you take charge of the boat, turn on channel 16, and stand by. Ann, get the VHF walkie-talkie. You are coming with me. I will row. Take the painter. David and I will launch the dinghy."

David reported that all three compartments of the inflatable dinghy were hard. The Old Man threw in a couple of white floatation cushions, took the oars and climbed in, followed by Ann who sat in the stern. As he rowed off the Old Man told David to get the outboard ready.

I could see dimly through the fog as they got to the other boat after a minute I heard on the VHF, "*Dancing Girl*, this is *Dancing Girl* Two. Shift to 13." When I came up on 13 Ann came on and said, "There is a woman here who just tipped a boiling pot full of chowder all over herself from the waist

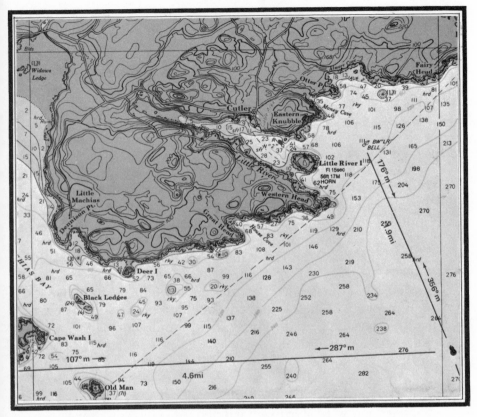

Cutler and Environs

down. She jumped in the water to cool it down. The Old Man and the man on the boat are trying to get her aboard. They do not have a boatswain's chair. I am coming over. Have David ready with our boatswain's chair and the medical kit. We better find out from the Coast Guard where there is a hospital, where there is a doctor, and what the ambulance situation is. I will be right there. Out."

She came over at high speed using the little short strokes that make a rubber dinghy fly. David had the outboard ready when she arrived. I took it and he climbed in the bow holding on as I passed the safety line and then the motor to Ann in the stern, she tied it to the dinghy and clamped the motor to its rack while David balanced the boat and prevented it from rearing up with the weight so far aft. The motor started with the first pull and they were at the other boat in short order.

I went to work on the radio and as usual the Coast Guardsman on duty was efficient. After some minutes he came back to report that the nearest hospital was in Eastport, about an hour away by road. The ambulance was there but there was a doctor who would be on the radio in 15 minutes. They would call us when he was available.

About 10 minutes later Ann came on and we shifted to 13. I told her what I had accomplished and she said she thought she had a story complete enough for the doctor, but that she doubted if she could reach the Coast Guard with the walkie-talkie limited range. I went to 16 and told the Coast Guard we would be on 13 and then went back to 13. When she and David got to the boat the Old Man and the husband had turned the woman with her back to the hull so the burns would not get rubbed as they tried to bring her aboard. They had not been able to lift her in that position but David and Ann between them had been able to balance the dinghy and arrange the boatswain's chair under the woman's butt, and the husband had taken the lower mainsheet block off the traveler and hooked it to the the chair. They dropped the life lines and were able to get her aboard and below. She had been barefoot and in shorts when she had tipped the whole pot of chowder as it started to boil over and she grabbed to take it off the stove. She was short and her front from her waist to her toes had been coated with a nice thick soup that was boiling hot. She had been smart to go over into the cold water for the cooling had come soon enough to prevent permanent damage. The fronts of her legs looked like they might have first-degree burns, but there were definite second-degree spots where her shorts had held the chowder against her. The tops of her feet had really taken a beating, and Ann thought they were at best second degree. Although being wet and cold concealed or duplicated some of her symptoms, it was agreed that she looked like she was going into shock. Her husband and the Old Man had agreed that a Demerol from *Dancing Girl*'s kit was indicated. There were only tablets aboard, but, aside from being a little slower to act as a syrette, one table would serve to reduce the pain that was putting her into shock.

Ann said she was going ashore to see about transportation to the hospital and to see what would be the best way to move the patient. She asked that I have a hockey puck and a course to the best landing spot ready for her as she came by for them. The other boat was *Rosemary* and would also be guarding 13.

The fog was dense, with less than 45 yards visibility, but the *cruising Guide* made it clear that Niel Corbett's wharf was the place to go ashore. The course was 078 from *Dancing Girl*. I checked the tide table which showed that we would have high water in hour. I gave the information and the compass to Ann and she was off into the murk, the little outboard purring like an eggbeater.

About then the Coast Guard doctor called and the Old Man took over on *Rosemary*'s VHF. He reported briefly on the patient's condition and said she had been given one 50 mg Demerol table 21 minutes before, and although it had helped a lot he thought that a second might be better. The doctor agreed. The second-degree burns were all covered with sterile gauze pads wet with water which had boiled for ten minutes and to which enough salt water had been added to make it taste slightly salty.

O. M. reported that he had run out of sterile pads but was planning to use clean bath towels wet with saline to keep everything wet. He further said he had Tetracycline in 250 mg capsules aboard, and if he had been out of reach of medical help he would have started her on that. The doctor said "Great! Go ahead with that but be sure to tell the doctor at the hospital about every medicaton. You are taking her to the hospital, aren't you?" The Old Man assured him that we were working out the details at the moment. He also said that he was going to push fluids and at the moment had found a bottle of Gatorade which he thought might be just the thing. The doctor agreed that that would be fine and reminded us that we should keep the patient warm.

At this point Big Ann cut in from the beach asking if she could check with the doctor on what she had arranged. She had had the good forture to run into a nice man who was about to drive over to Eastport on business. He had suggested that he would be glad to take them in his camper instead and would have room for the patient in a bunk and for her whole family. She had also arranged for *Rosemary* to be left on a mooring that another man was making available. The doctor approved and suggested that the hospital be notified of the patient's ETA. Ann said she would and the Old Man thanked the doctor very much for his help and the Coast Guard signed off.

Ann said it seemed to her that the patient could best be passed ashore over the rail on a floor board from the cabin sole, and that they should plan to come in port side to with fenders out. She would be on the dock to indicate the best place. There were a number of people ready to help. The Old Man said that they would be set in fifteen minutes and that he would give one long blast on the horn when he got underway. Ann said she would make the arrangements with the hospital and would keep the VHF on so that she could be raised if necessary and signed off.

I heard the long blast when *Rosemary* got underway and started putting the finishing touches on our lunch so that it would be ready in the icebox when our people returned. About a half hour later Ann called. The patient and her family had gotten off without a hitch and the Old Man and David were taking *Rosemary* out to her mooring. There was a good deal of cleaning up to do but they would return to the ship for lunch first and then go back and make things presentable for the family's return.

David's lobster salad made lunch a special occasion when we needed one and a bottle of Chateau Latour Martillac Graves 1980 that had been properly chilled in its bilge stowage struck me as an appropriate complement to the meal. The charcoal glowing in the fireplace added warmth and cheer. Somehow a tablecloth and a well-set table adds a sense of well-being to a foggy layday.

The troops were ready for a change of scene when they returned and although pleased by what they had accomplished were delighted to be back aboard. The Old Man said, "You know I have been dreading for a long time the events that we witnessed today, but I feel relieved to have gotten it over with. I am glad they were not at sea out of reach of medical advice or assistance. I was glad the Coast Guard doctor thought well of what we did. I guess we would have done all right on our own. It was lucky that poor woman was able to get into cold water so quickly. It is my guess that if she had not she would have been much more severely hurt. As it was she was suffering a lot and really needed those two Demerols. By the time she was in her wet dressings wrapped in garbage bags, dressed in warm sweaters and zipped into a sleeping bag she was beginning to rest more easily. The plywood bunk bottom she was tied to with sailstops made her a good shipping package. I think she will be all right."

"I have always considered your requirement that the cook wear a lobsterman's apron and calf high boots to be sort of worry wart," said David, "but I have been thinking a bit during the past hour and it is obvious to me that any cooking done on a gimballed stove is by definition unstable even in calm waters. In this case I checked and the stove had slipped in its hangers and was hanging tipped forward 60°. Improper maintenance on the stove compounded the risk of the improperly dressed cook. Her instinctive grab to save her chowder put her into it literally. I am glad it was not my front at risk."

Ann raised her glass, "I have two toasts. May we we always be able to help others who have had accidents that we are able to avoid." We all drank, and then she toasted again, "May we always live in the style we achieve at this simple repast." There was prolonged applause after we drank to that.

XII

~~~~~~~~~~~

Fire and ...

Dancing Girl had worked a long day but was now anchored in 40 feet in the Cross Roads, Strangford Lough in Northern Ireland on the Irish Sea. We had gotten under way from our assigned mooring at the Howth Yacht Club in Howth Harbor at 0626 but the winds had been fickle and it had taken us 12 hours and 11 minutes to push 59.23 miles under our keel. We had used most of the sails in the forward compartment and had sailed aggressively but we had missed the slack water when we arrived off the mouth of the Lough.

The wind died completely and we started the engine and headed in. Although there was reported to be only a rise and fall of 3.7 feet there was a large area to drain and at maximum ebb we had been told to expect over 7 knots against us. We did not want to spend the night out and were very interested to watch our progress upstream. There was not a breath of air and the sails were furled but Old Smoky put his heart into it and we kept a good 6.5 knots through the water. The Old Man kept us in the right hand side of every eddy and we were making good but diminishing progress. We kept checking by taking bearings on objects abeam on the beach. We stopped gaining momentarily from time to time as we got into an opposing eddy but we still looked like we were going to make it. The alternative would be to turn tail and run with the flow to a night offshore.

Then our hopes fell. We were in a particularly turbulent section and we started to lose ground. Our 6.5 through the water was countered by the water's 7 knots in the opposite direction. By twisting and turning we could find patches of favorable water but they were of short duration. We were dropping downstream and the current was still on the increase.

"Get the Main on!" shouted the Old Man. "Just felt a breeze on my cheek." Moments later the sail was drawing and the wind although variable was building. In true melodrama fashion a whirlpool opened up to starboard and we started to drop back. The skipper came right 10° and we started to edge over to the right. We passed just below the whirlpool's throat and I thought it gagged at us. I was glad we had water to spare under us. Then we were on the right side and moving upstream. It was easy after that but we were happy when we got both our hooks down in 40 feet.

Although the anchorage was protected from the current I did not want to swing around a hook in these waters. I wanted no midnight anchor drill with an anchor fouled by its own rode or even broken out by the boat's swinging around it.

The only other boat in the anchorage was a beautifully kept white Concordia yawl, a lovely sight, riding against the bright green of the Irish countryside and flying the Stars and Stripes. "I envy him his little bright wooden dinghy," said the Old Man. "I think my inflatable is more practical for me, but his is a lot prettier and easier to row."

We had the rum bottle out and were sitting around killing it as an appropriate sacrifice to the sea gods who were watching over us so well. I proposed a toast, "With cruising duties to be done, to be done, A sailor's life's indeed a happy one."

"We are going to have a visitor," said David.

It was a nice young man in his mid-forties rowing alongside in the bright dinghy, "I apologize for intruding, but could you possibly sell me a little stove alcohol? The baby got sick and we are using the stove more for him than for me, my wife, and our two teen-age boys combined. We will be able to get stove fuel in Howth day after tomorrow for sure."

The Old Man invited him aboard but he thanked him and said he had promised to get right back. David said that he had an almost full gallon of Truheat that we would not be using because we had adjusted the stove to the local stove fuel. The Old Man asked our visitor if Truheat was all right and was told it would be great. O. M. said, "Take this as a get well gift to the baby. If you can think of anything we can do give us a shout."

After profuse thanks the man rowed back to his boat. The Old Man said, "You know I bet he has one of those 10-gallon pressure tanks for his stove. They let you forget your alcohol consumption the way you never will putting fuel in a pint at a time. Besides, I am old-fashioned about having alcohol around under pressure. A leak in the flexible hose can give you a nasty fire. Remember when that boat burned to the water at Padanaram? Alcohol under pressure did that. Alcohol fires are easy to handle as long as they are small. All you have to do is put enough water on the fire to dilute the the alcohol below 100 proof and cool it so it does not produce vapor, and of course stay out of the steam."

"Fire is terrifying anywhere when it gets out of control," said David, "but that spray bottle you have sure makes it easy to get most fires out before they get started, and because it makes so little mess the cook is not afraid to use it at the first sign of need. Speak of the Devil. Look at the yawl!"

There were flames shooting up the companionway. The Old Man said, "David, you and Ann blow up the dinghy and put the oars in, David will row. Ann will take charge of *Dancing Girl* and guard 16. Give me the walkie-talkie set on 16. Professor get all five of the buckets from the lazaret and empty the stuff out of them in the cockpit and give them to me. Then take the big piston pump and get in the stern with it. I'll get in the bow with the buckets and a hank of quarter-inch line."

He went below and was back with three flotation jackets by the time that David was sitting down in the dinghy. The Old Man was cutting lengths of line and tying one to each bucket that did not have one.

"Professor," he said, "your job is to organize a line of full buckets coming into the cockpit and I think you can use the two boys. David, you and I will get that woman and her baby into their dinghy and send her on her way to Ann. She will know what to do. Then we get the owner up on deck and start throwing buckets of water all over the stove and at any low flame."

I grabbed the yawl as we came alongside and the other two went up. The mother and baby had come up the forward hatch followed by two teen-age boys and all were standing bewildered on the foredeck. The man had used his two dry powder extinguishers but there was too much alcohol around. David took charge of mother and child and rowed them over to *Dancing Girl* and came right back to help. The Old Man got the owner up on deck and started throwing buckets of water at the stove, jumping back to escape the steam. He passed the empties back to the deck boy for refilling. He explained that he wanted to get all the fire above the cabin sole extinguished completely before the fire in the bilges went out, because he was afraid of vapor accumulating down there and then causing an explosion when it ignited. We should try to stand clear of the companionway because of the risk of an explosion sending a column of flame up through it. He was puffing hard, so David relieved him of the water throwing detail. He asked for the big piston pump and set it in the largest bucket and with the owner's help started pumping to see if it could be used as a fire hose to deliver water more precisely. It looked as if it would work but for the time being the bucket brigade idea seemed to be what was best.

The owner thought of his engine room exhaust blower which he had kept when he converted her to diesel and all agreed it should be turned on. David reported that the cabin sole was awash and a few more buckets would assure that here were no fumes, explosive or not in the bilges. We then shifted to the pump, one person holding and another pumping, the latter job being particularly tough. At the Old Man's suggestion the owner went below and took over the hose from David who came up and got on the pump handle. We kept the bucket which supplied the pump filled from the other buckets.

The galley area was a charred mess but the owner agreed that now he had to go through the boat and make sure that there was not a spark or bit of smoldering material any-where. There must be nothing that could reignite.

I suggested that the Old Man call Ann on the walkie-talkie and let them know that the fire was out, no one was hurt and that there was naturally going to be a big clean-up job. She reported that the mother was nursing the baby in the for-ward compartment where she had set up housekeeping and to tell Daddy that the baby's fever was down from the night before. She was going to need diapers very soon.

Daddy was pleased with the message and explained, "My wife and the doctor agreed that for the boat life that baby should be nursed as long as she could feed him. He is 14 months now. This was the first time he has been sick so the system must be working." The Pampers were in a box in the forward compartment. At the Old Man's suggestion Ann rowed over and got them, taking the yawl personnel's sleep-ing bags back with her.

"By the way," said the Old Man, "My name is Obadiah Mayhew, named after an ancestor who was a rather success-ful whaling ship captain. As a little kid I decided that O. M. was a lot easier name to carry and that was the basis for my schoolmates labeling me Old Man, which is what most people call me. I retired 8 years ago and spend a lot of my time cruising in *Dancing Girl*."

"I am sure glad to meet you." said the owner. "I am Jack Barrett and have been a retired Air Force colonel for the past four months. This yawl, *Freedom*, has been the center of our planning for the past three years and is now our only home. It's lucky that I am handy with tools because you peo-ple saved her before any structural damage was done. Unless the fire starts up again I can make all the necessary repairs, maybe even in time to spend the winter in the Aegean as planned. Things are a stinking mess, that's for sure, but think of where we would be if you had not anchored here this eve-ning and been so savvy about fire-fighting. By the way how did you get to be so organized?"

"Jack, thanks for being so complimentary. I spent five years in the Navy in World War II, mostly in command, and I got indoctrinated to the 'Watch, Quarter, and Station Bill' approach to life at sea. As a retired Air Force colonel friend of mine used to say, 'Plan everything. Then if it goes wrong we will know it was because we planned it that way.' What we did this evening was planned and written up while *Dancing Girl* was being build 14 years ago. This is the first time we have had to use it but every person who cruises with us is expected to read our 'Bills and Duties' folder. Every now and then the system pays off."

It was agreed that it was now safe to pump the bilge and designated the two boys to man the cockpit bilge pump. They began to tire after a couple of turns each so I took a turn and then David did before giving the job back to them. When the water level had been pumped down far enough to eliminate risk of splashing Jack tried the diesel and it started as though nothing had happened.

The Old Man said, "I think someone should sleep aboard *Freedom* in case there is anything that might start to smolder but most of your people will do better sleeping aboard *Dancing Girl*. Why don't you nest alongside us? You can use a drink and by that time I am sure we will have dinner ready. I'll call Ann and tell her we will be alongside, starboard side to, in about fifteen minutes, if that is all right."

"*Dancing girl*, this is *Dancing Girl Two*, over."

"This is *Dancing Girl*, shift to 70."

"This is *Dancing Girl Two* on 70. We will be alongside you to port in about fifteen minutes. We'll use your fenders and lines. Over."

"Okay, I have figured on dinner for eight. Everybody ought to be hungry."

"Good. *Dancing Girl Two* out."

It was after sunset and I noticed that Ann had made colors and turned on the anchor light. I did the same for *Freedom* and relieved the boys on the pump so they could handle the anchor for their father. *Freedom* had chain in British style and the windlass permitted both boys to pump it at the same time. The plow was soon nesting in its roller and Jack ran over to *Dancing Girl* making a good landing so that David and I merely had to take the lines when Ann handed them to us and secure each in the appropriate place.

Ann had had water at the boil when O. M. called, and she had made up a batch of freeze-dried chicken and rice for the boys while we were coming over. There was also a big bowl of salad, a pitcher of lemonade, and a bowl of fruit so that they could eat while we drank. We had had a full day but the damage to *Freedom* and the contemplation of what might have happened cast a long shadow over our evening drinks. The boys had thirds on chicken and Ann added a little more to the batch being prepared for us. They were a little dubious about the salad but really pigged out on the fruit until Betty, their mother, called a halt. We were all starving by the time it was our turn at the table. Jack and Betty were impressed by the ease of preparing the chicken, but when they tasted it they were really converted to the idea. The rest of us just ate and were happy.

Ann slept forward with Betty and the baby. The boys each had an upper bunk. Jack had the firewatch on *Freedom*, the Old Man was in the quarter berth, and David and I had the other two. We were crowded but cozy and everyone had a bunk of his own. Pretty good, I thought, but I went to sleep too fast to think very long.

XIII

Overboard

Dancing Girl tugged restlessly at her tethers, secure but nervous in the 6-knot current. She was being held by a bow line to mooring ring on the middle pier of the Punte Neuve in San Vicente de la Barquera on the Biscay coast of Spain. As the ebb had approached maximum we had had to ease our stern line to the mooring buoy so that we would not be holding the weight of the buoy and also the weight of the trawlers hanging from it. Adjusting the tension on the stern line to control our swinging had been simple. The wheel was locked tight so that the rudder would stay amidships and the pier protected us from any large floating hazards coming downstream.

It had been an interesting day since we had left our assigned mooring at the Real Club Maritimo in Santander, the north coast's center for elegant yachting. The night before the Old

Man had gone ashore to present his credentials in full uniform with white cap cover and spotless white bucks but reported that he had felt we were a trifle scruffy for the liveried attendants and general opulence of the clubhouse. The winds had been Force 4 most of the day but the direction had changed enough to keep us changing sails once or twice an hour. The coast had been beautiful in the sparkling sunlight.

I was below writing letters at the table and beginning to think about what I was going to prepare for lunch. The Old Man was at the chart table working at his navigational duties. We were on starboard tack on a close reach with the triradial pulling like a Swiss mountain locomotive. Big Ann was on the wheel and David was hand tending the sheet. O. M. remarked that with these calm waters the boat was making better than 6.5 knots which was pretty good for 12 knots of wind over the deck. I noticed David cleat the sheet and go aft, presumably to relieve himself.

I went back to my writing and almost at once heard a loud bellow followed by Big Ann in a voice as penetrating as a trumpet, "Man overboard! Man overboard!" I instinctively repeated the call and shot up on deck followed by the Old Man who had hesitated just long enough to punch the hold button on the loran to preserve our position and to start his stopwatch. Ann had already scaled a cushion life preserver out, hitting David's arm, and released the starboard man overboard pole buoy and horseshoe life ring, and was heading down enough to put the apparent wind abeam. As we went forward the Old Man said he would keep David in sight and take care of the spinnaker halyard. We agreed that we could get the spinnaker down without setting a jib first to blanket it and told Ann what we were going to do.

I grabbed the takedown line and stood in the forward hatch. The moment I said "Ready," the O. M. let go the halyard on the run so that for a moment it was floating unloaded in midair. That was my moment and with full arm swings I got all but the foot of the sail down the hatch and out of the wind. I clipped the two sheets and the halyard together and the skipper who had run back to the cockpit pulled them taut. I grabbed the foreguy and, pausing to secure the halyard as I went by, brought the foreguy to starboard and out-side of everything back to the end of the boom as Ann came over to port tack and put the apparent wind abeam. I got out a couple of heaving lines and a length of line to throw to David if needed. The skipper rigged the end of the star-board genoa sheet with two loops in it to the two starboard winches to give David a couple of footholds to use climbing aboard.

Ann said, "Trim the foreguy hard and cleat it and you two stand by to grab David as we go by. I want to get him on the first pass."

Most of our preparations were unnecessary for the main, backwinded by hauling the boom forward with the foreguy I had secured to it, stopped us right over David where Ann had placed us so that all he needed to do was grab the toerail with his right hand, swing the cushion aboard with his left and, putting his foot in one of the loops, climb aboard.

Ann said, "Release the foreguy and stand by to pick up the man overboard pole and horseshoe. Let's get the spinnaker ready to go up as soon as I get squared away on starboard tack."

The Old Man and I went below and turtled the spinnaker in its bag while David picked up the pole and its attached equipment and returned everything to its proper place. I secured the foreguy and the sheet, guy, and halyard, making sure that each was properly led. David came forward and took the halyard and O. M. took over in the cockpit. When all reported ready, at the word from Ann, David two-blocked the halyard while I saw that the chute came out of the turtle untwisted and did not open until it was under control. In no time we were rolling along as though nothing had happened.

Ann beckoned David over to her as though she wanted to whisper to him. When he was close enough she grabbed his head and kissed him very hard on the mouth. "If you ever do that to me again I will strangle you with my bare hands. By the way," she said, "you might consider zipping up your fly and getting into some dry clothes." And then she went back to steering the boat.

Dinner that evening had been a magnificent paella that David prepared and served with Rioja which I had procured in our own bottles from the bodega. Dessert had been a perfect melon, and now we were lingering around the table savoring our coffee and Fundador, discussing the accident.

"Today everything went perfectly. Murphy must have been passed out in some saloon. Everything requiring precision went without a hitch and you, Ann, did not make a false move. No one could have done better. Of course we all know this drill on this boat and have all thought about it and discussed it together. If David had planned to do this stupid thing he could not have picked a better team to rescue him. There was no need for argument or discussion. Very few can toss a cushion as accurately as Ann did today. The pole and horseshoe went over so quickly that we did not need the second pole to give us a line. I was at the chart table and could punch the hold button, start the watch and log the time with much less than normal lost time. The Professor and I have worked together so much that we were safe in not taking time to set a jib. We knew he could have the chute gathered before it filled and we knew I could drop it so fast because I knew it would not drop to the water before the belly line had it aboard.

"If there had been more wind we would have had to take time to set a jib. That is why we always have a usable jib on the rail when a chute is up. If the wind comes up a smaller jib must be made ready. If David had been unable to swing himself aboard we knew the various steps we could take to retrieve him. If it had been rough I would have had to concentrate on keeping my eye on David, and the Professor would have done a solo takedown. Now suppose you had been alone on the boat with David, Ann, what would you have done?"

"First I believe that with only two aboard and a spinnaker up both people wear safety harnesses clipped on, but let's just say that David's suicidal machismo has him in the water and me with a mess to clear up. I think I would release the sheet, the guy, and the halyard in that order and try to steer to clear them in the water. The sheet and guy should run free and it would be a question whether it was quicker to untie the bitter end of the halyard from the bail or cut it with my knife. I certainly would drop both man overboard poles to give me a line and would try to keep track of times and courses run so that I could sail back to the victim. I would be quick to start the search plan if I got to the point and found my boy was not waiting for me. I am assuming that the weather will be lousy on this day and so am following worst case procedures. As soon as I could be absolutely sure that there was no chance of a line in the water I would seriously consider securing the main and starting the engine, feeling that the time consumed would be made up by better maneuverability later."

I added to the discussion. "I understand there is a project on, testing racing boats with full crews using traditional proceedures such as ours compared with heading into the wind, fighting down all sails. With the spinnaker up they are heading the boat and intentionally broaching to stop the boat. While she lies on her side they secure the sails. In either case, when it's certain there is no line that can get in the water, the engine is started. There are those who claim the new system is better. I am not sure, and am not sure whether being short-handed makes the new method more desirable or less. It is certainly worth thinking about though.

"Most people have man overboard drill by throwing a cushion in the water and picking it up with a boat hook. Most people do not drift as fast to leeward as a cushion does and most people will resent the devil out of being picked up by a boat hook under the chin. I think that a proper drill requires that you use a log for a victim so that it will not blow on the surface, will be as difficult to spot as a man would be, and will be hard to get aboard once it is located.

"Good preparation for a man overboard consists of first, thinking the problem through and writing up good procedures; second, frequently discussing and reading to get the thinking of others; third, practicing; fourth, thinking through the problem every time you have the wheel."

The Old Man said, "David, do you care to tell us exactly what happened to put you in the water and us over the hurdles?"

"Sure. It was easy. My zipper jammed and when I released it, it bit me, not on the hand. By the time I pried its vicious teeth apart, I was airborne. I assure all concerned that there is no permanent damage."

"If you had not been picked up, you know, you would have permanently wrecked my life," said Ann.

XIV

〜〜〜〜〜〜〜〜〜

Bodies

After an early departure from the guest mooring in Bidde-fore Pool *Dancing Girl* had been beating all morning in light fog and moderate easterly winds hoping to spend the night in the inner harbor at Small Point. The water was compara-tively calm and we were making good time on the 3.7 oz #1, trimmed inside the lifeline to the block on the 8° track and the main with a flattening reef and 3,800 pounds pressure on the backstay. The draft of the jib was 45 percent and the main 50 percent. We had worked the twist so that we thought the telltales were reacting perfectly from top to bottom on each sail. We had the loran duplicating our DR and piloting with 10 waypoints in use. As we were crossing the approaches to Portland Harbor we were guarding channel 16. Mostly though we were just striving to see how perfectly we could sail the boat. About 1100 there was a sudden loud shout of "Made" on the VHF as though someone had keyed a trans-mitter by mistake, very loud but nothing else. About fifteen minutes later David called, "Something in the water dead ahead, about a mile, looks like a reef!" I looked at my watch as the Old Man logged the time. It was 1117. There was no way we could be approaching any rocks.

The Old Man answered, "There is nothing out here but water, unless we are really lost. Turn on the depth finder, though."

"We've got 61 feet. There is nothing out here but Witch Rock and that has 21 feet on it," said Ann after a quick check. "Could it be seals?"

Old Man looked through his binoculars, "It looks like there is a skiff surrounded by floats. It's right on course, and we'll find out soon enough."

As we got closer we could see that there were about twenty people swimming around a skiff with five people in it. We were about to tack to avoid interfering with whatever they were doing when they saw us and started yelling. I could not tell whether they were telling us to stay away or yelling for help.

"There's something wrong," said the Old Man. "I am going to try to find out what. Drop the jib and stop it to the starboard upper lifeline with one stop. Hook the foreguy to the end of the boom so we can really back the main. Get our heaving lines out of both cockpit lockers. See if we can make out what they are saying."

"One of these guys is making sense. He says that the party boat *Lulu and Sue* has just sunk and they are the survivors."

The Old Man told Ann to get out a Mayday and took the wheel. I rigged the swimming ladder on the starboard side. O. M. had David rig a vang from the end of the boom with a loop in it that a person could put his arms through and get hoisted aboard..

"Mayday, Mayday, Mayday," Ann's voice was hard and clear.

"Vessel calling Mayday this is U.S. Coast Guard Portland," said a female voice.

"Coast Guard, this is *Dancing Girl, Dancing Girl, Dancing Girl* WZQ7393. We are a 37-foot blue sloop sail number 3933. Our loran position latitude 4337 point 41 north 7009 point 32 west. We have around us in the water possibly twenty-five survivors of the sinking of the party boat *Lulu and Sue*. There are four of us. We urgently require assistance. Acknowledge. Over."

"*Dancing Girl*, Coast Guard. We have your message on tape. You are in position 4337.41 N 7009.32 W. Please stand by. Over."

"I will stand by but expect to be busy. Keep trying if you need us. We will keep you informed. This is *Dancing Girl* WZQ7393. Out."

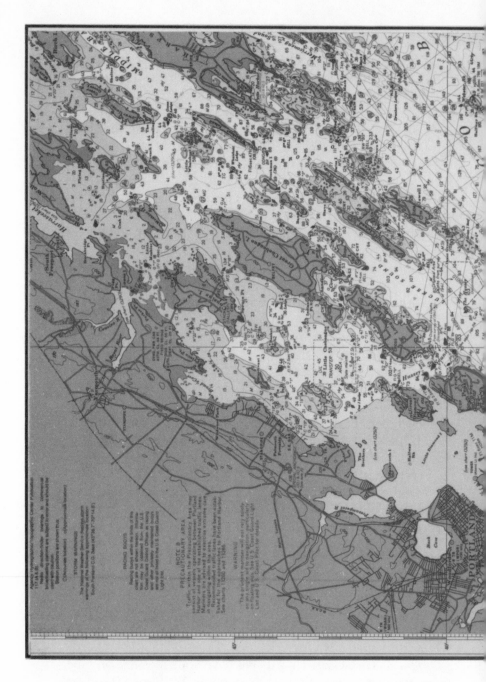

Marine Patrol *is in the far north portion of the chart south and slightly west of South Freeport. The 41-footer is reported to be in the vicinity of Wood Island in the southeast corner of the chart. Witch Rock is about in the center of this chart. The Coast Guard Station is not far from the D in Portland.*

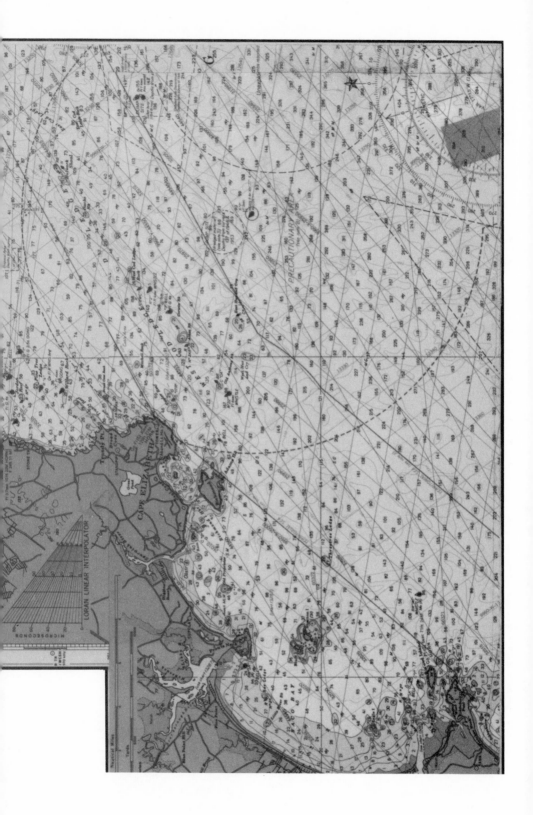

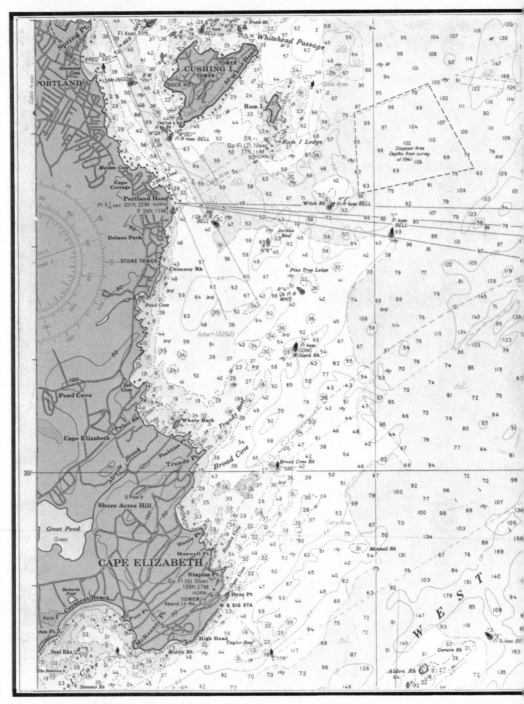

Cape Elizabeth to Portland

"*Dancing Girl,* Coast Guard. Understood. Out."

"Pan Pan, Pan Pan, Pan Pan. Hello, all stations, this is United States Coast Guard Portland Station. Break. A party boat with approximately twenty-five persons aboard is reported to have capsized and sunk at 4337.41N 7009.32W in the vicinity of Witch Rock. All mariners in the area are requested to keep a sharp lookout and assist if possible. This is the U.S. Coast Guard Portland. Out."

The Old Man told us he was going to windward of the biggest bunch of people and back the main and we would lie there dragging people aboard as fast as we could. We were going to have to get any of these people to help who could do so but with the water temperature at 49°, as it was when he checked earlier, they were going to be too cold to do much. We got out our eight cockpit cushions and tossed one to any person in the water we could reach who did not have a life jacket and then we did the same with our nine horsecollars. There were only three or flour flotation jackets that we saw in the crowd. When everything was under control on deck I put in the chimmney and went below and lit the cabin heater stove and the Seaswing with a full kettle of water on it.

"*Dancing Girl,* this is *Marine Patrol.* We have your Mayday. I figure you are about a mile east of Witch Rock. We are up north of Cousins Island. We will be there in 20 minutes. Over."

"Marine Patrol, this is *Dancing Girl.* Affirmative. We are a mile east of Witch Rock. Thank you. Out."

With the Captain's approval I went on Channel 16. "Coast Guard Portland, *Dancing Girl,* Over."

"*Dancing Girl,* Coast Guard. Over."

"Coast Guard, *Dancing Girl.* These people are very cold. We are not equipped to handle hypothermia in these numbers."

"*Dancing Girl,* Coast Guard. Understood. Our 41-footer is on its way to you from the vicinity of Wood Island. Its ETA 4337.41 7009.32 1216, I repeat 1216. Over."

"Coast Guard, *Dancing Girl.* Roger. Out."

"Vessel calling Mayday, this is the dragger *Isabella Grande.* Our ETA 1148. Come back."

"*Isabella Grande,* this is *Dancing Girl, Dancing Girl, Dancing Girl.* We are a blue sloop sail number 3933. There is a lot to do here. Thank you very much for your help. This is *Dancing Girl* standing by on channel 16. Out."

The Old Man brought us into position with mainsail flapping and the foreguy holding the boom so that we made leeway but neither headway nor sternway. David hauled the skiff alongside the ladder. There were five women in it and he organized a crew of two of them and himself to drag people out of the water and get them up the ladder to the deck. The Old Man helped them up the ladder, took their flotation from them to throw to others, and Ann got them down the ladder to me. Many were dazed and speechless with cold and fear. I sat the first ten on the bunks facing each other. There was one very fat woman who would have had trouble moving about in dry clothes at the dock, but she was cheery and joking about her size and seemed to give a boost to the thinner ones, who lacked her protective coat of fat and felt the cold more. She ended up sitting next to the head door which I thought might be a problem but she was too big to shift around. The eleventh man down was one of the crewmen. He was younger and in better shape and asked if he could help. I put him in the head in charge of the toilet and of the buckets which Ann passed down to me. He knew how the toilet worked, and I told him it was his job to see that nobody clogged the head or threw up except in a bucket. He laughed and said, "Wish me luck. I'll do my best."

He packed all the sails in the forward compartment way forward and somehow or other stowed five people in there. I cleared all the stuff stowed in the upper bunks and got two small men into each by explaining to them that they would be warmer there.

There was a lull below and I went on deck. The skipper of *Lulu and Sue* had just been picked up and was talking to the Old Man. "There were forty-eight of us aboard when we shoved off, me, the mate, the crew and forty-five paying passengers. I planned to fish on Witch Rock for a while. The first man to get his jig over had about 2 fathoms of line when he started yelling he had a big one. The mate figured, 'Oh well,' went over to be nice about it, and damned if the line was not hooked onto something solid but moving slowly. He looked over the side and damned if the jig had not snagged the fin of a big whale shark. I mean big. Big as my boat at least. A lot of people saw it at the same time and started yelling, and then everybody was crowding and yelling to get a look. The mate shouted for them to get back, that it was only a shark, and then everyone was screaming, 'Shark! Its attacking us!' and rushed to the other side to escape "Jaws". That did it.

"We had shipped a little water to starboard and when she came back she rolled all the way to port to put her mast on the water. I got out a Mayday and almost did not make it out of the pilot house before she was under water. My crew got the skiff free but the life rafts and most of the life jackets went down with the boat. There were five women passengers and he got them all in the skiff. One of them must weigh 250 pounds. I don't know how he was able to get the others to balance the boat then roll her aboard, but he did and then got in the water to give the boat a little freeboard. I couldn't do a thing but tell people to stay together."

O. M. interrupted to say, "Professor, there are three sea-cocks in the head, one under the galley sink, and one in the lazaret. Get them closed, before we get any deeper in the water. I am timing our roll and if you keep the weight down low we may be able to handle a lot more people before our metacentric height gets too low."

I took care of the lazaret and the galley sink. I noticed that the stove had the cabin warming up like a steam bath as I swung my way forward like an overage Tarzan to the head. I pointed out the three valves to my man in charge and he closed them. When I asked him he said his name was Jimmy and things were going okay. There were two people holding buckets and being sick in them and he was afraid we might have trouble later on because a number of people had swallowed a lot of salt water and it was beginning to go through them. The head was too crowded for people to move around in but with big Nora's help and his experience with his baby daughter, he thought they could handle it if I would stop blocking the line. I told him he was great and to keep it up but call me if I could help. I told Nora she was wonderful and keep up the good work. "You're pretty cute yourself Professor, darling," was her reply. As I left I heard her tell an old and very pale man, "Darling, let Mummy take your pants down so Daddy can put you on the pot." He just said, "Hurry."

The cabin sole had people sitting on it, packed like rolled anchovies in a can. I called to Jimmy, "See that no more than two people stand up at a time. We have to keep the weight low or we will have to stop picking up anymore. Nora, you help see to that, will you?"

"Count on me. I don't want to go in the drink again. My doctor says if I have more than one bath a day I may wither away to skin and bones."

I counted twenty-three people in the cabin and three on deck. The Old Man said that we should get our weight as low as possible because we had to bring more aboard and he was not sure how many we could handle on deck before we began to run into stability problems.

The last people we picked up were pretty far gone from the cold and needed a lot of help to do anything. I went on deck and took the helm Old Man went below to the VHF: *"Isabella Grande, Dancing Girl.* Over."

The VHF blared on full power. "This is *Broad Jumper,* calling *Sexy. Broad Jumper,* calling *Sexy. Broad Jumper,* calling *Sexy.* Come back, Jack if you're not too hungover."

"Hey Pin Head, you were sure burning with a blue flame last night. Lots of healthy exercise cured my hangover, if you know what I mean. How'd you do?"

"Broad Jumper and *Sexy,* channel 16 is a calling and distress frequency, and there is a Mayday in progress. Get off the air!" The Old Man's tone of voice helped carry his message.

"Isabella Grande, Dancing Girl. Over."

"Go ahead, *Dancing Girl.*"

"There are another twenty people in the water. We cannot bring many more aboard, but will pick up any we can in *Lulu's* skiff and our rubber dinghy. The cold is getting to them, and they cannot help us help them. Maybe when you are near us you could take some of ours so we can take on more. Over."

"Roger, we just have sighted you through the fog. We will pick up all we can see and then take the people from your skiffs. Let me know when you get anymore and we will let you know how we are doing. Over."

"Roger, we are drifting down from the northern edge of the people. Why don't you start at the southern end and we'll work toward each other?"

"This is *Isabella Grande*. That sounds good. We'll do it."

"This is *Dancing Girl*. Roger. We will be standing by on 16."

The Old Man went back up on deck and relieved me. Ann and David had inflated and launched the rubber dinghy and it was riding on its painter against the port quarter. Ahead of it was *Lulu*'s skiff riding against the two fenders which had been hung one on each side of the boarding ladder. All of our guests but five were below sitting as low as possible. The Old Man said, "I do not want to sail with our stability reduced when we have taken aboard as many as we may have to. We have picked up everyone within heaving line range and there are no more people to leeward. Let's put the #1 in its sausage and furl the main with a good tight furl so that people can hang on it if they want to." We left the foreguy attached to the boom end in case we needed to use it as a crane using the vang to get some really helpless person aboard. We made sure that there were no lines over the side or that could get over the side. When everything was shipshape the Old Man told us he was going to start Old Smoky and zigzag back and forth to make sure we did not go by someone too weak to yell or wave as we made our way south towards *Isabella Grande*.

I went below and told our guests what we were going to be doing and gave them a report of our status. Most really were not interested. But I did not want the engine noise to startle them, and I wanted to prepare them for the idea that they might be transferring to a USCG boat for the ride into Portland.

"This is *Marine Patrol*. We have a blue sloop in sight. Do you have your sails down? Over."

"*Marine Patrol*, this is *Dancing Girl*. Affirmative. There may still be fifteen people in the water between us and the *Isabella Grande*. We see a small, very fast vessel with two aboard to the north of us coming very fast. How fast are you, anyway?"

"This is *Marine Patrol*. We were doing 50 when we sighted you. We understood you and the *Isabella Grande* are working the crowd. We will circle to make sure we don't miss any."

Lulu and Sue's skipper and mate were the last two below

and there was no room for them to sit so they had to stand, but their weight was lower than it would have been on deck. I did not think we could get many more below. "That *Marine Patrol* are sure willing to beat the hell out of themselves to get to the scene when they can help."

The skipper said, "They are good guys. Its the old story though: the no-good fishermen complain about them, but those of us who are fishing right and making a living like them."

The coffee pot was boiling and I put the mate in charge, "Make it good and strong and heavy on the sugar. Put enough cold in it so that nobody can get burned. We only have nine mugs so it will be three people to a mug. It may make them feel better."

"*Dancing Girl, Dancing Girl, Dancing Girl.* This is United States Coast Guard 413008. We expect to be in sight of you in five minutes. What is the status of rescue operation at this time? Over."

"Coast Guard, *Dancing Girl.* We have twenty-nine survivors aboard, very crowded, and many in need of better care than we can provide. The last people we have picked up may be critically hypothermic. Our maximum speed in this condition is probably 4 knots. Suggest our survivors be transferred to your vessel because of your better facilities and speed. Over."

"Roger, stand by one."

"413008, this is *Isabella Grande.* We have six victims aboard, all in bad shape. We can carry ten more but can't give medical care they need. Our best speed 15."

"Roger, stand by one."

"413008, *Marine Patrol.* We have five critically hypothermic victims aboard. We can carry three more and still do 45 but we can do nothing for them. These people need help now. Over."

"Roger, Stand by."

"413008, *Dancing Girl.* This is the skipper. Try to get to a position due west of us, distance 50 feet, slow to 3 knots, and turn to 270° magnetic. We can rig fenders, come alongside your starboard quarter and control our position well enough to pass survivors to you if you have two experienced men to receive them. We can have skipper to skipper communications on Channel 6 VHF. I have no other channel on my portable VHF. Once we are in position we can increase speed to 4 or maybe 4.5 knots to improve our handling characteristics. I used to fuel coast guard cutters from my DE in World War II at 12 knots and have exchanged personnel with Coast Guard vessels underway at sea recently. I believe *Dancing Girl*'s bow will more closely approach the height above the water of your stern than vice versa."

"*Dancing Girl,* this is United States Coast Guard Portland. We have medical personnel standing by. They suggest it is important to get victims under medical care without delay."

"Coast Guard, *Marine Patrol.* We will be at dock in five minutes with five survivors and will return to scene, Over."

"*Dancing Girl,* 413008. We are taking position on your port beam as you suggest and will turn to 270° and slow to 2 knots to let you get in position."

"This is *Dancing Girl,* Roger."

"All vessels at the scene this is 413008. Shift to 22."

"*Dancing Girl* shifting to 22."

"*Isabella Grande* shifting."

Marine Patrol going to 22."

"David," said the Old Man, "rig four fenders one forward of the shrouds all extending above the toerail. We will transfer just abaft our shrouds. We may find that it looks practical to ride to a midships forward spring running from our forward genoa car to some stanchion base or other point and back to us so that we can release whenever I want, but we have to make sure that it does not drop in the water and get around the screw. You take charge of that whole business. Skipper, if you and your mate and Jimmy can take charge of handing these people up to the Coast Guard one at a time I will either stay in position or swing in and out each time when you are ready. Lets get the sickest ones over first. Professor, you organize the troops to come up into the cockpit one at a time. Ann, you get them up into the cockpit and out on deck to the skipper so there is no delay. Set the walkie-talkie on channel 6 and give it to me so that I can talk direct. Tell 413008 that I am on 6 and I will test."

All was done as planned and the Old Man was holding *Dancing Girl* just off 413008's quarter. He took the VHF out of his jacket pocket and transmitted, "I think we would have better control at 4.5 knots, what do you think, 41?"

"Agreed. Going to 4.5 knots. We are ready when you are."

"Coming in."

The first man was just about out, unable to help himself at all. Ann and I had to drag him up the companionway and into the cockpit where he sat slumped against the cabin. Jimmy and Ann slid him along the deck house to where the mate and the skipper could get him ready to transfer. *Dancing Girl* was brought in with her fenders against the other boat's quarter, the victim was lifted to his feet and the two coast-guardsmen grabbed him and practically snapped him aboard. They were good and they were strong. They each had on safety harnesses and our team had lines around them secured so they could work with both hands. The Old Man swung out till we had the next man ready. That part was taking a lot of backbreaking effort.

The Old Man spoke to David, "Forget about that line. We will do better without it. We really need some strong hands getting these people to the launching pad. See what you can do to help Ann and the Professor."

We tried various systems, including draping the victim over David's back and having him climb up to the cockpit with his passenger riding there. Finally we decided on the third one that Ann and I in the cabin and David in the cockpit worked best. It was not easy but we worked well together and each of us had the same understanding of the problem. It was something like bringing an extra heavy and big sail up to bend it on a rough day.

The Old Man said three in the cockpit was enough and that he was ready to go in. David and Jimmy worked as a team getting the first man to the launch pad and the second to the ready seat in rapid order. This time when the Old Man went in we worked like clockwork, getting the three trans-ferred as we got the fourth to the ready seat. Before that one could be transferred, the Old Man had to bring *Dancing Girl* out. He would use only 2° or 3° of course change to move the boat in or out and adjusted the speed by tapping the throttle with his foot. Ann and I were now getting better results mov-ing people toward the deck and by the time O. M. was ready to go in again, we had three more in the cockpit and a line of people starting to become continuous. David and Jimmy were working so that before people could settle down in the cockpit they were on their way to the ready seat. This time in we got eight people transferred before the boat took a shear and we had to pull out till she settled. The Old Man said that if he could have controlled the throttle more easily and had more power it would have been easier to get in and out but that with our limitations and the reasonably calm seas he was doing fine just using the wheel.

He later said that the secret was to keep our stern clear to permit us to swing out with 10° to 15° of rudder if we had to, but to use only 2° or 3° going in. With 413008 steering 270°, he never steered to the left of 260° but when he needed to get out he would come right as far as 290°.

The only people left aboard *Dancing Girl* now were in pretty good shape and could do a lot to help themselves. The captain of the 413008 said he was getting pretty heavily loaded and that maybe if he had all the people who needed medical help aboard he should run this load in and return immediately to help here. He could make 30 knots and should be back in 15 or 20 minutes. *Marine Patrol* was back and was off-loading *Isabella Grande*'s six sickest people for a quick run ashore. He said he would be back.

We were about 200 yards from *Isabella Grande*, who had picked up five more since our last check, and our count showed that there were still three people to be accounted for. The Old Man started the simple spiral search plan he had made up years ago and always kept pasted inside the cover of the current log book. It was very simple to understand but required some discipline to carry out. It merely required that the boat turn right 90° after each leg and that each leg be 15 seconds longer than its predecessor. It made for pretty fast action for the first few legs but got easier later on. It resulted, at 6 knots, in the track of each leg being 50 yards outside the track of the leg four turns before. With good lookouts this would produce thorough coverage of the area searched. Ann went up to the bow with a good pair of binoculars. I set the navigator's timer for 15 minutes to remind me to relieve her.

There were eight guests aboard including the skipper, the

mate, Jimmy, and Nora. Although the cabin, because of the stove, was like a steam room they were all in wet clothes and far from too warm. David asked them if any of them could go for some hot soup and a sandwich and they all said yes, thanks, or words to that effect. David got both burners going on the stove and got enough soup for twelve started in two pots. He gathered all the used coffee mugs and washed them in cold water with a little extra Clorox in it.

The Old Man called down to me, "Professor, find out how many people know CPR. The next one we pick up is sure to need it." The skipper and the mate of *Lulu and Sue* had both completed the refresher course 6 months ago, Ann and David had taken it 4 years ago, and I had been a qualified instructor at school about 5 years ago but had let another master take over and had not bothered to recertify. The bell rang, and I went up to relieve Ann as lookout resetting the timer for 15 minutes as I went by. She was swinging the glasses up to the horizon and down to 20 feet ahead and back and forth to 45° on either bow, like an automaton. It would be hard to get more thorough coverage. I was not sure I could be as disciplined. As she went below I told her, "We used to have a Resuscitube aboard. I bet it still is in the first aid kit. It might come in handy."

The Old Man had a stop watch around his neck and had been making precise 90° turns with what seemed to be unnecessary frequency but now our spiral was expanded to where the next leg was 3 minutes. As the end of my turn approached the Old Man told Ann if she would relieve him he would relieve me. I was glad to be able to relax when he took over.

"Ann, come left 10°. I see something."

"Coming left to 260. . . . Steady on 260."

"It looks like a person but he does not look good. We better pick him up."

David and Jimmy ran up on deck and as Ann slowed, climbed into the skiff.

"Swing out the boom we are going to do a vang pick up."

The Old Man ducked below and made his log entries to keep track of our search and came back on deck to help me with the the boom and vang. With the foreguy and the sheet we were able to get the boom end right over the skiff and lower the vang. David tied the line under the victim's arms and around in front of him with a reverse surgeon's knot. The Old Man and I two-blocked the vang and swung in the boom. I had to knock open the pelican hook with my pliers to drop the upper life line. The man was cyanotic and gave no sign of life as I lowered him onto the starboard cockpit seat and untied him. The skipper and the mate dumped a lot of water out of the man as they rolled him over and got him below. They stretched him out on the cabin sole and arranged themselves in the galley area as they started to work. Their instructor would have been proud to see them. Calm, quick and efficient. The skipper was glad to use the Resuscitube and the mate's counting seemed like incanted magic, if only it would work. David said he and Ann would be ready to take over when the first team got tired.

"*Dancing Girl, Marine Patrol.* We will be there in a couple of minutes. What's the status?"

"*Marine Patrol, Dancing Girl.* We have one more aboard. We do not know how *Isabella Grande* is doing. We are giving CPR to one victim. No results yet."

"*Marine Patrol, Isabella Grande.* We have picked up one body about ten minutes ago. No one aboard knows CPR, but this guy was floating face down when we got to him."

"*Dancing Girl, Marine Patrol.* It looks like your victim has the best chance. We will be over to help with him. We will come alongside you to port and one of us will come aboard you. Then we can decide whether to transfer him to us with the CPR team for a fast run to the beach."

"Roger, we will have fenders over for you. Suggest that at 5.5 knots we will be easier to land on. Over."

"Roger. We are coming in now."

The operation went quickly and well and the victim was put back aboard *Marine Patrol* along with Jimmy and his skipper maintaining the rhythmic CPR. They took off at 50 knots.

"*Dancing Girl,* we have just found another one. By our count that is all. We are heading for the barn."

"*Isabella Grande, Dancing Girl.* We agree with your count.

We have one aboard we cannot transfer at sea. We are headed in and will see you at the Coast Guard Base in about 50 minutes."

We lifted the rubber dinghy aboard and deflated it and, putting the skiff astern on a lead long enough to get it sliding on the second wave, took off at 6.5 knots.

"I think we will spend tonight on a mooring at Handy's. Then we can go into the float and clean up in the morning," said the Old Man.

Appendix

The appendix describes the organization of *Dancing Girl* and the way situations will be handled as they arise. It falls into three sections: 1. Duties 2. Customs. 3. Sails 4. Special Situations and Emergencies. Persons joining the boat for a cruise will be lent a copy of the appendix so that all aboard may be familiar with its contents and share common approaches to common goals.

Duties

CAPTAIN

The captain is responsible for the boat. Although he cannot be expected to be an expert in every field in which a problem can arise, he, if expert advice is not available, will have to make the decision based on his own experience. A decision to do nothing or a decision to act must be made and will have a greater chance of being correct than indecisiveness. Any plan is better than no plan.

If time permits the captain may discuss the problem and solution with the ship's company. Although making no claim to know all the answers, the captain is responsible for the decisions regarding the boat. The more stressful the situation, the more important that the captain's decisions and instructions be carried out by all hands. All hands should remember that the less informed a person is the more liable he is to differ with the captain's orders.

Experienced seamen know that there are many differ-
ences of opinion as to the best solution to any problem, but
that when they come aboard a vessel they do so knowing that
although the captain has weaknesses, they will follow his orders
regardless. They should know that to do otherwise will
endanger the safety of all. They should remember that there
are eight different ways to do each job and that any one will
succeed and any two will fail. The captain may delegate
responsibility to others in the ship's company he considers
particularly qualified, but he is under no obligation to do so.
By coming aboard, those who do so accept these conditions.

WATCH CAPTAIN

The watch captain is responsible for the operation of the boat
from the moment he or she relieves the person previously
running the boat until relieved by the captain, another watch
captain, or some other person known to be judged by the
captain to be competent to do so. Before allowing anyone
else to relieve, the watch captain should get the captain up
on deck so that he can take the responsibility before that person relieves. The watch captain should abide by the ship's
rules and the captain's instruction, keeping the captain
informed at all times, particularly if departure from the rules
seems to be required by the circumstances.

The captain should be kept informed of everything that
happens that can affect the safety or welfare of the ship. The
range and bearing of a vessel or other object, a change in
wind direction or strength, or in the condition of the sea's
surface, or the color of the water or the range of visibility are
typical of matters to be reported but do not exclude other
equally significant circumstances.

The watch captain will keep the navigator, who often will
be the captain, informed of everything that happens that might
affect the navigation of the vessel, including the sighting of
a light or the loom of a light, hearing the sound of a nava-
gational aid, or not observing such an aid or object when
expected. If possible the range and bearing as well as the
time should be observed. Often the time that the light comes

over the horizon or dips below it gives the distance and thus increases the value of the bearing. All such information should be logged with the time, without which the value of the observation is greatly reduced. It is far better to log too much rather than too little.

When in any doubt, consult the captain without delay; he will get more sleep if you call him for every little thing than if he is worrying that you will neglect to notify him of something significant. In times of emergency act, but at the first opportunity call the captain up on deck. There will be circumstances when the watch captain should call all hands on deck and then tell the captain what is happening.

Every hour, on the half hour, and at the change of the watch, the watch captain should enter in the log, or have his watch stander do so for him, the significant events of the preceding hour that were not entered at the time they occurred. Most important are estimates of course and speed made good, including an evaluation of the current. The navigator will be needing set and drift evaluations to improve his dead reckoning and your observations are essential.

The watch captain should mentally review the Rules of the Road frequently to be clear as to what action they dictate in each circumstance. It is also important to go over the emergency bills so that if a man goes overboard or a fire breaks out, correct action will be taken without delay. In many cases promptness is a desirable substitute for more drastic action later. The more serious the circumstance the more important it is that instructions be given in calm, clear tones that will inspire confidence in others. By thinking ahead, the watch captain can be prepared to project the air of efficient competence that will ensure that all perform at their best.

The watch captain should see that sails are at all times trimmed to their most efficient performance. Cruising is most enjoyable when the boat is sailing at peak efficiency and this is the watch captain's responsibility. Subject to the limitations imposed by being shorthanded the velocity made good to the next mark within the bounds of good seamanship is the measure of how well the watch captain is fulfilling his responsibilities.

The best watch captain is alert and foresighted. Problems are met before they get started. An extra hand needed for a sail change is called before the situation deteriorates to the point where two people are needed. In the simplest words, the watch captain should run the boat as though it was his boat while keeping the captain informed at all times.

NAVIGATOR

The navigator is responsible for the definition and identification of the boat's environment and its relationship with this environment and for the charts, publications, instruments, and equipment used in determining this relationship. This responsibility includes the existing relationship and the prediction of future circumstances, the utilization of outside sources of information and the procurement and maintenance of all materials and devices contributing to the successful fulfillment of this obligation. In the final analysis, the safety of the boat depends on the navigator and he or she must be the judge as to how best to use talents and abilities to provide the information that will permit the ship's company to make the best of circumstances.

The ship's compass mounted in the binnacle is usually adjusted professionally every year. The navigator, however, will check the deviation whenever possible, such as when an amplitude or azimuth can be taken or when crossing a navigational or other range. Two compasses, on the navigator's desk and another in the bilge, are an integral part of the ship's electronic dead reckoning system. Both should be adjusted to correspond with the ship's compass. Care should be taken to insure that no magnetic influence, be it a quartz watch, a sharpening steel, or a pocket knife be allowed to come close enough to any of the compasses to cause a false reading.

There are also two hand bearing compasses aboard. They should be checked against the ship's compass from time to time as they are the sources of the bearings of navigational aids that are used to fix the ship's position. One of these is normally carried by the watch captain for taking bearings of navigational aids or vessels as they are sighted. The other is normally reserved for the navigator.

Aboard *Dancing Girl* there are two lead lines in the starboard cockpit locker and these are used in confined waters, particularly when the charts are of doubtful accuracy, and to back up our electronic depth finders. Depth is primarily obtained from the digital depth finder which has a transducer on the centerline in the forward bilge forward of the speedometer rotors. Readings are displayed over the navigator's bunk and may be displayed on any of the digital displays in the cockpit or below.

For backup we have an old and long trusted flashing depth finder which has a transducer on the port side just abaft the galley sink drain. This instrument is mounted on an arm which permits it to be swung around so that it can be read either from below or from the cockpit. Next to the compass these are our most important navigational tools for coastwise cruising.

In the lazaret there is stored an old-fashioned taffrail log with two spare rotors, which is streamed whenever the distance run through the water is particularly important for navigation. Most of the time the distance run provided by the electronic system is sufficient. There are, however, occasions when drifting grass or other subsurface flotsam foul the rotor and cause a falsely low reading.

The boat's electronics include a masthead unit which gives relative wind direction and speed at the masthead. It takes this information and the input from its speedometer and compass to compute much useful information, including true wind direction and speed. Its operation is described in the instruction booklet on the navigator's desk.

On *Dancing Girl* we have a loran C which takes continuous loran readings and uses them to compute course and speed made good over the ground, course and distance to destination and much other information useful to the navigator. One of its most vital, but we hope least used, functions is to freeze the record of the boat's position when the hold button is pushed. This is used when someone goes overboard to aid in retrieval. The instruction book is kept on the navigator's desk at all times.

We have a radio receiver which covers from 150 to 4,500 kHz and with its hand-held unit permits taking accurate radio direction finder bearings on transmissions in its frequency range. The corrections to be made to bearings taken at the navigator's station are given inside the back cover of the ship's log book.

The VHF is the communications radio of choice with stations with antennas within line of sight. (The higher the antenna the greater the range.) It has four channels that receive the NOAA continuous weather broadcasts. It is useful for bridge-to-bridge communications with other vessels, communications with drawbridges, shore facilities, including the Coast Guard, and for telephone calls ashore.

A single-side-band radio communicates with stations outside VHF range. It is wise to monitor the various applicable frequencies to determine what stations and what frequencies can be expected to provide the best reception. Various frequencies work better at different times of day and at different ranges. When the proper frequency is used this radio will provide the input for the weather facsimile printer which provides up-to-date weather charts including prognoses and satellite photos. These are particularly valuable when we are out of range of the regular NOAA forecasts. As a backup to provide input to the fax we have a receiver which can also provide broadcast music to the speaker in the galley.

Other equipment includes a pelorus which lets us get accurate bearings of celestial and terrestial objects based on the ship's compass, a good micrometer sextant, and a three-arm protractor. There are clinometers at the nav station and in the cockpit to port of the companionway below electronic digital readouts. Running lights are controlled by switches on the board on the bulkhead abaft the icebox. We have a masthead triple unit for use under sail, and port and starboard lights in the pulpit and a stern light on the pushpit alternatively for use under sail. With the addition of the steaming light these lower lights are to be used when the engine is in gear. The masthead unit also includes an all around light which we use as an anchor light and a strobe which is controlled from a switch on the binnacle but is only to be used as a last resort to try to attract the attention of a vessel that appears to be headed for a collision with us. The bell, which is most frequently used to show inspecting parties from the U.S. Coast Guard, is available on the occasions when we are at anchor in the fog. It is in the bottom of the starboard cockpit locker.

The boat's navigation library includes *Bowditch* and *Dutton* and these volumes should be reviewed annually to keep fresh such skills as celestial navigation, the use of vertical angles or two bearings to determine distance off. Many mathematical tricks are only valuable if one is sufficiently adept to work them quickly and accurately without hesitation. There are many navigators who can pass detailed written exams but who fail at sea because they cannot hold on and use two hands on a sextant or because they cannot jam themselves against the chart desk and look up figures quickly in tables they have not recently consulted. In many cases slow navigation is useless because it is too late. It is hoped that everyone who comes aboard *Dancing Girl* will be inspired to become a good navigator. There are too few of them.

COOK

Any army is said to travel on its stomach but on *Dancing Girl* the cook is far more important than the old saying would suggest. The cook is not only expected to provide meals that will at all times build morale, but also, having regular contact with both watches, is expected to provide the ideal channel for communicating with them. The cook should know the ship's customs, rules, and orders and, by reminding the crew of them, help them to comply. The cook is also in the position to get the watches relieved on time and the watch standers in and out of their bunks without waste of time.

Dancing Girl's cook also has the responsibility of reminding all hands of the need for flotation, safety harnesses, and clipping on. Setting a good example is part of the job and the lobsterman's apron and knee boots must be worn when there is any sea running. The smart cook will be in safety harness and snapped on before the need arises. The job is a hard one, but often when a voyage is over it is apparent that the reason the cruise was a happy one was the cook.

The cook runs the boat except for the hull, the sails, the cockpit, and the engine. In addition the cook, ideally, is prepared to fill in wherever there is a need or a vacancy. The ideal cook does not get seasick and can so discipline himself that he sleeps in every spare moment. The cook, like the skipper, should be asleep whenever not really needed so that he will be rested to fill in when the going gets rough and the boat suddenly seems shorthanded. The cook must know the captain's plans and be able to represent him accurately to both watches at all times when the captain is sleeping or otherwise engaged.

The cook should plan the food, beverages, and water for the cruise after discussing overall plans with the skipper. Usually the attempt should be made to provide fresh food for as much of the trip as possible, using good canned goods to maintain the quality of the menu when refrigeration is exhausted. Food supplies must be tailored to the area and be flexible enough to feed well regardless of conditions. Water use should be monitored at least every third day to make sure consumption is not above plan. Normally a voyage will be planned to take a certain number of days with a margin of safety chosen after discussion with the navigator. In addition the boat should have adequate food and water to bring the crew home in a happy state under a jury rig if disaster strikes.

Stowage of food supplies should be such that a roll-over will not send cans and other heavy items out of the storage area. Food can be stowed by meals or by types of food or any other system that will permit the cook to lay hands readily on the ingredients of a good meal when the going gets rough. The cook should be able to present appropriate but appetizing fare that can be eaten from a bowl by an exhausted watch stander with an arm around a stanchion, when the boat is gyrating like a speared octopus. When the weather gods smile and the pressure is off the crew, they must eat well enough so that each meal will be a high point of the day.

The cook is responsible for seeing that the watch is relieved on time, for nothing so disrupts the morale of the ship's company as the emphasized disappointment when the end of the watch comes and goes without the relieving watch letting the watch standers get below to eat and get into the bunks they have been longing for. The cook therefore has to judge with the help of the oncoming watch when each must be called considering the state of the weather and what clothes will be needed. Watch standers must be called in good time but not too early. Dramamine and a cracker can help the sleeper get to the cockpit before nausea sets in. Food and hot soup or coffee should be ready and if a meal is not scheduled, snacks should be available. An empty stomach is more likely to churn. Watch standers should be on deck, dressed, fed, and in harness with time to look over the boat and relieve no later than 5 minutes before eight bells strikes. A skilled cook can rush a potentially sick person through the danger zone and up on deck before mal de mer can destroy him, but also give the on-comer time to check the navigation and the log before going topside. The cook should be the best source of weather information.

When an extra hand is needed in the cockpit for a jib change, the cook ideally should be able to take the wheel and save the sleep of the rest of the ship's company. When the navigator needs a fathometer curve, the cook should be ready to start the timer and log each reading on schedule. The cook also keeps an ear cocked for the radio. The cook should handle scheduled weather broadcasts to be sure that they are recorded for future use. If the cook is not the head captain, and he normally should not be, he has the responsibility to see that the head captain's job is being done properly. Somehow or other the cook must enlist the cooperation of the gorillas so that their cage does not become a sty, and so that the off-coming watch finds the hot bunk awaiting him is ready for occupancy. Great tact will be required to get people into their bunks rapidly so that every person can have enough sleep stored up in case conditions deteriorate.

As the boat approaches its destination, the cook must have lists ready so that stores can be replenished without delay. All the ship's company is expected to assist with the provisioning, but a visit to a new port can be much more enjoyable if time is not taken up with disorganized provisioning. The crew should be directed so that the cabin is picked up, cleaned, and ready for port activities. Then all can get ashore with minimum delay. Shopping is different in every port but the cook will find that ingenuity and charm can get the cooperation of forces ashore and ensure that the ship's company will eat as well on the next leg as they did on the voyage that started at home. The personal contacts the cook makes shopping ashore often can play a large part in determining how the local people regard the boat and its crew.

Rules and Customs

DRUGS

In many of the waters in which we sail the possession of illegal drugs can cause the authorities to confiscate the boat in which they are discovered. Aside from all other considerations this is reason enough to require that under no circumstances will any illegal drugs in any amount be brought aboard.

The ship will furnish alcoholic beverages in keeping with local availability but those who require special drinks should let the cook know, preferably when the voyage is in its planning phase, so that they can be provided in one way or another. The problem is complicated by customs requirements in the various countries we visit. We do comply with the letter of the law and should plan ahead to avoid problems.

Dancing Girl is sailed precisely and fast with the result that pressures are great and mistakes can be serious. Alcohol affects alertness, coordination, and judgment. For this reason we do not consume any alcoholic beverage when the boat may be expected to be under way before the effect wears off.

Those who smoke are asked to do so with consideration of those who do not, particularly when the cabin is closed up and the going rough. Particular care must be taken to eliminate all risk of starting a fire. There can be no smoking in bed and every hot ash must be carefully extinguished. A boat seems to make a burning butt more liable to fall in a dangerous place at the same time it makes the hazard from fire greater.

HEADS, ETC.

Men should pee over the side whenever conditions permit. They should remember, however, that this is statistically one of the most dangerous activities performed on a boat. The rule should be "One hand for the backstay and one for the hose." At night and when it is rough the safety harness should be clipped onto the backstay for no one should be moving around topsides without being clipped on in these conditions. If it is rough enough so that there is running water in the cockpit it is recommended that men pee in the cockpit if their oilies permit. If they use the head they should be seated or kneeling. Any others standing, whether or not they splatter, will be considered by a grateful electorate to have just completed a successful campaign for head captain.

Dancing Girl's head is trouble free for years on end unless some crew member attempts to improve on established routines. One such person had to take it totally apart five times in one cruise to get it back into operation. When she got home she removed the head from her own boat and used a bucket thereafter. Under the sink at deck level there is a valve which controls both the outflow for the sink and the flushing water for the toilet. This valve must be open when the head is to be flushed. By the after port corner of the toilet there are two valves. The inboard valve is open when the macerator-chlorinator is to be used and closed when we are at sea and by-passing this battery-killing device. The outboard valve is closed when the MSD is in use and open when it is being by-passed. At the base of the toilet at the starboard forward corner there is a pedal which when depressed permits flushing water to flow into the bowl. On the port side of the toilet there is a pump handle which when swung forward and back at a moderate pace removes water from the bowl and discharges it either to the MSD or over the side depending on the valve settings. As the foot pedal is depressed, flushing water is brought into the bowl at each stroke. As the pump's piston powers both these functions there is a mixing of dirty and clean water. It is better to use the pedal to let flushing water run into the bowl and then, releasing the pedal, pump the bowl dry, repeating the procedure until the water in the bowl is clean. At this point the user should depress the pedal and pump twelve strokes to make sure that all dirty water has gone overboard. The bowl should be left clean for the next person which sometimes necessitates wiping up spots in the bowl with toilet paper which is flushed in the usual way. The operating instructions for the MSD are posted under the sink near the pump handle.

Anything except toilet paper should be processed by the user's alimentary system before putting it in the bowl. Forbidden are paper towels and Kleenex (which before being so treated have wet strength sufficient to jam the machinery), cigarette butts, cotton swabs, tampons, bobby pins, nail clippings, etc. All belong in the the trash bag, not the toilet. Keep the cover down to prevent undesirable material from falling in.

SAFETY AND SAFETY HARNESSES

Often we will be sailing shorthanded and alone, where darkness, rough water, cold, or fog make the danger of going overboard much greater. For this reason at sea we have jack lines rigged to permit all personnel to be clipped on topsides when conditions indicate. There is a wire jack line on the foredeck running from the forward end of the cabin to a pad eye by the mooring cleats. There is another on each side of the coach roof running from the forward to the after corner. There is also another on each side of the cockpit under the edges of the seats. The transparent drop board in the companionway permits a person coming on deck to time the opening of the slide so that he or she can clip on before coming on deck without letting water pour down into the boat.

Persons coming aboard without their own safety harnesses should each immediately borrow one from the boat's supply for the duration of the voyage. Without delay the harness should be fitted to the individual and two pennants for each should be selected from those made up by previous crew members. There is a supply of carabiners to be used with these harnesses but those chosen should be checked over and lubricated before being used to ensure that they are worthy of the trust placed in them. There is a supply of 3/8-inch twisted nylon line available for those who do not have confidence in any of the existing pennants. Most people feel that six tucks are desirable in splices in safety harness lines and some like to whip the splice besides to reduce the chances of the splice working loose.

Safety harnesses should be worn and clipped on whenever there is any undue risk of going over the side or any extra risk that a man overboard will not be retrieved. Crew members should clip on when the boat is bouncing or there is risk of a green sea coming over, when there is ice or snow on deck, or when bundled up so that agility is affected. When shorthanded or operating in the dark or fog, particularly when there are extra sails set, the difficulty of getting back to the victim and keeping him in sight make clipping on particularly wise. All personnel topsides should wear safety harnesses and be clipped on when sailing shorthanded with a spinnaker or other sail reducing maneuverability, when alone on deck, when the wind over the deck is over 22 knots, and when it is rough or foggy or the water temperature is below 45° Farenheit.

People should look ahead so that they will be wearing their harnesses when conditions require them to clip on. Each crew member has a responsibility to see that his or her shipmates do not have cause for worrying about man overboard or a shipmate lost at sea.

NIGHT VISION

Below decks *Dancing Girl* has in addition to regular white lights red lights and red light flashlights of the proper color to minimize any ill effect on the night vision of the ship's company. All should be acquainted with the location of these lights and use them after dark at sea to ensure that no one's night vision is unfavorably affected.

LOG

Dancing Girl's log is important in many ways. It contains inside its front cover for ready reference information frequently used or that may be seriously needed at infrequent intervals. Photos of the pages are shown here so that crew members may have a clear idea of what is available. The first page gives the search plan to be used in that desperate situation when a man overboard is not found in the area where we expected to find him.

The second page has a variety of useful information. First the standard terminology used to describe the density of fog to assist in writing up the log accurately. Second is a table giving the dew point for various wet and dry bulb readings used for log entries and for estimating the likelihood of fog. With a sling psychrometer the navigator or his assistant gets the wet and dry bulb readings and, using the table, determines the temperature at which fog is liable to occur. Third is the most recent deviation table under power prepared by a professional adjuster. It has no great usage if the deviation is zero but becomes valuable when deviation has to be applied to courses to be steered. Fourth is the table correlating the time of 50 flashes on the taffrail log with speed through the water. This is often a more accurate way of determining boat speed than the electronic log. Fifth we have a graph showing the percentage speed increase necessary to justify a given number of degrees off course. This is particularly valuable in making tactical decisions when the information is not being computed and displayed electronically. Sixth is the amount of Clorox to be added when filling each of the various water containers aboard *Dancing Girl*. This will keep the water sweet without giving more taste than the filter system can remove.

The next page covers the Beaufort wind scale and gives photos of cloud formation to help those writing up the log to describe weather conditions accurately. Following that is the page describing the fuel filtering system and the water filtering system. More important, on this page, although we hope it is going to be used far less often, is the procedure for sending out a Mayday. Presumably when this information is needed it will be valuable to get it right the first time.

In the back of the book is a page giving the signal flags and pennants with their meanings and their Morse equivalents, to be available when communications problems bring them up. The page before that lists the call-in letters and in Morse code and the frequency of each of the aeronautical RDF beacons in our operating area between New Jersey and Massachusetts, giving the latitude and longitude of each. It also gives the corrections to be applied to all RDF bearings taken from the navigator's station. The pages before this were left empty to be ready for notes of people's names and addresses, service companies phone numbers, customs information, bridge schedules, and whatever else might be useful.

Before this comes a section devoted to the time checks made for each of the boat's chronometers giving the current rate of each and the station from which the accurate time was obtained. Several pages before this are devoted to the radio log giving the date, Greenwich Mean Time, local time, station heard or called, channels used, remarks including details of all Maydays received and the signature of the operator. The section preceding this is devoted to the weather facsimile receiver giving the date, Greenwich time, local time, station heard, frequency used, and remarks. This type of information can all be of great value at some future time when conditions are similar.

The log itself on *Dancing Girl* should contain a record of all that happens each day that there are people aboard the boat. It should have entries for wet and dry bulb thermometer readings and the computed dew point, it should have barometer readings, a notation of the barograph trace, a description of cloud and visibility conditions and the weather according to the Beaufort scale. A quotation from significant radio weather forecasts is also helpful. These entries are normally made by the captain or navigator at 0800 each morning. When we are standing watches the watch captain will also make them at the end of each watch.

The navigator will normally do all his work and computations, including celestial lines of position, in the log so that they will be a part of the boat's permanent record. Sail changes, weather and sea changes, the use of running lights, fog horns, the fog bell, the sighting of navigational aids or other significant objects should all be entered as they occur. These entries should include the time, the mileage reading from the electronic or the taffrail log, and the depth of water. Particularly important are the bearing and estimated ranges of vessels sighted that may come close to us. When the anchor is hoisted aboard it is good to enter a comment as to the character of the holding ground for future use. Illnesses or damage to personnel or equipment should be entered promptly and in appropriate detail.

The preciseness and detail with which the log entries are made will depend on the number of people in the crew and the boat's demands on them. At least a summary of events can be written up at the end of each day or at the end of each watch. Future value of this book can be greatly enhanced by entering in it names and addresses of people aboard or met elsewhere. Details of harbors and pilotage will be useful if we return to the waters covered.

When the paper in the barograph is changed the completed chart should be pasted in the log book. It will add detail to our record of the barometric pressure experienced and when the sea is rough the motion of the boat causes the tracking arm to vibrate giving an indication of how rough the going was.

The log is a serious legal record and must be kept that way. Its completeness may some day be invaluable. It also enhances our recollections of our cruise by preserving details that time might have led us to forget.

ANCHORS

Dancing Girl carries four anchors. First are two 12-pound Danforths which are our primary system of anchoring. We use both, in a seaplane moor, spaced so that the angle between their rodes is about 60°. We also carry a Paul Luke 65-pound Herreshoff disassembled in the bilges for use where kelp or other conditions make the Danforth ineffective. Finally we have a 35-pound Danforth as hurricane anchor. We have a 10-foot chain pennant for each anchor and carry two 25-pound "angels" to slide down the anchor rodes when we want to keep our anchor line deep to avoid damage from passing boats or to make the rode more closely parallel the bottom.

We carry our anchor rodes cut into 100-foot lengths with an eye splice, thimble and shackle at each end, in nylon mesh laundry bags holding 300 feet each. For the small anchors we use 3/8-inch twisted nylon and for the heavy we have 1/2-inch. When conditions are really demanding, we will put out all four anchors in a gull-foot pattern shackled to a swivel in the center with proper scope line leading from that to the boat. There is vinyl chafing gear in the starboard locker for protecting the rode as it rides in the chock. Our mooring cleats are through bolted to a heavy backing plate and are calculated to be stronger than the lines we are using.

We like to anchor with about 10-to-1 scope and to be sure that we will have at least 5-to-1 at the highest tide. We carry our 12-pound anchors with their rodes in mesh bags, but attached, laid out on the forward bunks on canvas mats below the forward hatch, one on each side, ready for immediate use. The line is stowed in each bag three hand-sized loops at a time carefully packed so that it will run freely without kinks when needed.

ENTERING PORT

When approaching port from sea it should be the objective of all aboard *Dancing Girl* to get everything set up so that the ship's work will interfere to the minimum with activities ashore. The principle is the same whether you are coming in from a month or an hour at sea. The good sailor tries to leave the boat a little better than when she came aboard and to be ready for the next trip with minimum delay. Knowing how long the ship's stay will be in the port ahead and how long it will be at sea or away from support facilities when it leaves can make planning much easier.

The cook will have to know how many days before the next supplies can be acquired and have a pretty clear idea as to the number and type of meals that will have to be prepared from this provisioning. Normally it pays to pack the ice box solid with ice on arrival and to plan to bring in frozen and other perishable foods at the last minute before departure with a cold box ready for them. Water and fuel tanks and jugs should be filled immediately upon arrival with plans to top off at the last moment before departure. Staples and boxed and packaged goods can be gotten aboard and stowed on arrival. Provisions to be consumed before departure should also be brought aboard without delay. Scrubbing and cleaning up that could not be done at sea should be gotten out of the way as quickly as possible.

The same principles apply to hull work, engine work, and the innumerable hardware items that seem to demand attention in the navigation and communications areas. Early scheduling can reduce the number of items that will remain undone when departure time comes. Sails needing repairs should be ready for sailmakers on the beach when the boat arrives. Charts and publications needed should be listed for procurement. Laundromats and showers should be located in order to be available to ship's company early upon arrival.

If every person has his or her list ready the captain will often be able to obtain information from customs or yard personnel, or dock attendants and onlookers that will save much duplicated effort and much time for every one. The more experienced and capable the sailor the better the details of entering port are handled.

DEPARTURE

As the scheduled time of departure approaches all hands should make lists of items that can be completed before the ship departs. The cook will be thinking not only of water and ice, but of fresh vegetables and bread and of meats that the local butcher has frozen for the boat. The lists that were ready when we entered can now be checked to see which items, including laundry, have been taken ashore and have not yet returned, which items are not yet done which can be left undone when we leave and which items will delay departure unless extra attention is given them.

Phone calls from local phones are cheaper and sometimes more satisfactory than those made by radio. A voyage plan should be filed with *Dancing Girl's* secretary giving expected routing and the times at which what frequencies will be guarded. If all goes well, items will be checked off in large numbers as the deadline approaches and finally the captain will pay any outstanding bills and we will be off. If nothing is forgotten or mishandled it is the mark of a good crew and a good ship which is what we aspire to be.

FUEL

Dancing Girl has an integral fuel tank which holds 23 gallons and extends down into the keel. She also carries in the cockpit rack two 5-gallon jugs into which all fuel coming aboard the boat is normally placed. Operating as she does in faraway places it has been found from time to time that friendly, well-intentioned people unwittingly deliver fuel heavily contaminated with water, algae, and other sources of time-consuming engine problems. Our solution is the filtering system, which is mounted on the forward bulkhead of the port locker. The heart of the system is an ordinary truck fuel pump, such as a Bendix or Facet electric fuel pump. This is arranged so that it can take suction either by means of a probe from one of the jugs, or from a suction at the deepest part of the fuel tank itself. This fuel is then forced through two filters in addition to the filter in the pump and delivered to the top of the fuel tank or to the engine.

Under power *Dancing Girl* uses about 0.8 gallons per hour, usually making about 6.25 knots. If we use 7.5 miles per gallon we will not be far off. We figure that we will get about 180 miles to the full tank. When charging batteries she uses only 0.2 gallons per hour. When we are away from support facilities we will transfer 5 gallons from a jug to the tank whenever there is room. We try to arrive at a fuel pump with the tank full and the jugs ready to be topped off, with the proper amount of diesel additive in each.

When the engine is running we usually also take suction on the bottom of the tank with the filter system and recirculate our fuel through the filters back to the tank. When it is time to fuel we set the valves, connect the probe to the aircraft quick connect fitting under the companionway seat in the cockpit and insert the probe into the delivering jug. If the weather is wet the screw cap is used to prevent water from getting into the jug. The overflow vent for the fuel tank is the pencil diameter hole in the base of the starboard secondary winch island. As the computed capacity of the tank is approached we have someone watching the overflow armed with an oil-absorbent pad. By being alert we can stop the fuel pump before the vent releases more fuel than the pad can easily absorb. With this system fueling can be accomplished in rough weather with everything buttoned up tight. By having jugs and tank full whenever we depart shore facilities, we minimize worries about running out. We log engine hours run whenever we stop the engine and try to refill the tank every time it has room for the contents of one of the jugs. Every time the engine is started we calculate the fuel supply and act accordingly.

Occasionally we will be in an area where there is no risk of dirty fuel and where our need for fuel is so great that we will have to take fuel directly into the tank without passing it through our filter system. The steps and precautions required in these circumstances include all those needed when we fuel from jugs and others only required when we are fueling conventionally.

1. Clear deck of everything that can be damaged by oil.
2. Put all cushions below.
3. Loosen cap on tank and have sounding rod handy. Compute how much fuel we can take at this filling.
4. Hose down decks, wetting the teak thoroughly to prevent deep stains.
5. Clear water from fueling cap area.
6. Have rags and paper towels handy for spills. Oil absorbent mats should be used.
7. Assign responsibility for sounding, tending fuel hose nozzle, reading gauge on pump, and stopping pump.
8. Log fuel taken.
9. Wipe up, clean up. Mark sounding rod secure. Leave dock smartly if not permitted to stay. Do not hang on dock awaiting stragglers on the beach. Plan ahead.

10. CHECK TO SEE THAT CAP HAS BEEN PUT BACK ON FILL PIPE TIGHT.

Sails

The sails we use and the way we trim them aboard *Dancing Girl* are similar to the practice of other boats but it is helpful for a person coming aboard for the first time in several years to be informed as to our current thinking. Absolute precision is not possible because the boat will perform differently and have different needs when it is light and when it is ballasted with voyage stores or when it is carrying a full expert crew. This section will describe what will generally work best but as a cruise progresses we may define our thinking as to how to improve performance.

MAINSAIL

The main is cut to be hoisted as high up the mast as possible without having the halyard foul the block at the masthead or the backstay or topping lift. The foot is cut with an ample shelf to give us optimum fullness off the wind. The flattening reef is rigged with extra blocks inside the boom so that an ordinary person can adjust it without a winch. The outhaul is not needed to adjust sail fullness. The cunningham is used to control sail shape by preventing heavy winds from moving the draft further aft than 47 percent or when we think that boat speed will be improved by moving the draft as far forward as 43 percent, giving us a wider groove. The roach is cut full requiring careful control of the leech line and vang in order to achieve optimum speed for the conditions. When beating the main is trimmed to produce maximum VMG and particular attention is given to weather helm. We always try to sail the boat so as to achieve the best speed to the next mark, feeling that then we can best appreciate the pleasure of a well-sailed boat. The wheel is marked to show every 2° of rudder from 2° to 8°, port and starboard. Ideally we would like to sail the boat with a weather helm requiring 4° of rudder and under most circumstances we consider 8° to be an indication that the main should be flattened and the traveler eased. As long as the leech telltales are streaming the luff can lift without slowing the boat.

The backstay hydraulic is tensioned at 1,000 pounds for maximum fullness in light air and can be pumped up to as high as 3,800 for maximum flattening in heavy air. There is a vang tackle which when not in use is kept hanging from the movable ring which can be slid fore and aft in its track along the under side of the boom. Once the boom is rigged to leeward of the leeward end of the traveler the vang's block which carries the cam cleat is hooked into an idle genoa car on the toe rail placed to give control of sail shape and trim and to ensure that the vang will not affect the freedom of motion of the boom when the sheet is slacked in a knockdown or for any other reason. The cam cleat is angled so that it can be released from the cockpit even if the boat is standing on its ear.

The mainsail is cut so that when the clew is hauled to the end of its track the shelf has maximum fullness. The flattening reef can control the fullness of the foot of the sail all the way from maximum depth and power to board flat. In mirror calm when we have to spit in the water to detect forward motion, the flattening reef is tensioned to remove 60 percent of the shelf. The traveler is eased all the way to leeward, about 9 inches off the centerline. The sheet is trimmed to make the leech parallel to the leech on the jib. In these conditions we try for a neutral helm and are lucky to be able to tack in 100°. The secret is to keep the boat moving no matter what the direction and to use no more than 5° of rudder. Both sails are trimmed for moderate draft but must not become board flat or lifeless. Crew weight is to leeward and forward enough to prevent lee helm and everyone is careful to cause no shaking of the sails. As the boat begins to move the boom is brought in to the 14° line, carefully avoiding any action that would cause any undesirable motion.

As long as the water remains glassy and the anemometer stays down around 1 or 2 knots the helmsman is going to be hunting the shifting zephyrs and we must be quick to ease

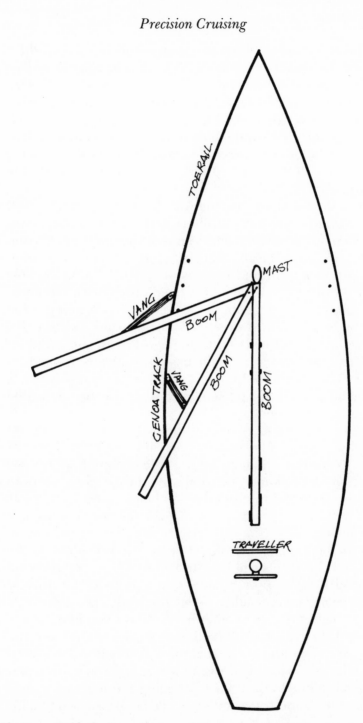

The Vang Holds the Boom Down and Forward, and with Tension Against the Mainsheet Controls Sail Shape.

the sheets and go hunting air. In very light air no more than half the shelf can be used without the airflow separating from the lee side of the sail. Most of the boat's power will come from the jib but the main must be handled to waste no available propulsive force. As the boat gains way its motion creates its own useful wind which must be held onto when the true wind fades. The precisely sailed cruiser will be moving when less skilfully handled boats are drifting helplessly in uncontrolled circles.

From the moment that the wind is strong enough to lift the telltales on the leech at the end of each mainsail batten, it is essential that these telltales be kept streaming at all times. If they are not it means that the main is stalled and rather than producing lift and drive is merely serving to heel the boat and push it sideways. The main's top batten should be kept parallel to the boom at all times except when the full main is being used in over 22 knots of wind with the #3, when it may be opened slightly to provide twist and to reduce weather helm. By watching the position of the draft the trimmer will be able to help determine proper trim. The draft should always be at 50 percent even when the main is luffing back to the batten ends.

When the wind increases to 6 knots it is time to increase backstay tension. The steadier the wind the more precisely sail shape can be optimized. For a rule of thumb we can say that from 6 to 10 knots apparent wind the flattening reef can close the shelf and the backstay can be pumped up to about 3,000 pounds, watching to see that the sail does not become lifelessly flat.

As the boat gains way, it will be able to sail closer to the wind and the sheets will have to be brought in. By the time the wind is up to 6 or 7 knots over the deck, the traveler should be moved to weather so that the boom's position causes the sail to give us 4° of weather helm. With 12 knots of apparent wind the traveler will be 4 inches to windward and the sheet should be adjusted so that the main boom is just kissing the centerline. Backstay pressure will be at 3,800 pounds and the boom hauled down hard flattening the main to control weather helm and backwinding by the jib. As the wind builds the flattening reef goes to maximum tension. Enough cunningham should be used to keep the draft at 50 percent regardless of how unfavorable the conditions. The sheet and traveler are adjusted to keep the boat on course with no more than 6° of rudder. By the time the wind has built to 20 knots over the deck, unless the water is smooth and the helmsman is feathering well, it will be time to put in a single reef to gain an increase in boat speed.

The mainsail on *Dancing Girl* is rigged so that we can optimize its shape to handle the infinite variety of wind and sea conditions that we find at sea. Because we have a short traveler, dictated by the demands for usable space in the cockpit, we must use a vang to control the height of the boom end once we are sufficiently off the wind to have the boom outboard of the traveler's end. The vang is necessary for maximum control of the leech curve which we are trying to make it conform to the shape of the genoa leech.

The vang is usually secured to the spare genoa car at the forward end of the genoa track on the toe rail or to the base of the stanchion located at the chains. The cunningham line permits hauling, by brute force, the cunningham hole closer to the tack grommet, further tightening the luff and bringing the draft forward. Our cunningham goes around through its two grommets three times to give adequate mechanical advantage.

The flattening reef line is secured to the flattening reef grommet and goes from there to the flattening reef block which is attached to the boom end. The line then goes back through the grommet down to the block which has been mounted on the port side of the boom as far aft as possible. From there it goes through a cam cleat at the forward end of the boom to a cleat. If the main sheet is given a quick, complete slack a man standing ready at the cleat can haul in the flattening reef with a quick arm motion, permitting a person in the cockpit to retrim the now flattened main without delay.

Depending on conditions we may carry one or more reefing lines reeved in. This means that the line goes from the cam cleat that will hold it, to the block mounted on the side of the boom slightly aft of the point to which the reefing

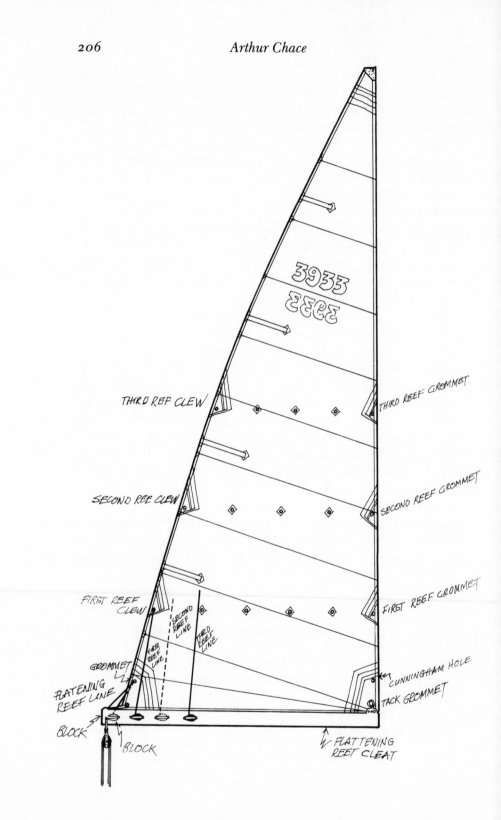

THIRD REEF CLEW

THIRD REEF GROMMET

3933

SECOND REEF CLEW

SECOND REEF GROMMET

FIRST REEF
CLEW

FIRST REEF GROMMET

SECOND
REEF
LINE

THIRD
REEF
LINE

FIRST
REEF
LINE

GROMMET

CUNNINGHAM HOLE

TACK GROMMET

FLATTENING
REEF LINE

BLOCK

BLOCK

FLATTENING
REEF CLEAT

grommet will be brought down then up through the reefing grommet and back down to the foot of the sail. Here it goes through the appropriate slot in the foot, around the boom where it is finished off with a bowline around the standing part of the line permitting the line to tighten around the boom as pressure is applied. To reef, the halyard is dropped to the mark which indicates that enough slack has been given to permit the person making the reef to hook the tack grommet over the pigtail at the gooseneck. When this is done the reefing line is hauled taut, using a line tensioner if necessary, and the halyard is then hauled taut. A lacing line makes a neater reef but is not used if time is short. A second and third reef can be put in over the first and in each case will produce a mainsail with a good flat shape.

The mainsail was made with slab reefing for three reefs and normally at sea we carry, in addition to the flattening reef, reefing lines rove in for the first two reefs. The first reef can be put in if needed with the #1 genoa at the top of its range, but it normally will not be needed with the #3 until the apparent wind is over 25 knots. By the time the wind is about 30 knots the second reef may give us better speed and we certainly should reeve in the line for the third reef. At about 32 knots we would normally reef the #3. Ideally we like to keep the boat heeled over between 22° and 26° for once it is heeled 22° it cannot go any faster and when it is at 26° it starts to slow down. With 36 knots over the deck the third reef will almost certainly give better speed as well as an easier helm. It pays to keep an eye on the clinometer, the rudder angle marks on the wheel, the anemometer, and the speedometer.

To reef the mainsail, the main halyard is eased till we have gone about a foot past its mark for the next reef. The reef tack is then hooked over its pig-tail hook at the goose neck, the mainsheet is slacked and the reef line is hauled tight using the halyard is then hauled taut to the reef mark and after that the reef line is also winched tight enough to give good sail shape. The sheet is trimmed, making sure that the leech of the main again parallels the leech of the jib.

A triple reefed main will work well with a reefed #3 and after that appears to be too much sail, with the storm jib.

When the wind is much over 40 over the deck, the trysail should replace the main which should be carefully furled. If the winds are expected to go much higher the free end of the mainsheet should be used to put tight half hitches around the furled sail and boom no further apart than 9 inches to make certain that there is no way the sea or wind can catch a hold of it.

Headsails

Dancing Girl's drive is derived mainly from her jibs. Because she never races, her sails are selected without concern for rating or handicap. Because she is used for fast cruising, her sails are designed to move her well in light winds without concern for the fact that reefing or shifting down to a smaller jib wastes time allowance. To reduce somewhat the need for sail changes her sails are heavy enough to be carried beyond the wind velocity that the boat can use for maximum speed towards the next buoy or turning point. We reef or change to a smaller jib, not to prevent distortion of the sail, but rather to increase *Dancing Girl*'s velocity made good toward the next mark. Her canvas is designed to get her to faraway places at good speed in a seamanlike way regardless of the conditions. *Dancing Girl* carries the headsails: shown on the opposite page.

The deck layout of *Dancing Girl* permits some precison of sail trim and this sketch is designed to make it easy to understand the system we use. The sheets of the Solent jib are led through blocks appropriately positioned on the 9° track to the heel blocks and thence to the primary winch. For identification these sheets have three whippings at each end. The sheets for the #1 genoa, which are marked with two whippings at each end, can be led in one of three ways depending on conditions. When it is rough or the winds are varying and we are not trying to point, the sheet goes outside the life lines to the block in the proper position on the toe rail and then through the heel block to the main winch. If we are trying to get a bit closer to the wind the sheet is led inside the life lines instead. When conditions are ideal and we can really work to

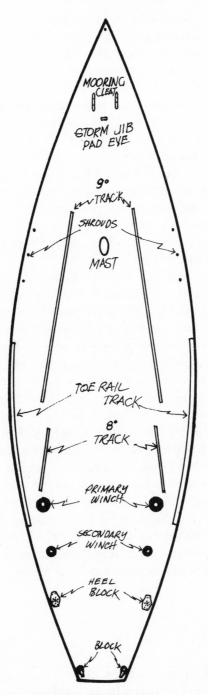

Dancing Girl's *Deck Layout*

weather the sheet goes to a block at the proper point on the 8° track and then as before.

The reacher uses the spinnaker sheets, which have only one whipping on each end and which are led through the blocks on each side of the counter to the main winches.

The storm jib is tacked to the pad eye aft the mooring cleats which are also the connection for the forestay. This pad eye is connected by a rod with turnbuckle to the keel. The forestay has a detachable wire pennant to get the wire to the winch so that the splice need not carry a heavy load. When the pennant is removed this line is used as the topping lift for the spinnaker pole. The halyard for the storm jib does extra duty as the topping lift for the reaching strut. The storm jib uses the same sheets as the Solent but led through the blocks moved to the after part of the 9° track.

The sketch on page 211 shows a matched set of three 40-foot sloops anchored at high tide in an area with 20-foot tides. To clarify our thinking each is anchored at low water in 10 feet and we have depicted the path of the bow of each as the tide came in. Boat A's bow would be at a' at low water, a" at mid-tide, and at a'" when the tide was full. The bow positions of B and C are similarly indicated. Note that were A and B to have anchored in line there would have been a 20-foot overlap at low water although they would have barely cleared at high. Note also that A's anchor rode will be straight up and down at high water, breaking itself out on the first wavelet. The relationship between B and C is much happier, but at high tide B would only have 2.5-to-1 scope which will greatly reduce the holding power of its anchor, particularly in rough water. The arcs described by each of these anchor rodes as the tide changes should be kept in mind when anchoring in restricted water, where there is an unusually high tide, or in areas where wind or current can put heavy loads on the anchor.

SOLENT JIB

This is our #3 genoa, a masthead 91 percent jib with reef points spaced 12 inches apart. It was made ten years ago from

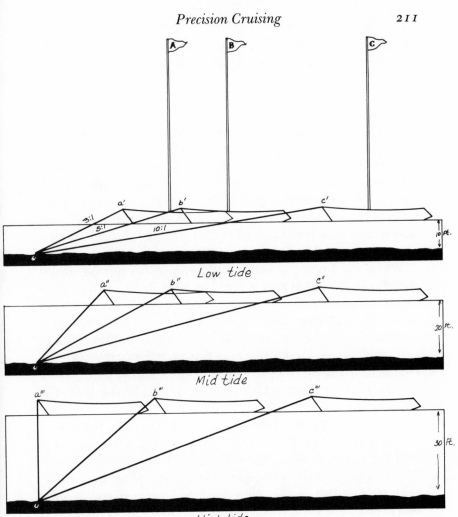

Low tide

Mid tide

High tide

7.25-oz. Dacron and has been a workhorse since the first day it came aboard. It is the jib of choice in conditions where we are suffering from crowded or confined waters, fog, gusty winds, lobster pots, inadequate charts or insufficient navigational aids. In negotiating poorly marked narrow channels the Solent used alone will give the boat forward motion but not enough speed to interfere with the work of the lookout and leadsman in the bow. In such maneuvering we would normally have an anchor lead out through the weather bow chock and hung in the pushpit, ready should kedging off appear appropriate. The Solent would provide minimal interference with spinning the boat around in such a circumstance.

In winds under 3 or 4 knots when the slop will shake the wind out of the #1, the Solent holds its shape and the wind. The jib is cut so that with 1,000 pounds on the backstay to give the main proper fullness, it will develop maximum power in these light zephyrs. The original piston hanks have been repaced by Wichard snaps which permit one-handed bending on of the sail in roughest conditions. Normally when beating it is sheeted to a block at the sixth hole on the 9° track which is abreast the turnbuckle of the upper shroud on each side.

When the wind becomes steady enough to permit use of the #1 the Solent is either sent below in its bag or is furled to the lifeline, ready for future needs. Usually the apparent wind will have risen to 21 knots or more when the Solent is rehoisted and the backstay will be at 3,800 pounds. It will probably pay to shake the reef out of the main when this change is made but the first and second mainsail reefs will be in when, at 32 knots of wind over the deck, the Solent is reefed.

To reef the #3, it is lowered to the deck to give the necessary control so that the reefing tack grommet can be snapped into the tack shackle at the stemhead. If the reefing clew is lashed tightly to the clew, threading the reefing line in the reef clew through the clew at least three times to give mechanical advantage, the sheets will not have to be shifted to the upper grommet. All lines are tied with reverse surgeon's knots which will not flog out easily and yet can be untied when the time comes. It is particularly important to roll up the idle sail in as tight a furl as possible and arrange the furl so that there is enough spare sail available to fold down over the furl, so that when the points are secure there is no way for the wind or the sea to work its way into the furl. Careful folding in the tack and clew areas is needed to maintain the furl's integrity. As soon as all is secure the halyard goes up smartly with heavy tension and the sheets are trimmed promptly to avoid unnecessary flogging.

#1 GENOA

The 165 percent #1 genoa is made from 3.7-oz. laminated Mylar and Dacron and has more dimensional stability than the 5.0-oz. Dacron it replaced. It is the performance jib for apparent winds from four to twenty-one knots but should not be subjected to more than twenty-two knots over the deck. It has two speed stripes with "hash marks" indicating the location of the draft 45 percent back from the luff. The sail is made with a tacking grommet halfway back in its foot. When beating, if there are three or more people on deck, it pays to snap the foreguy into this eye and assign one person to haul the sail smartly forward as soon as it luffs each time the boat comes up into the wind as she tacks. This not only speeds the tacking process but also reduces significantly the wear caused by the sail dragging across the spreader end.

When conditions are ideal with calm waters, steady winds and a good helmsman the halyard can be slacked till the #1's draft goes aft to 47 percent. When conditions are unfavorable about 3 inches of extra halyard tension will move the draft forward to 43 percent and provide a wider groove in which the boat can be sailed more easily. Putting more tension on the luff than is needed to position the draft at 43 percent runs the risk of causing ruinous permanent distortion of the luff of the sail. Although not a deck-sweeper, this sail demands a continuous conscious effort on the the part of the helmsman to see what is behind it. If conditions are demanding it will pay to designate a member of the crew to keep a sharp lookout in this blind sector so that the helmsman can devote all his attention to getting maximum performance from the boat.

In light air the #1 is sheeted to a block on the toe rail outside the life line and trimmed so that the patch is eight inches off the spreader end. As the boat begins to move with increasing wind the sheet is moved progressively to the same block inside the lifeline and then to a block on the 8° track with the patch in to 2 inches off the spreader and the foot against the shrouds. In pinching up it may pay for short periods to have the sail on the spreader but the helmsman should be careful to note the first signs of hobby-horsing, that short pitching motion that indicates that pinching has been carried too far.

As the wind and seas increase it may pay to let the clew move up and out to provide proper twist and a more powerful shape remembering that the leech curves of jib and mainsail should be parallel. With the apparent wind approaching 22 knots a skilled helmsman can keep the boat driving with less rudder and less angle of heel by feathering up in the puffs and at the same time be sure he has maximum sail to keep the boat moving at her best in the lulls. Before the wind over the deck gets to 22 knots the #1 is replaced by the Solent.

When changing jibs we make every effort to minimize the time we are bald-headed. The oncoming jib is snapped on the headstay below the snaps for the jib that is working, the sheets are bent on and made ready to shift to the primary winches. The jib halyard is freed to run and when all is ready the jib to be doused is lowered and unsnapped as it comes down. The dropped sail is stopped to the lower lifeline, the halyard shifted to the new jib which is immediately two-blocked and its sheets put on the primary winches and trimmed. The foredeck and mast area is tidied up quickly and the crew gets its weight back in the cockpit.

Sometimes it pays to put in the first reef at eighteen knots apparent wind to keep the boat sitting up in confused seas but usually it is better to delay reefing until the Solent is hoisted and there is 24 knots of wind over the deck. The second reef will be put in the main at about 28 knots and at 32 the Solent is reefed. The third reef is in the main before the wind is reading 38.

By the time the wind is over 40 knots over the deck there are many strategic decisions to be made and it is well to give more serious consideration to avoiding damage to boat and personnel than we would if we were racing. Speed made good to the next turning point is usually less important when cruising. On the other hand we always want to maintain good steerageway so that the helmsman can avoid hazards showing up suddenly and near. It is also good to remember that we will take less of a beating if we move the boat out of troubled waters than if we choose to bob up and down, under-sailed in troubled waters.

STORM JIB

Usually before the anemometer reads 45 we will have set up the forestay and set the storm jib on it. For the forestay we use the wire spinnaker pole topping lift with a wire pennant, which is stored under the mattress on the starboard bunk in the main cabin. This brings the wire halyard down to the winch with enough to spare to give five turns around the winch and put the rope-to-wire splice between the winch and the cleat. This wire shackles to a pad eye through bolted about 25 percent of the way back from the tack fitting to the mast. Under the deck the pad eye is connected by a rod and turn-buckle to the keel. The reaching strut topping lift is used as the storm jib halyard. It is sheeted to the car on the toe rail just forward of the after end of the deck house. If more twist is desired because of heavier winds or rougher seas or both, the block can be moved further aft. If the storm jib is to be set on the forestay with neither mainsail nor trysail the mast will require balancing support and the running backstays must be set.

Dancing Girl has beat to windward under storm jib and try-sail in moderately sheltered waters in winds that were constantly pushing the anemometer past 65. In winds of this velocity, however, the trimmer and the helm must work together and they will find the work heavy. It is a struggle easing the sheets and feathering up as necessary to keep the boat from heeling more than 26° or losing steerageway. At the same time they must prevent the sails from flogging themselves to pieces. In the open ocean there is also the problem of threading a path around the most troublesome waves or other hazards.

STORM TRYSAIL

The storm trysail is carried at all times at sea bent on its own track, alongside the mainsail track in its special bag snugged against the base of the mast. Spliced into it is its tackline which is rigged by going around the mast through the reaching strut pad eyes. There is a blue mark on the line to indicate where the line is to be snugged to the first pad eye, which is the starboard one. After both pad eyes the line goes through the tack cringle, around the mast again, very tight, and is then secured with a clove hitch to the tack cringle. The sheets are both spliced into the clew and each goes to a block snapped into the bail at the forward end of the port and starboard turning blocks. Each sheet then goes to the primary winch on its side and is cleated. The sheets are both kept cleated to maintain control of the sail and prevent unnecessary flogging, but are adjusted to give optimum sail shape on each tack.

The chart on page 217 collects in one place our latest thinking about the use of each of our sails when going to windward. The exact positions of halyard mark and block must be varied to give more power when resistance to progress is great as in a choppy sea and provide a wider groove when the boat cannot be sailed with the precision that the variable conditions demand. On the other hand with steady winds, calm water, and a good helmsman we should have our draft farther aft and a flatter sail because we can stay in the narrower groove resulting while maintaining good speed closer to the wind. Studying this chart until we are able to recall and apply every bit of it to the conditions we encounter will make it possible to increase the artistry of our sailing, but if we cannot find time to do the necessary studying we can use it as a reference whenever possible in the hope that we will be brought eventually to the same point.

The trysail is not used more than once or twice a year but when it is needed it should be ready to be set without delay. The winds that demand its use may occur within a mile of home as readily as 2,000 miles away. The good sailor is prepared to make a good showing against the worst the sea can produce wherever a boat may be.

Dancing Girl's spinnaker is a 1.5-oz. triradial made in 1975 and delivered to the boat in Spain. It has clocked a lot of miles, many under tropical sun and was rebuilt once in 1983 after a broach off the coast of Newfoundland in 20 knots of wind. It is a work-horse, forgiving and powerful. We can carry it from 60° off the wind but from 150° off to dead astern

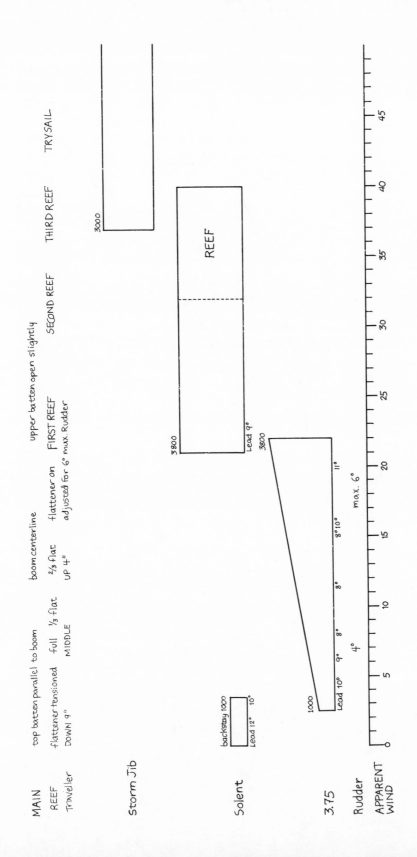

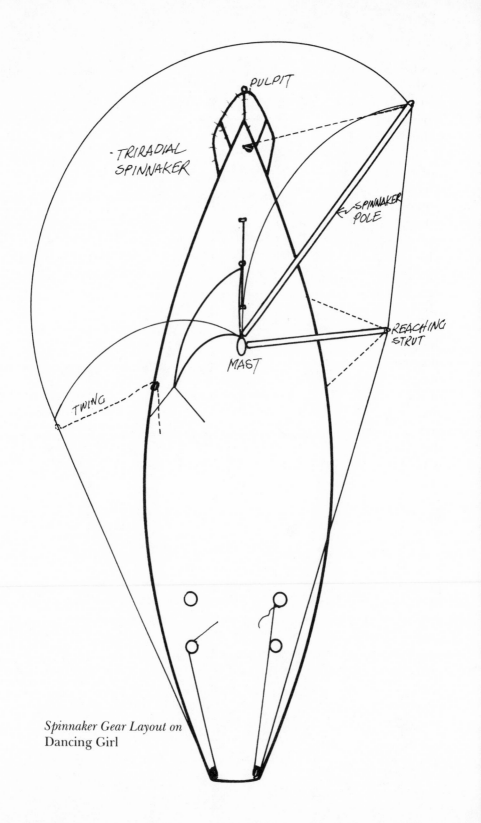

PULPIT

-TRIRADIAL
SPINNAKER

SPINNAKER
POLE

REACHING
STRUT

MAST

TWING

Spinnaker Gear Layout on
Dancing Girl

it is not being allowed to do its best for the boat. It has held its shape well, but sunlight does weaken nylon. Although we carry a 165 percent #1 genoa, the spinnaker does not have a penalty pole for we feel it is big enough for shorthanded sailing without that.

The pole inboard end drops into a fitting on a sliding pad eye mounted on the face of the mast, its height from the deck is controlled by a line through blocks above and below it. Both ends of this line are to be secured at the same jam cleat below the slide. The pole lift clips to its outboard end on top and the foreguy clips to an eye on bottom of the pole end. The topping lift cleats to the mast and the foreguy goes to a clam cleat at the after end of the deck house. The hooks at each end of the pole are closed by gates controlled by lines which each extend almost to the opposite end of the pole. The guy goes through the hook at the end of the pole, around the open block on the end of the reaching strut, to the weather block on the counter and is handled by the main winch. The reaching strut is mounted into one of the rings on each side of the mast, and is controlled by a topping lift, tended at a cleat on the front of the mast and two guy lines, one of which goes to the head of the stanchion forward of the shrouds and the other to the stanchion head abaft the shrouds. The strut is normally rigged before we set a spinnaker regardless of relative wind, to prevent us from finding ourselves on a close reach unable to control the pole's position until we rig the strut and fight the guy out around the block at the end of the strut.

The spinnaker sheet goes from the clew of the sail to the leeward block on the counter to the secondary winch. (The primary leeward winch will probably be in use for the sheet of the jib.) The person on the sheet ideally will be stationed on the weather rail near the shrouds and will be assisted by a grinder at the winch. In sloppy conditions a twing (a line snapped around the sheet and tended from a block mounted at the leeward shrouds which can be tightened quickly when the chute starts to collapse) can greatly improve the efficiency of the sail. The objectives of those tending the chute should be to have the clews as high as possible and to keep the pole parallel to the water's surface. When the wind angle

is 60° the pole is on the headstay. For each 10° the wind moves
aft the pole comes aft 5°, until the wind is at 120 and the pole
is perpendicular to the wind. Thereafter the pole is perpendicular to the wind.

When the halyard and the sheets are not in use they are
attached to the ring attached to the pulpit forward. The halyard once performed valuable service in this position when
the rod headstay failed due to stress corrosion. Present rod
rigging is, we believe, made from better steel.

THE STAYSAIL

In *Dancing Girl* the staysail is tacked to a ring which can slide
forward and aft on the jackline rigged between the forestay
pad eye and another just forward of the deckhouse. One line
from the tack of the sail goes through the ring forward around
the base of a mooring cleat and back to the stanchion base
forward of the weather shrouds. Another line goes from the
tack aft through the same ring to the same stanchion base.
Adjusting these lines controls both the height of the tack above
the deck and its position fore and aft. The staysail is sheeted
to the hand rail on the deck house and to the leeward life
line. Adjusting these lines permits precise clew positioning.

TRIRADIAL

Dancing Girl carries only one spinnaker. This is a 1.5-oz. nylon
triradial of moderately conservative cut. It carries telltales 15
inches in from the edge on each side of the sail's horizontal
stripe. If the seas are calm, it may be possible to carry it on a
close reach in winds as low as 4 knots as far foward as 60°,
apparent, off the bow. It can be carried on a run with 20
knots over the deck unless the seas are rough. In this much
wind if there is a broach or near broach, it is necessary to get
the load off the sail quickly by slacking the sheet until the
boat is moving and we have regained attached flow on the
rudder. The chute is always carried ready to hoist in its worm,
a long, tube-shaped sail cover with a full-length zipper with
a Velcro strap which goes through the swivel at the head of
the spinnaker holding the worm up to the head of the sail
which is bunched with its leeches together in a long rope and

when the zipper is closed from the top it covers the sail down to the clews.

After the spinnaker has been flown it is taken below, untwisted, and the luffs cleared and put parallel. To facilitate this the head is hung from a hook, placed, for this purpose, at the top of the forward bulkhead of the cabin, by the mast. The worm is slipped over the head, with the zipper top under the sail. Worming is best done by two persons. One who, holding the luffs together and on top, chokes the sail down to as small a rope as possible. The other person holds the worm and chute in one hand above the closed zipper and pulls the zipper down over the roped sail held by his teammate. A little practice will develop the teamwork necessary to make the process go smoothly and rapidly. The wormed sail is bagged untwisted with the head and the clews available at the mouth of the bag.

Well in advance of the hoisting of the chute when there is any chance that the wind may be forward of 130° apparent, the reaching strut is placed between the after and forward lowers in its pad eye on the side of the mast and the strut topping lift taken from the bail at the base of the mast and clipped to the end of the pole, passing forward of the forward lower shroud. There are also two light guy lines spliced into the outboard end of the strut. One goes to the stanchion base abaft the shrouds and one goes to the base of the stanchion forward. These three lines fix the strut so that it will not move regardless of whether the chute is flown high or low. When the pole is well forward the strut is essential for a proper lead for the guy which without the strut would be exerting a force largely compressing the pole against the mast. When the strut is needed, we will not have time to wait for it to be rigged.

The guy is led over the sheave at the end of the strut and at this time the crew should check to see that it has a fair lead. The pole is also removed from its holders on deck, attached to the topping lift and foreguy, and its base is placed in the trumpet on the slide on the track on the front of the mast. The slide is then hoisted to the double mark which indicates that the outboard pole will be able to clear the pulpit and headstay.

As the time for the set approaches, the bagged spinnaker

is brought up the hatch to the foredeck and tied to the weather stanchion base. The hatch is closed. The guy which is secured to the ring in the foremost point in the pulpit, called the bull nose, is passed through the fitting on the end of the pole. It is then snapped to the tack of the spinnaker which should be arranged with the zipper down and forward. The tie-down tape is tied to the lifeline to keep the worm aboard after the set. The sheet is taken from the bull nose and snapped into the other clew. The halyard is taken from the ring and snapped into the head. To prevent the halyard from taking over in a puff, the stopper is set and the halyard is cleared to hoist. The helm is notified that the sail is ready and on his instruction, the chute goes up, the guy is trimmed part way, the sheet is taut but under no load. When the okay is given to break it out, the slide is pulled down and off to open the zipper, tension is put on the sheet, the worm is given a shake if it needs it, the zipper falls open to the head and the worm drops to the deck, with the bow man's help, and the chute fills. The worm goes down the forward hatch as soon as possible and then the hatch is closed. Normally, the jib is then dropped to the deck and stopped to the lifeline ready to be hoisted if needed to provide a lee for the spinnaker at the takedown.

The spinnaker has a belly string which provides the preferred method for dousing it. The genoa is hoisted and trimmed as the boat is brought to a reach. Keeping the after-guy and the sheet taut, the spinnaker halyard, which has been flaked down and its stopper opened in readiness, is cast off and the takedown man, standing in the forward hatch with his feet on the leeward bunk, brings in the string with full arm swings under the genoa, stuffing it down the hatch in front of him. As he has it almost entirely gathered, the sheet and guy are eased from the cockpit. He unsnaps each as he climbs on deck and clips them together. He stuffs the sail down the forward hatch and closes it. The foredeck is then cleared and secured.

As soon as they can be spared, two people go below and make up the spinnaker so that it will be ready for the next opportunity to use it. The setting and dousing of the chute are maneuvers that must be carried out at racing speed for when the sail is going up or down it must pass through phases where there is risk of something going wrong such as hour-glassing or wrapping around the headstay before it is trimmed and full, or scooping water before it is gathered aboard and sent down the hatch. It is essential that each step be discussed and planned ahead to make sure that nothing is left to chance.

An alternative that may be preferred, particularly when there is only one person available to do all the jobs in connection with the douse, is for the crewmember who is to imitate an octopus to snap a retrieving line on the sheet and secure it to the lifeline about 6 feet abaft the shrouds where it will be handy when the time comes to gather in the sail. If conditions are sloppy and the chute is in danger of collapsing, its performance can be improved by the use of a twing, a line with a snap shackle at one end which goes around the spinnaker sheet. The other end goes through a block and is tended by a crewmember who by hauling in hard at the crucial moment tightens the sheet down enough to keep the chute flying. If a twing is rigged, it will serve well as a retrieving line.

The crewmember:

—moves the sheet to the secondary winch and puts the jib sheet on the primary and cleats it at a slack trim;

—goes forward, releases the stopper, and clears the halyard to be sure it will run freely;

—checks to see that the topping lift and foreguy have the pole's position tightly fixed at the height that can be reached without difficulty;

—takes the stop off the jib, clips on the halyard, hoists it smartly, and jumps to the cockpit to adjust the jib sheet a trifle over-trimmed to give a good lee;

—goes forward and releases the guy, keeping clear of the pole, grabs the halyard, holding it by the forward hand, and runs back past the mast, gathers in the sheet with both hands and as much of the foot of the chute as possible and holds it tight against the lee side of the main;

—eases the halyard and the sail simultaneously as fast as possible;

—clips the halyard and sheet to the life line while holding the tightly bundled sheet between the knees, throws the sail down the companionway as far forward as possible, and cleans up the foredeck preparatory to tacking or the next spinnaker set;

—when all is secure on deck, goes below and worms and bags the chute and stows the bagged sail in its proper place.

It is of course more efficient and safer to have all these evolutions handled by a team of several capable people.

The first concern when trimming the chute is to keep the air flow attached over as much of the sail as possible. This allows the trimmer of the sheet to add significantly to the boat's speed. The sheet must be eased constantly to the point where the luff is about to curl. On a run, so much of the sail inevitably will be stalled that there is less opportunity to gain but the pole can be squared to the apparent wind and the sheet trimmed to produce the greatest area-to-wind. Reaching and broad-reaching, the pole should be raised so that the upper and lower luff telltales lift at the same time as the helm brings the boat closer to the wind. If the pole is too low, the upper telltales will lift before the lower ones and if the pole is too high, the lower woolies will lift first. In light air, however, when the chute is starving for enough air to maintain its shape, a very low pole may save the situation, but the pole should be carefully raised as the wind fills the chute. If a hand is available, this pole height control should be his assignment. Close-reaching demands a low pole which will not only level the tack with the clew but will also move the draft forward. Raising the pole slightly from this position will increase the power by sagging the upper luff to leeward and closing the leech while moving the draft aft. Moving the sheeting position forward controls the fullness of the lower part of the sail. Lowering the pole and clew has the same effect on the upper part of the sail. If the sheet goes over the boom, the sail will have an open head and a flat foot which is desirable in heavy air. In underpowered conditions it will be better to have the sheet pass under the boom for a shape that will be more powerful and easier to control because it will be deeper. Whenever we have sufficient personnel, we can derive considerable enjoyment from keeping the chute in its ideal trim at all times. If we are cruising shorthanded we will have to do the best we can with what we have.

The triradial can be carried as soon as the relative wind reaches 60° and may be carried dead down wind (180°) but the VMG will probably be better if we do not let the relative wind get above 150°. From 120° upwards, the pole will produce the best results by being trimmed square to the apparent wind. As the wind comes forward, the pole will make a better sail shape by being perpendicular to the true wind. For a start you can set your pole in relation to the apparent wind according to the following table:

RELATIVE APPARENT WIND	POLE'S DEGREES OVER SQUARE
100°	5°
100°	10°
90°	15°
80°	20°
70°	25°
60°	30° (touching headstay)

If the pole presses too hard against the headstay when the guy stretches in a puff, forces may be set up that will break the pole. For this reason we try to use lines with minimum elongation under load for our spinnaker guys.

Dancing Girl has a loran that computes the VMG which makes it easy to select the course that will get her to her next turning point in the least time, but if we are short of power or for any other reason are unable to use the electronics, the table in the front of the boat's log will give you the percentage increase in speed through the water necessary to justify a given number of degrees off course. Thinking about these relationships will improve your sailor's eye and applying it precisely will be worth the effort.

In sloppy conditions with light air it will pay to rig our rope spinnaker net on the headstay using the jib halyard. It has prevented a lot of wraps. In heavy air and difficult conditions the Solent jib trimmed flat amidships will serve the same purpose and also help to prevent the boat from rounding up. Many times we have used the triradial successfully when there were only two of us aboard, but when conditions are difficult, extra hands can make the sail perform more enjoyably for all.

POLELESS SPINNAKER

This is a masthead, free-luff balloon jib set with a single spinnaker sheet in place of the spinnaker. It is more forgiving in sloppy conditions and easier to trim than the chute when we are shorthanded. It is made of 1.5-oz. nylon spinnaker cloth and can be flown in apparent winds of from 2 to 25 knots. It is tacked to the foreguy which permits adjusting the height of the tack above the stemhead (4 feet is right most of the time). There is a snap at the sail's tack to provide a sliding anchorage to the headstay at this point. With the wind abaft the beam this snap can be released to permit the tack to move out ahead and to weather. It is hoisted on the spinnaker halyard and although forward of the beam it is usually two-blocked, it sometimes benefits from about 2 feet of slack when the wind is abaft the beam. The sheeting position is moved so that the luff breaks evenly from head to foot. Normally, the block should be opposite the main winch on the toe rail. It is set in a sock, a narrow sleeve which completely contains the hoisted sail. The device has a rigid, loose-fitting ring at its mouth with a control line which, when the crew is ready, hoists it as a compact bunch to the sail's head, allowing the sail to fill. When the sail is to be doused the control line is used to pull the sock down over the sail as the sheet is eased. The sock does not work as well when wet and when soaked may not work in winds over 15 knots apparent. If the wind suddenly rises above this level the Gennaker is taken down in the lee of the main, preferably with a jib hoisted to produce additional blanketing, like an ordinary spinnaker. As a back-up it also has a belly line which permitted a very tidy takedown once when the sock jammed above the sail's head. Under ordinary conditions, however, it is pulled up or down as easily as a windowshade and under ideal circumstances the sail has been effective beam-reaching with 25 knots of wind over the deck.

The foreguy is worked from the cockpit using the clamcleat mounted on the cockpit coaming. It is led through a

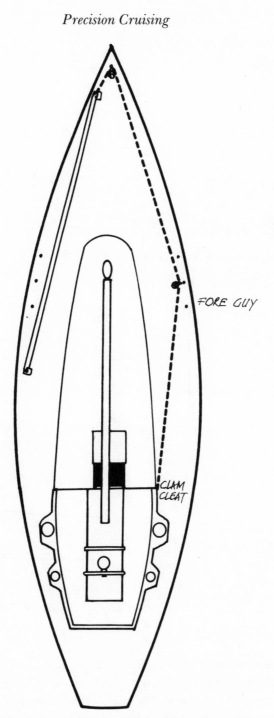

FORE GUY

CLAM
CLEAT

Spinnaker Pole and Foreguy Stowed When Not In Use

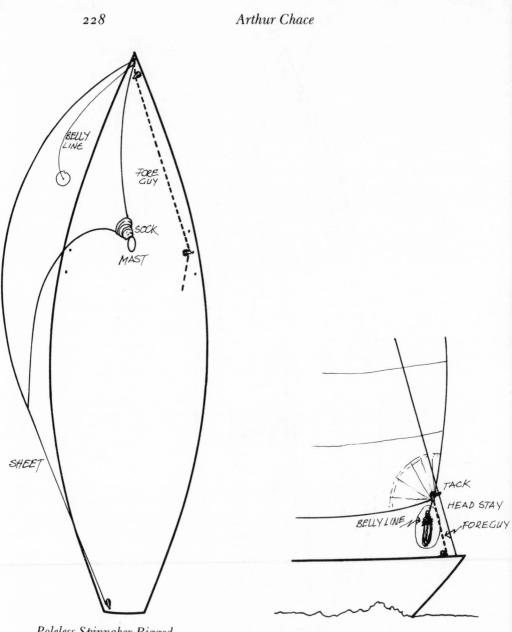

Poleless Spinnaker Rigged

block mounted on the stanchion base at the chains to give a
fair lead and then goes to a block at the stem head. When
not in use it is clipped to the bail of the spinnaker pole chock.
This line when clipped to the eye on the under side of the
end of a working spinnaker pole, prevents it from riding up.

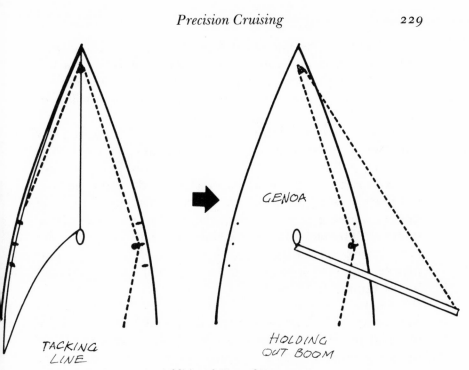

TACKING LINE

GENOA

HOLDING OUT BOOM

Additional Uses of Foreguy

As it in part opposes the pole topping lift and the guy, it must be trimmed in coordination with them. The foreguy and the topping lift must both be taut when the bowman releases the tack of the spinnaker in a conventional under-mainsail take-down to prevent the pole from clubbing him when the sail is released. When the foreguy is cleated under heavy load the resident gorilla may find that even when he is seated with his feet braced against the after bulkhead of the cabin he is not strong enough to release it. Taking the line to the primary winch may make it possible to lift the line out of the cam cleat.

The foreguy when snapped into the grommet in the foot of the #1, serves as a tacking line, hauling the sail forward as the sheet is released. In this way tacking is accelerated and wear on the sail reduced.

The poleless spinnaker is usable when the wind is from 050° to 150° relative. It is equipped with a sock that can be slid down over the sail to furl it and up off the sail to set it. It is important that the sail not become twisted. To make checking for twist easy the luff tape is blue, the leech red and the foot white. The free end of this line when not in use is secured to the tack grommet with enough slack to make sure it will never adversely affect sail shape. The sail is best set and doused with the boat headed down wind so that the main will provide a lee.

The Gennaker used the spinnaker sheets and blocks. Only one sheet is used at a time. The sail is never tacked. It is jibbed by pulling the sock down over it before jibing, changing the sheet to the new tack and when ready, after the boat has jibed, raising the sock. The foreguy is snapped into the sail's tack giving easy control of the height of the tack above the deck. The tack has a snap which is usually clipped to the headstay except on those occasions when there are enough people aboard to attempt to get slightly better air for the sail by unclipping the tack and letting the sail move away from the headstay as much as two feet. The luff of the sail has woolies on it like a genoa to assist the helmsman to avoid the cardinal sin of over-trimming when close-reaching. Ideally the sail is trimmed to carry a slight curl along its luff. Once the wind moves aft to a beam reach the telltales are no longer of use because the flow of air becomes too turbulent. We do, however, want to keep a slight curl in the luff for maximum drive. The foreguy is trimmed to put the tack 2 feet off the deck when the wind is at 50° and is gradually eased so that on a very broad reach it may give the best speed by letting the tack rise 10 feet off the deck.

Setting this sail is very simple. One need only make sure the sock is not twisted, bend on the sheet and halyard and two-block it. The sock control line is long enough so that it can be secured to the life line without unnecessary tension, ready to be used. When the order comes to set, the sheet is tended in the cockpit and the sock control line is hauled, hoisting the sock smartly as the sail is trimmed. Do not hoist the sock higher than is necessary to free the sail. In extreme cases this action could jam the device above the head of the sail. The douse would then have to be accomplished using the belly line. Normally the sock makes setting and furling the poleless chute as easy as pulling up and down a window shade.

When heaving-to, as in a man overboard situation, when it

is essential to avoid forward or backward motion, the fore-guy can be snapped to the end of the main boom and hauled taut till the boom is on the leeward lower shroud. With the helm hard a lee any forward motion results in the boat heading towards the wind with the result that the wind pushing against the back of the mainsail stops the forward motion and pushes the boat slightly back and to leeward. As soon as she has settled down the boat just lies there with only leeward motion.

STAYSAIL

Dancing Girl's staysail usually adds about 10 percent to the boat's speed when it can be used properly. It is most effective with the relative wind at 60°-90°. In this range it is tacked to a ring which slides on the jackline between two pad eyes on the centerline of the foredeck. There are two lines on the tack. The longer one is led from aft forward through the ring, through the base of the weather mooring bitt and then back to be secured to the stanchion base on the weather side forward of the shrouds. The shorter line goes from forward aft through the ring and directly to the same stanchion base. By adjusting the tension on these two lines, the tack can be placed where desired fore and aft and at the desired height off the deck. Normally, for best results the staysail leech should clear the spreader by about 6 inches. The tack should be high enough to put the clew at the same level as the mainsail gooseneck. There is a sheet spliced into the clew long enough to permit trimming to the stanchion head by the shrouds and then barberhauling it to hand rails, lifelines, or whatever is available to position it correctly. The spare jib halyard provides the best hoist and enough tension is applied to place the draft as far forward as the conditions require. The more motion the seas impart to the boat, the further forward the draft should be to keep the sail working. Clew position is adjusted so that the staysail slightly constricts the flow of air to leeward of the mainsail.

The staysail can be flown effectively with the spinnaker or the #1 or the Solent. One of these last two combinations can be used on a reach instead of setting a chute when that seems to be too demanding. Occasionally with a spinnaker flying we have gained speed using the staysail and the Solent. This requires moderate winds and fairly smooth seas, but it is fun when it works and the gain in VMG is enough to add to the fun.

Drills Aboard Dancing Girl

Drills must always be called as such. No False Alarms. Call "Man Overboard Drill" or "Fire Drill in the Galley." A stop watch can tell a lot about efficiency and comparison with previous practices. After each drill it is usually very productive to have a discussion of how the drill went and how the procedures should be modified to have a better result.

Although circumstances will always be different from each incident, the fact that the crew has run through an exercise of a similar imaginary incident can produce considerable saving in time and confusion.

MAN OVERBOARD

Man overboard is an all-hands maneuver of the utmost seriousness.

When someone goes over the side, everyone should shout "Man Overboard" loudly and all hands come on deck without delay. The watch captain will be in charge until relieved by the captain. The helmsman will immediately throw one or more life preserver cushions to the victim. The other watch stander will put over the man overboard poles, horseshoes, and lights and KEEP AN EYE ON THE VICTIM. The helmsman will immediately bring the boat to a course with the apparent wind abeam. The navigator will start a stopwatch, punch hold on the loran to store the coordinates of the place where the man went over, and log the reading on the electronic log.

Regardless of course at the time of the accident, the helmsman will come so that the apparent wind is on the beam. As soon as possible to come about with way on, he will do so.

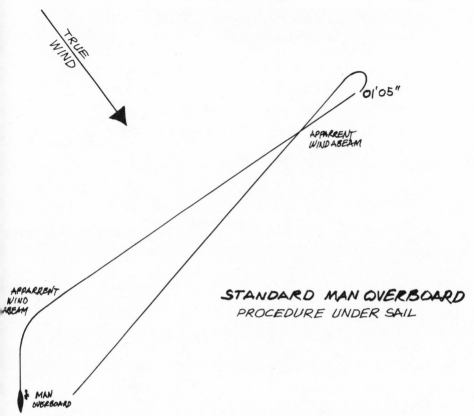

TRUE WIND

01'05"

APPARRENT WIND ABEAM

APPARRENT WIND ABEAM

MAN OVERBOARD

STANDARD MAN OVERBOARD
PROCEDURE UNDER SAIL

These courses will head the boat to leeward of the victim so that heading into the wind will kill headway as the victim is brought alongside to leeward. If there is a spinnaker up, this must come down and be stowed first, but the objective is to get around on the other tack with the apparent wind abeam as soon as possible. After tacking, the foreguy will be immediately attached to the boom so that it can hold the boom forward. The jib will be lowered and stopped to the rail. If a genoa is bent on, it should be remembered that the clew of this sail can be dropped overboard to provide a hammock into which an injured man can be towed and then used by winching in the sheet to hoist the man up to where he can be rolled aboard. Ideally, the victim is still in sight, but if sight has been lost, every effort should be made to regain it without delay. This means good binoculars and good eyes for-

PROCEDURE UNDER POWER
WILLIMSON TURN

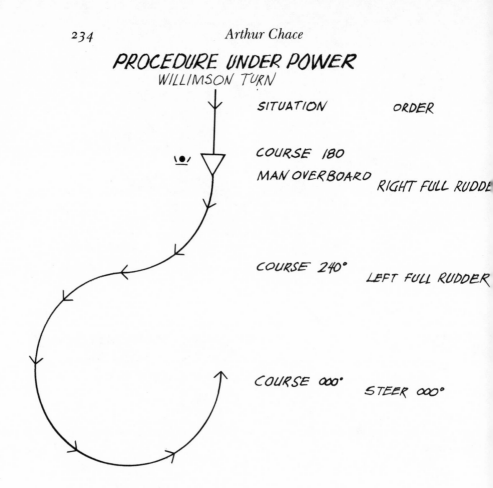

SITUATION   ORDER

COURSE 180

MAN OVERBOARD   RIGHT FULL RUDDE

COURSE 240°   LEFT FULL RUDDER

COURSE 000°   STEER 000°

ward. The pole should provide an indication of direction and, if two poles have been gotten over, they will give a line indicating of the direction in which the victim lies. A further clue will be available if the cook has been able to break open a dye pack and flush it down the galley sink providing a trail of dye in the water. With the man in sight, the helmsman steers to place him 3 feet to leeward at the shrouds with the wind on the opposite bow.

If the boat lies with the wind on the opposite bow, then, with the main held out, any time the boat moves up to windward, the wind will push back on the main and push the boat down. If the boat heads down, the sail will immediately push it up into the wind. Obviously, this will be most effective if all headsails are stowed.

A strong swimmer should be ready to go, with a life jacket and a line, to the victim and secure the victim to a tackle hanging from the end of the boom. The victim is then two-blocked and the boom swung in, the victim released and dropped into the cockpit. In the excitement do not forget that the swimmer should also be brought aboard as soon as possible.

A system that we are evaluating is to check that there are no lines in the water, start the engine in neutral, secure all sails, and then proceed under power to recover the victim.

If the boat is under storm jib and trysail when the accident occurs, the same procedure is followed but, obviously, the stronger winds will produce a number of problems. It will probably be very difficult to hear communication and, therefore, it is particularly important that all communication be directed to a specific person who acknowledges when he understands. The trysail probably will have to be poled out in order for it to work as we have described above. Even with the mainsail furled, the main boom can be used to hoist the victim aboard. If sight of the victim is lost, the line of the two man overboard poles will be very valuable, as will loran coordinates. It should be kept in mind that in stormy conditions, the sea surface moves downwind at 3 knots or so during an ordinary gale and far greater speed during a storm. Tidal currents will also carry the victim away from the geographic spot where the accident occurred.

The engine can be very useful in some many overboard situations, but it is essential that the watch captain does not permit the key to be turned on until he is absolutely certain that there is no line that can get into the screw. Again, before the clutch is engaged, a check should be made. If the recovery is being attempted under power, the same course should be followed but all hands should be particularly aware of the tragedy that could result if the victim is thrown in contact with a spinning propeller.

Once the cook has left the dye marker trail, hot water should be made ready for soup and warm towels. If the man is conscious, hot soup will help warm his inner core, but an unconscious man or a man too cold to swallow should not have hot liquids poured down his windpipe. It is wise to taste everything before giving it to the victim to make sure that he will not be burned by it. A garbage bag for all the victim's wet clothes will keep things a lot better below. A fire in the cabin heater stove will help warm the cabin. Towels should be available to dry the victim quickly, being careful to avoid being too rough on his or her skin. A dry, warm sleeping bag will be of great assistance in warming a victim, particularly one that has been carefully dried. If the victim is in serious straits, two warm members of the crew should strip down and get on each side of the victim in a sleeping bag, or two sleeping bags, to transfer heat as rapidly as possible. Care should be taken, however, not to do anything to accelerate the return of the cold blood in the extremities to the inner core. An additional way to warm the victim is towels dipped in hot water and wrung out. Again these should be checked, probably with the cook's elbow, to make sure they are not too hot.

If the victim is not located promptly, a logical, analytical approach is indicated. In the absence of any other clues, go to your best guess where the person was last seen and follow the search spiral diagram in the front of the log book. Notice that each leg is 15 seconds longer than the leg before, but that the elapsed time from the start of the search plan is shown on the chart.

Although there have been many cases where good seamanship and good luck have returned a man overboard quickly to the boat unharmed, the odds are sufficiently poor so that every possible step must be taken to insure that he is recovered. Even more important is to see that everyone stays aboard. All hands must remember that it is their most important concern to see that they do not leave the ship unwillingly. Feet must be set down carefully, hand holds must be used and every effort made to stay aboard.

As conditions start to get rough, it is important to get the safety harnesses on and clipped on early. Men peeing over the side should remember that this maneuver has been the cause of a great many man overboard accidents.

The final advice is don't go overboard, but, if you do, shout to attract attention, grab a cushion as soon as possible, and swim with it to the horseshoe where you may be more likely to be found. Breaking open the dye packet on the strobe light will increase the victim's visibility and the whistle attached

MAN OVERBOARD
SEARCH PLAN

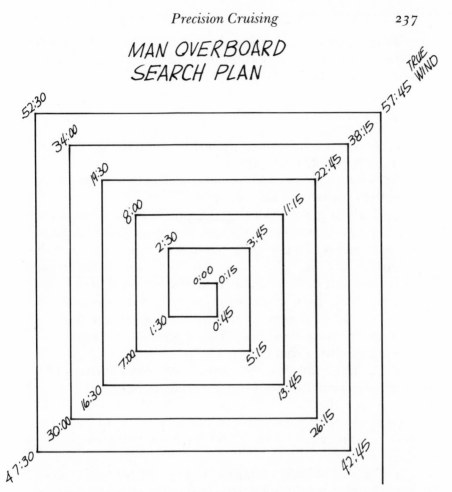

A copy of this search plan is posted inside the front cover of the log for ready reference in time of need. Boat alternates between close and broad reach, Each leg is fifteen seconds longer than its predecessor. At six knots this produces a spiral with fifty yards between tracks. Slower speeds put tracks closer together, faster further apart.

there will be useful when the boat returns within earshot.

The man overboard poles, one on each side, are secured to the upper lifeline abreast of the cockpit and are connected to the horseshoes in their racks at the forward end of the pushpit. Also lashed to each horseshoe are an automatic strobe light, a drogue to reduce drift, a whistle to attract attention, and a dye packet. The entire rig on each side is held aboard by a pair of metal pins that are easily released by pulling on a ring connected to them by a wire line. The ring and the pole are each secured to the lifeline with a spinnaker elastic band which, if it deteriorates, is replaced by the oncoming watch captain before he relieves.

FIRE

Whenever fire is discovered aboard the boat, the word should be passed rapidly giving the location.

All hands should pass the word and gather at the scene. The following steps must be taken:

1. Make all preparations to abandon ship. If the situation requires, then send out a Mayday promptly with an accurate navigational position and description of your vessel and the nature of the fire. Even if you do not require immediate assistance and think you may be able to save the vessel without outside help, it is the better part of wisdom to have the Coast Guard or others notified as to what you are doing so that, in the event that things take a turn for the worse, you will not pass up a chance to get help.

2. Upon the discovery of a fire, if possible, deprive it of as much air as you can until you are ready to fight it.

3. Attack the fire at its base with the dry powder extinguishers located in the starboard cockpit locker, in the galley, and at the forward hatch. If the fire is electrical turn off the ship's power.

4. Use all available containers to bring water to the scene. Place water carefully at the base of the fire where it can effectively cool and smother the blaze. Do not use water with an electrical or oil fire until that aspect of the fire is eliminated.

5. Use wet swabs, broom, wet blankets, and towels to smother and cool the blaze.

6. Isolate all burning combustibles. Anything that may even possibly harbor a smoldering spark should be isolated on deck and extinguished for certain or submerged over the side. Do not dump blazing materials in a harbor where they can ignite oil or other combustibles.

7. Be calm when cooling and smothering. Wetting down the endangered area and preventing the spread of the fire can save the boat. You can use a water-soaked sweater to scrub out a fire that excited incompetence can spread. Don't put

water on grease or oil. Smother these or use dry powder. Do not put water on electrical fires. Use dry powder. Calm courage will work in many situations but do not hazard personnel in a lost cause. Get off the ship if you can't save it. Don't panic.

8. When the fire is under control, get every possible hiding place for a spark smothered and wet down and opened up so you can be sure it is really out and cold. Pull out every bit of charred kapok or other stuffing. Check every crack.

9. Electrical fires require turning off the current as soon as possible and not turning it on until you are certain that all insulation has been restored and all chances of reignition has been eliminated.

Dancing Girl has a two-burner alcohol stove without an oven and without an external pressure tank. When she was built, this was considered to be the safest way to handle the cooking problem.

The fire rules for this stove are: 1. NEVER FILL A STOVE UNTIL IT HAS COOLED DOWN. 2. If there is any loose alcohol around, shut down the stove immediately and clear up the alcohol before tragedy occurs. 3. As water works very well with alcohol fires, we keep a garden fogger, holding about two quarts of water, by the galley sink, where it is handy in the event of fire. This is pressurized before each meal so that, in the event of a flare up, all the cook has to do is reach for the pressurized jug. Fog emerges when the trigger is pushed. Direct it at the base of the flame. These pressurized garden sprayers can produce a very heavy, wet fog if properly adjusted. It is almost a spray and, played back and forth over the base of the flame, has a very good cooling effect. It can also be played back and forth over areas being reached by the flame to keep them cool enough so that there is no risk of further combustion.

On the few occasions when we have had a fire, the cook has calmly picked up the spray bottle and applied it to the fire until the flame was extinguished, then refilled the jug, repressurized it, put it back in its stowage and started to get the stove ready to relight so that dinner would not be delayed. In the event, for some reason, the fire gets away from this provision, the next step is to use the canvas bucket secured to a long line by the companionway to start bringing buckets of sea water up which can be poured on the fire to dilute the alcohol and to cool places that have gotten too hot. If the fire has gotten too large for fog to make satisfactory progress, dry powder extinguishers should also be used.

Crew members who review the characteristics of the various fires that may be encountered and think through the best way to fight them will find that, should an emergency occur, they will have the proper answers for minimizing the problem.

COLLISION

1. As soon as you have evaluated your situation, make all preparations for sending out a Mayday in the event that this should become necessary. Write down the name of the other vessel involved in the collision and all that you can remember about it. Regardless of the vessel, this information should be gotten out on the radio, depending on the damage.

2. Locate the damage. If there is any hope, man the pumps. Use buckets to set up a bucket brigade.

3. Sleeping bags, mattresses, pillows can be stuffed in a hole controlling flooding so that pumps can keep up.

4. A collision mat on the outside can be very effective. Sails are well designed for this work. *Dancing Girl*'s collision mat is in a marked mesh bag in the starboard locker with a sheet spliced into each of its four corners. The sheets hold the mat in position over the leak or hole.

5. Doors, locker tops, floor boards, etc., can be very effective as temporary repairs. Use everything you have. A patched boat is better than a life raft, but if the boat is lost, everything with it is lost. We are better off to bring it in wrecked than run the risk of losing it whole.

6. Holding the bow in the cut in the side of the vessel struck can slow flooding and give personnel time to plug the leak.

ABANDON SHIP

In any disaster situation, immediate steps should be taken to insure that all personnel have the best chance of survival even if the ship cannot be saved. When this concern is in process of being brought under control:

1. Send out a Mayday if damage creates doubt of survival. The procedure which is written out with the other important data in the front of the log book.

a. Set the transmitter on Channel 16 high power.

b. Call "Mayday Mayday Mayday. This is *Dancing Girl* Whiskey Zulu Quebec 7393.

c. My position is latitude _____, longitude _____ by loran. (Or give the loran coordinates or the range and bearing from an easily identified object or if you have nothing better give your dead reckoning position.)

d. There are _____ persons aboard.

e. We are on fire burning out of control. OR Have hit ice and are leaking faster than pumps and bucket brigade can handle. OR Have been rammed by _____ OR Are dismasted and our engine is out of commission and we are drifting toward _____ rocks so rapidly we do not expect to have a jury rig operating in time to keep us off.

f. *Dancing Girl* is a 37-foot single-masted sailboat with blue hull, white decks, mahogany trim, sail number 3933.

g. This is *Dancing Girl* Whisky Zulu Quebec 7393. Channel 16. Over."

If there is no answer check to see that the VHF is operating properly and repeat. After three transmissions without an answer warm up the SSB and go through the same procedure on 2182 giving that frequency when signing off. Keep trying to get your message out. Someone may read you but not be able to transmit.

2. Do not abandon ship except as a last resort.

3. As time permits, launch life rafts, each with a boat tender to hold on to the boat and to go with the raft if the ship sinks. Better too soon than too late. Do not turn life rafts loose unmanned. Do not let them get adrift. The person going with the boat should have oars or a paddle and a clear understanding of how little progress will be possible in a blow. Boat keepers should hold on to the ship as long as it is available and make sure that all ships personnel are accounted for and aboard before it sinks.

4. All hands should be in life jackets with extra sweaters

and warm clothes with shelter from the sun and weather.

5. All available drinking water should be in each boat, as much as possible. Food also can help. Flares, seasick pills, knives, fishing gear, etc.

6. Charts and the course to nearest land may prove essential.

7. Take the horseshoes, poles, and strobe lights.

8. All hands drink as much water as possible before abandoning ship.

There is only one exception to the rule that you never leave the boat until you have to climb up to get in the dinghy. That exception is when the flames do not give you a place to windward of the fire where you can remain without burning. The rubber dinghy and the canopied life raft are both wonderful inventions, but no one in his right mind would choose them in preference to a vessel such as this. Concerns for visibility, seaworthiness, comfort, and survivability are best answered by staying with *Dancing Girl* as long as she is available.

STORM AT SEA

Start preparing at the first indication of a possible storm. Follow the weather reports, log the true wind direction and the barometer readings every hour, and when the storm gets closer every half hour. Keep a plot of the center of the storm. In the Northern Hemisphere tropical storms rotate counterclockwise and if you face the wind the center of the storm will be 10° behind your right shoulder. If the bearings are decreasing the center is passing to the right of you and you will be in the least dangerous semicircle. If you forget, simply analyze that because the rotation of the storm is counterclockwise and the course of the storm is usually curving in a northeasterly direction, the velocity of wind is added to the velocity of the storm on the right side of the track and subtracted from that velocity on the left. With a storm having, for example, a speed of advance of 20 knots, vessels in the dangerous semicircle will experience winds 40 knots greater than those to the left of the storm's track.

If the bearing of the center decreases you are where you want to be and should make knots to distance yourself from the disturbance. If the bearing is increasing you are going into the dangerous semicircle and you had better plot the best course to reduce your problem. If the bearing is steady you are going pass through the eye of the storm if you do not push hard to get away from the projected track. If the situation is dicey, logging the bearing of the center every 10 minutes may give you an early indication of the possibility of an improvement in course. *Bowditch* recommends for the Northern Hemisphere that if you are in the track of the dangerous semicircle you put the wind on your starboard bow, and if you expect the navigable semicircle to run over you put the wind on your starboard quarter.

While the navigator is working to minimize impact the rest of the ship's company should be taking all possible steps to reduce vulnerability to storm damage:

a. Check all stowage to see that the boat can take a 360° roll.

b. Secure everything below that can be put below and lash securely on deck all that must stay topside.

c. All hands should dress in warm dry clothes, sea boots, flotation jackets or vests, and oilskins with a towel at the neck and sleeves and trouser legs tied to prevent water getting in. Safety harnesses should be checked, worn, and clipped on.

d. Check to see that all jacklines are in place properly secured with shackles moused or taped.

e. Check all topside gear to be sure that it is protected from past or future storm damage.

f. Rig the forestay and bend on the storm jib, ready for use when needed.

g. Check the trysail and make sure it will be ready when needed.

h. While maintaining maximum speed toward safer waters, be prepared to take as needed the steps necessary to prevent being over-canvased.

i. When the main is finally furled, lace it with tight half hitches 9 inches apart using the end of the mainsheet.

j. The storm trysail is usually carried stowed in its sack but bent onto its own track. If not make it ready. As you are racing to be in the safe semicircle or at least to get as far away from the center of the storm as possible, you will not want to reduce sails too soon, but do as much preparatory work as you can before the seas get rougher.

k. Prepare stormy weather rations and make provisions for hot food, if possible.

l. Issue seasick pills to all hands using them. There is a limit to what even the toughest stomach can stand.

m. Check to see that life jackets are in a readily available place and that the dinghy and the emergency raft are ready to be used but securely lashed to the boat so that they will not be carried away by green seas.

n. *Dancing Girl* has never been in a situation where streaming warps seemed to provide a desirable result. A storm at sea is a very dynamic situation and a skilled helmsman can avoid a great many of the dangers that could overtake a vessel lying ahull without steerageway.

o. *Dancing Girl* will always have someone on the wheel, and the boat will always be handled so as to have way enough so that the helmsman can steer to avoid disaster. *Dancing Girl* can make good 120° off the wind under bare poles and, under most circumstances, will have enough speed through the water to permit a skilled helmsman to avoid getting into the spot where she will be rolled over or where she will have to stick her nose into a green sea. Remember lying broadside in a trough is dangerous because the right wave can come under you, pick you up, and roll you over. Just before it does, you will be impressed how much it resembles a large apartment house about to fall on you. Running straight downwind, you are liable to go too fast and stick your nose into the back of a graybeard with the risk that you will pitch-pole.

p. After the storm has been blowing for several hours, the waves will become quite large and the vessel will find itself becalmed in the trough between the waves but fighting incredible noise and motion when up in the wind. Sails will have to be adjusted to maintain steerageway.

q. Hatchways and lockers must be latched when not in use to ensure that they will not open or be open when green seas are seeking a way into the boat.

r. Take every opportunity to refine your navigational position so that in the event that you require assistance, you can describe your location well enough so that potential rescuers will have confidence that they can find you.

s. *Dancing Girl* has been maintained with the thought that she will have to face any storm at sea and, although we should not be overconfident, we should realize that a well-found, well-maintained, carefully thought-out vessel can survive all but the worst spot in the ultimate storm.

STORM IN PORT

Although everyone is involved in preparing the vessel to withstand a storm in port, good seamanship will normally see that the preparations are made sufficiently in advance so that they do not have to be an All Hands maneuver under pressure.

1. At the first suspicion that a storm is approaching, get all weather reports. Check and record the barograph and barometer readings, wind direction and velocity at least every hour at the start but every fifteen minutes when the storm is close. Remember that the center of the storm is 10° behind your right shoulder when you are facing the wind in the Northern Hemisphere. Plot the storm center and try to evaluate its course.

2. Evaluate the present anchorage as against alternatives, not forgetting that, in some cases, getting out to sea and off-shore can be the safest course.

3. Ideally, the vessel should sit out Force 12 winds in a small, sheltered, sandy or clay-bottomed pond that is exclusively available to it with nothing to blow or drift down on it. While this is generally not available, we should always have a port to hole up in as similar as possible to this ideal.

Our hurricane anchoring system is as follows: We put out a 35-pound Danforth in the direction of the greatest expected wind with 100 feet of its regular rode to a swivel. In the opposite direction, we set our 65-pound Yachtsman, similarly connected to the swivel. On each side of the Yachtsman arranged the same way, we put out our two 12-pound Danforths, hoping to achieve equal strength to withstand all directions of wind. We place the 35-pound Danforth to take the load when we are heading toward the most heavy wind expected. To the swivel we shackle a length of ½-inch twisted

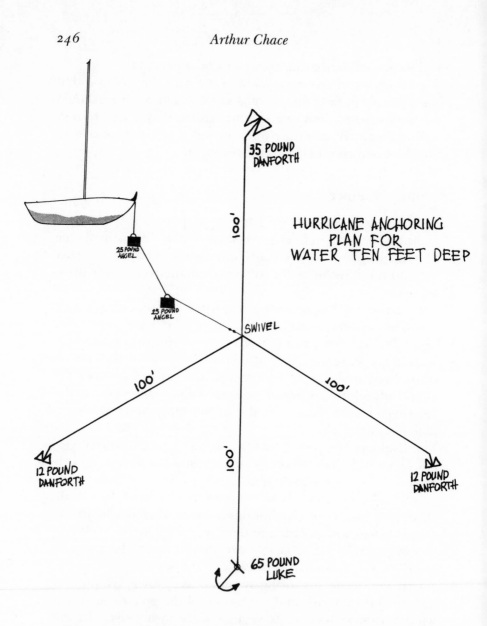

HURRICANE ANCHORING
PLAN FOR
WATER TEN FEET DEEP

nylon anchor line. (All anchor lines are made up in 100-foot
lengths, with a thimble spliced in each end. These are shackled
together as conditions require.) We use enough of this line
to insure 10-to-1 scope to whichever anchor the direction of
the wind dictates, with the rode cleated to the mooring cleats
and additional line ready so that the scope can be maintained
in the event of high hurricane tides. These cleats are heavily

backed and the backing is connected with a rod and turnbuckle to the keel, but we would run relieving line from them to the main winches to distribute the load.

4. Split vinyl chafing gear should be used and it should be lashed to protect the rode where it passes through the chock in a way that will prevent it from shifting its position. You should also have rags ready as supplementary chafing gear. It is wise to lash down the line so that it will not easily jump out of the chock and start sawing a groove through the toerail or further into the hull. We have two 25-pound weights, which the British call Angels, that we rig to hold the rode down and provide additional energy absorption. We place one about 6 feet from the swivel end of the rode and the other so it rides just off the bottom directly below the bow. Lines to shoreside rocks or trees that the storm cannot move can supplement this mooring procedure.

5. Sails, life rafts, horseshoes, poles, oars, or anything else that provides unnecessary windage or can be damaged or blown away should be struck below. The boom should be secured in the boom crutch, which is stored under the beam ends in the port locker. A line around the boom to the stanchion bases on each side by the main winches provides additional security.

6. Preparation for handling collision should be made, not only to fend off but to repair damage as it occurs. All hands should be properly dressed for any eventuality. Don't forget that the situation may deteriorate suddenly and you might find yourself in the water in need of flotation.

7. The engine may be used to control yawing and reduce the strain on ground tackle. It is absolutely essential that, under no circumstances, you permit any hazard of a line getting into the prop.

8. If you are staying aboard, remember that you may have to leave the boat because it is sinking without hope of staying afloat. You should, therefore, make provisions for abandoning ship, but remember, never leave the boat before you have to step up to the dinghy, unless fire forces you to.

9. After the vessel is battened down and in all ways prepared for a hurricane, it may be the best course to take all personnel to safe, high ground, rather than run the risk of

being lost with the vessel. Under no circumstances permit one of the following two hazards: First, that you get so frightened that you leave the safety of the boat for the dubious security of a fragile dinghy. Second, that you become so heroically dedicated to the saving of the vessel that you forget that human life is more valuable and that survivors can get new yachts.

RESCUE

1. In a rescue situation involving a large number of people, radio communication with the Coast Guard or other assistance should be established at once. You should have an accurate navigational position to give. If the job is too big for you alone, get help. If you can handle it, report your progress from time to time and don't forget that it is possible that you can be met at the harbor you have selected with sufficient medical support to handle the situation.

2. Stay far enough away from a burning vessel and to windward of it to make sure that it does not spray you with flaming liquid if its fuel tank explodes. If you are to weather when an explosion does occur, anything hitting the sails will probably drop in the water, whereas if you were to leeward, it will drop in the boat. There may be a situation, however, where you can come up on the weather quarter of a vessel in distress with your big fenders rigged on your lee bow and place yourself close enough so that the distressed personnel can be helped aboard quickly enough before damage occurs. If the boats are jumping too much, it may be possible to get close enough to get long lines over for each member of the crew to be rescued to tie a line around himself with a bowline and jump in the water to be pulled aboard *Dancing Girl*'s stern. A line through the bow chock with a man in tow can be winched in enough so that the victim will swing alongside and can be lifted aboard.

3. An inflated dinghy on a long painter can be let drift to leeward to pick up personnel. Uninjured people can hang on to a dinghy in pairs on opposite sides, four can be in the dinghy. Others can hang on cushions or rely on their life jackets. All swimmers should be told to stay together and with

the dinghy. They should be tied together if possible.

4. Any injured can be brought aboard but must be kept below in bunks or on cabin sole. Avoid overloading which can prevent care for the injured, make impossible ship handling, radio use, galley, and the ship's survival. All weight should be kept as low as possible for every bit of weight added above our center of buoyancy brings us closer to the point where capsizing is inevitable. As the boat approaches overload start timing her roll cycle and watch for any sign of sluggishness coming back. That sluggishness is the warning that she may be about to roll on over and that we, instead of being proud of the lives we have saved, will save none and instead add our names to the casualty list. In a major disaster a small vessel can do the most good by saving a few and calling in help. It will do the worst by overestimating what she can do and end up losing hope of radio communication and adding unnecessary names to the list of victims. After we have picked up all we can carry and given the others what flotation we can develop for them the only further contribution we can make is to provide radio communication.

A string of boats and swimmers connected with the ship while you are giving first aid to the injured and using the radio is possibly the best you can do in a major disaster. You must coldly decide against taking on board more people than you can safely save.

5. Try to provide seasick containers for all the rescued. The seasickness of those with weak stomachs can be contagious. A cabin with an inch of vomit over the deck could provide an atmosphere to disable most navigators or radio people. Instruct all newcomers as to how the head works and, if possible, have a reliable person in charge, particularly to check after each user.

6. Hypothermia can be a problem varying with the climate but we should expect to keep the cabin heater stove going and balance the need for ventilation with the need to conserve heat. We may have to provide more specialized care for the critically hypothermic. Hot but drinkable soup and coffee can be a real morale booster. Seasick medicine should be available and first aid for cuts and broken bones is essential. About all we can do for burns is to keep them wet in salt

water. We have a complete first aid library for our size and we will have to do the best we can in the circumstances.

FIRE AND RESCUE

When a fire occurs on a nearby boat in a harbor our procedure is to send at once by dinghy a party of up to three with our full supply of buckets each of which should be equipped with a line long enough to allow it to be filled from the harbor from on deck. The walkie-talkie set on channel 16 for calling and the big piston pump should also go. One person capable of getting *Dancing Girl* underway should stay with the boat.

The objective should be to get a bucket brigade going as soon as the fire is determined to be non-electrical, to get non-essential people off the boat and flood the fire. Actual procedures will vary as circumstances dictate. On the way over, the rescue party should individually review all the techniques that might be useful. Depending on where the boats are anchored it may be possible to get timely assistance by radio, but quick and effective response is the answer to most boat fires.

TOWING

There is a wide spectrum of circumstances in which *Dancing Girl* may find herself confronted by a vessel in need of a tow.

1. Consider standing by and calling by radio for help. The job may be too big.

2. First considerations are to save lives and prevent damage to both boats when considering a tow.

3. In calm waters with no more than moderate wind tow on the longest available anchor line. A combination of sails and engine sometimes will work, to give a faster towing speed, but do not overstrain boat.

4. Approach to throw a heaving line but keep ship clear of the distressed vessel. Make a particular effort to observe the leeway made by both vessels. You don't want to get into a situation to leeward of a vessel that is drifting faster than you

are. Remember that your drift decreases when we get in its lee.

5. If possible use a megaphone or radio to work out plans in detail.

a. Do not take them in tow until they understand what you are offering to do for them and want to be towed where you are planning to take them.

b. What tow line they will use. How we will pick up their tow. How it will be connected.

c. How we will communicate. VHF is best. Hand signals can work with a horn to attract attention.

d. They must follow in our wake unless told specifically to do otherwise. Cutting a corner can cause a collision, because with the towline keeping the towed boat from running a course parallel but inside ours, the shorter distance they have to run if they cut the corner means a sure collision.

6. Cast off (if necessary, cut) tow line if either ship is endangered.

7. Use a bridle through both stern chocks leading to spinnaker winches. Use chafing gear. Do not overload ship.

8. Plan ahead how you will handle your mission when you are in restricted waters. You may find that your progress through a harbor will be safer if you tow alongside. The state of the vessel towing can make a lot of difference as to how much they can do to help you take care of them. Don't try to do more than you can do safely.

9. If *Dancing Girl* is to be towed we will use one of our heavy anchor rodes. Shackle a heavy pennant into the end you send over to the tow boat so that the heavier line can take the chafe if they do not have chafing gear. Be prepared to use our heaving line to send the towline over or to receive the towing vessel's heaving line or a line from a line-throwing gun.

INDEX